Library Users
and Reference Services

Forthcoming topics in *The Reference Librarian* series:

Library Instruction Revisited: Bibliographic Instruction Comes of Age

Authors: See MANUSCRIPT INQUIRIES, copyright page.

Published:

Library Users
and Reference Services

Jo Bell Whitlatch
Editor

The Haworth Press, Inc.
New York · London

Library Users and Reference Services has also been published as *The Reference Librarian*, Numbers 49/50 1995.

The development, preparation, and publication of this work has been undertaken with great care. However, the publisher, employees, editors, and agents of The Haworth Press and all imprints of The Haworth Press, Inc., including the Haworth Medical Press and Pharmaceutical Products Press, are not responsible for any errors contained herein or for consequences that may ensue from use of materials or information contained in this work. Opinions expressed by the author(s) are not necessarily those of The Haworth Press, Inc.

The Haworth Press, Inc., 10 Alice Street, Binghamton, NY 13904-1580 USA

Library of Congress Cataloging-in-Publication Data

Library users and reference services / Jo Bell Whitlatch, editor.
    p. cm.
    Includes bibliographical references and index.
    ISBN 1-56024-731-2 (acid-free paper)
    1. Reference services (Libraries)–United States. I. Whitlatch, Jo Bell.
Z711.L56 1995   94-48326
025.5′2′0973–dc20   CIP

INDEXING & ABSTRACTING

Contributions to this publication are selectively indexed or abstracted in print, electronic, online, or CD-ROM version(s) of the reference tools and information services listed below. This list is current as of the copyright date of this publication. See the end of this section for additional notes.

- *Academic Abstracts/CD-ROM,* EBSCO Publishing, P.O. Box 2250, Peabody, MA 01960-7250

- *Current Awareness Bulletin,* Association for Information Management, Information House, 20-24 Old Street, London EC1V 9AP, England

- *Current Index to Journals in Education,* Syracuse University, 4-194 Center for Science and Technology, Syracuse, NY 13244-4100

- *Educational Administration Abstracts (EAA),* Sage Publications, Inc., 2455 Teller Road, Newbury Park, CA 91320

- *IBZ International Bibliography of Periodical Literature,* Zeller Verlag GmbH & Co., P.O.B. 1949, d-49009 Osnabruck, Germany

- *Index to Periodical Articles Related to Law,* University of Texas, 727 East 26th Street, Austin, TX 78705

- *Information Science Abstracts,* Plenum Publishing Company, 233 Spring Street, New York, NY 10013-1578

- *Informed Librarian, The,* Infosources Publishing, 140 Norma Road, Teaneck, NJ 07666

- *INSPEC Information Services,* Institution of Electrical Engineers, Michael Faraday House, Six Hills Way, Stevenage, Herts SG1 2AY, England

(continued)

- *INTERNET ACCESS (& additional networks) Bulletin Board for Libraries ("BUBL"), coverage of information resources on INTERNET, JANET, and other networks.* –JANET X.29: UK.AC.BATH.BUBL or 00006012101300 –TELNET: BUBL.BATH.AC.UK or 138.38.32.45 login 'bubl' –Gopher: BUBL.BATH.AC.UK (138.32.32.45). Port 7070 –World Wide Web: http://www.bubl.bath.ac.uk/BUBL/home.ht ml –NISSWAIS: telnetniss.ac.uk (for the NISS gateway), The Andersonian Library, Curran Building, 101 St. James Road, Glasgow G4 ONS Scotland

- *Library & Information Science Abstracts (LISA),* Bowker-Saur Limited, Maypole House, Maypole Road, East Grinstead, West Sussex, RH19 1HH England

- *Library Literature,* The H.W. Wilson Company, 950 University Avenue, Bronx, NY 10452

- *Newsletter of Library and Information Services,* China Sci-Tech Book Review, Library of Academia Sinica, 8 Kexueyuan Nanlu, Zhongguancun, Beijing 100080, People's Republic of China

- *OT BibSys,* American Occupational Therapy Foundation, P.O. Box 1725, Rockville, MD 20849-1725

- *Referativnyi Zhurnal (Abstracts Journal of the Institute of Scientific Information of the Republic of Russia),* The Institute of Scientific Information, Baltijskaja ul., 14, Moscow A-219, Republic of Russia

- *Sage Public Administration Abstracts (SPAA),* Sage Publications, Inc., 2455 Teller Road, Newbury Park, CA 91320

(continued)

SPECIAL BIBLIOGRAPHIC NOTES

*related to special journal issues (separates)
and indexing/abstracting*

☐ indexing/abstracting services in this list will also cover material in any "separate" that is co-published simultaneously with Haworth's special thematic journal issue or DocuSerial. Indexing/abstracting usually covers material at the article/chapter level.

☐ monographic co-editions are intended for either non-subscribers or libraries which intend to purchase a second copy for their circulating collections.

☐ monographic co-editions are reported to all jobbers/wholesalers/approval plans. The source journal is listed as the "series" to assist the prevention of duplicate purchasing in the same manner utilized for books-in-series.

☐ to facilitate user/access services all indexing/abstracting services are encouraged to utilize the co-indexing entry note indicated at the bottom of the first page of each article/chapter/contribution.

☐ this is intended to assist a library user of any reference tool (whether print, electronic, online, or CD-ROM) to locate the monographic version if the library has purchased this version but not a subscription to the source journal.

☐ individual articles/chapters in any Haworth publication are also available through the Haworth Document Delivery Services (HDDS).

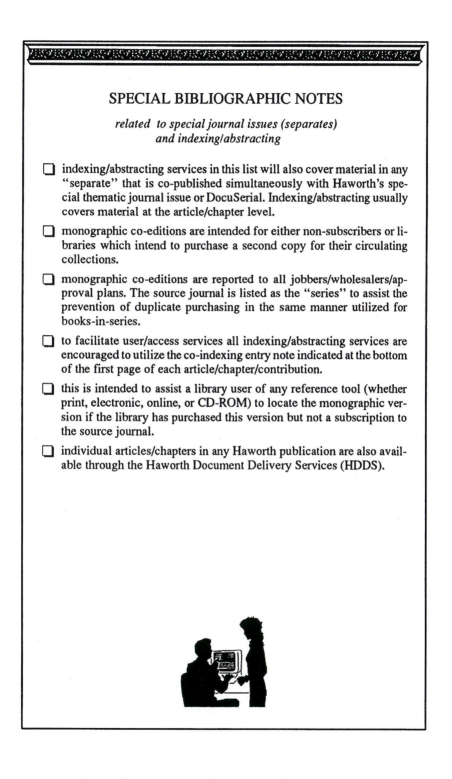

Library Users and Reference Services

CONTENTS

INFORMATION SEEKING PATTERNS: DIVERSE POPULATIONS

MEASURES OF USER SUCCESS

FUTURE

ABOUT THE EDITOR

Jo Bell Whitlatch is History Selector and Reference Librarian at San Jose State University, San Jose, CA. Her subject interests include evaluation of reference services, user studies in libraries and information seeking behaviors. She is the author of *The Role of the Academic Reference Librarian* and has published articles in *RQ*, *College & Research Libraries*, *The Reference Librarian*, and *Journal of Academic Librarianship*. She is Vice-Chair/Chair-Elect of the Management and Operations of Public Services Section of the Reference and Adult Services Division (RASD); she has also served as Chair of the Research & Statistics and Evaluation Committees of RASD.

Introduction

One of the themes of growing importance to society, and thus, to libraries, is the needs of the great variety of diverse groups in our society. Marcia Naurital argues convincingly that traditionally libraries have focused on meeting individual needs and not on targeting services for specific groups within our population. She believes that information available in libraries remains largely unexploited by many groups in our society because of the library's traditional focus on school-related needs or recreational reading and service to individuals. She proposes that libraries redirect a substantial portion of their services from individuals to groups. She also observes that–many attempts at special programs have failed due to underfunding, lack of community involvement, insufficient understanding of the life experience of target clienteles, and a reluctance to structure services to meet collective as well as individual needs.[1]

This volume begins by exploring customer service, economics of information, and marketing as key concepts which are used in studying information needs of specific groups in our population. Jo Whitlatch explores the implications which a strong customer focus will have for reference service practice. Jim Kuhlman develops a model with an emphasis on patron cost. If we adopt his model, we might make some service decisions very differently! For libraries interested in developing services directed at particular clientele groups, Gene Norman's chapter on marketing reference services contains much used information, including an overview of marketing and discussion of important concepts such as integrating strategic planning into marketing efforts and directing promotional efforts at specific groups.

[Haworth co-indexing entry note]: "Introduction." Whitlatch, Jo Bell. Co-published simultaneously in *The Reference Librarian* (The Haworth Press, Inc.) No. 49/50, 1995, pp. 1-4; and: *Library Users and Reference Services* (ed: Jo Bell Whitlatch) The Haworth Press, Inc., 1995, pp. 1-4. Multiple copies of this article/chapter may be purchased from The Haworth Document Delivery Center [1-800-3-HAWORTH; 9:00 a.m. - 5:00 p.m. (EST)].

The next section concerns scholars and students in the three broad academic disciplines: humanities, social sciences, and sciences. In the humanities, Judy Reynolds observes that electronic resources have the potential to dramatically change research habits of humanists; also, librarians have the opportunity to play a significant leadership role in the development of indexing and access to databases in the humanities. After reviewing the information seeking patterns and behaviors of social scientists, Mary Folster discusses the importance of developing specialized journal services for social science researchers, particularly current awareness services and electronic services related to document delivery. To effectively assist scientists in meeting their information needs, Marilyn Von Seggern envisions changes in the role of traditional reference librarians; information professionals will become familiar with the needs of researchers, may spend time in the user's environment, participate in problem solving activities to understand the context of the problem, and in response, offer specialized services such as education, finding and managing useful information, assembling technologies for use in scientific communication, and assisting with specific information problems.

The third section covers groups with special characteristics, such as age, youth, poverty, gender, or profession. Jill Mendle's case study at the University of Alabama will provide valuable information for those interested in developing specials services for persons with disabilities. Mengxiong Liu discusses key elements for effective reference service to multicultural populations, including effective communication, special program development, needs assessments, and training and recruitment. Elfreda Chatman and Victoria Pendleton indicate that both formal and personal sources are lacking practical information of the kind needed by poor people. They suggest that our profession focus on providing information which is perceived as more trustworthy, reliable, and relevant to the situation of the poor.

Connie Van Fleet offers a valuable primer of practical advice for librarians serving older adults. She believes that services to older adults can fit comfortably within our existing services, but that we must provide those services with increased sensitivity, awareness, commitment, and enthusiasm. Virginia Walter reviews the purpose and development of the *Output Measures for Public Library Service for Children*. She discusses the role that proper data collection and therefore, knowledge of the patterns of children's use of public libraries, could play in developing a more proactive approach to children's information needs. She stresses the importance of perceiving children as active consumers of information. Geraldine King looks at a population which actually represents a majority of library users–women–but has been little studied. She notes that in view of the increasing access through online services to practical fee-based information, public libraries also need to research the information needs of the average citizen.

In her review of the role of various types of libraries in meeting business information needs, Helen Josephine stresses the importance of gathering information and analyzing the needs of the business community, surveying perceptions of the business community regarding library services, and developing a strong marketing plan. Lorene Sisson and Donna Pontau assess the influence the traditional teaching paradigm has upon the perceived information needs of educators. With the change in paradigm, they note the exciting and challenging opportunities for librarians to design services in support of teaching in a learner centered environment.

The fourth section, evaluation, is one still too often neglected in our preoccupation with the every day demands of delivering service. Effective evaluation is, however, key to providing successful service to such populations. The primary intent of this section is to provide guidance in use of the most widely accepted measures for assessing reference effectiveness. Three important techniques for assessing whether library services meet client needs are included in this issue: (1) Reference Accuracy by Loriene Roy; (2) User Report of Success by Marjorie Murfin; and (3) Willingness to Return by Joan Durrance.

Finally, lest we forget the role of vision and leadership in planning for the future, Jim Rettig summarizes Faith Popcorn's ten major societal trends and its implications for redesigning future reference services. Now and in the future, information seeking can truly be said to be the other half of library use. Because of the increasing diversity of America's population, librarians striving to plan and deliver excellent reference services must enhance their understanding of the information seeking needs and behaviors of the diverse groups in their communities; librarians must also seek to learn how these groups see reference services as helpful or not helpful in meeting their needs.

Jo Bell Whitlatch

REFERENCE

1. Marcia J. Nauratil, *Public Libraries and Nontraditional Clienteles: The Politics of Special Services* (Westport, CT: Greenwood, 1985), p. 155-166.

SERVICE, ECONOMICS, AND MARKETING

Customer Service: Implications for Reference Practice

Jo Bell Whitlatch

SUMMARY. The past decade has seen an increasing emphasis on customer service in business research and management of companies. Two concepts which are very useful in understanding business customer service practices are the service encounter and Total Quality Management. This article discusses these concepts, highlights customer service research and practices in business, and explores the implications for reference service quality.

INTRODUCTION

Patrons, readers, consumers, customers, clients, and *users*–all librarians can remember staff debates about the most appropriate

Jo Bell Whitlatch is Reference Librarian and History Selector, San Jose State University, San Jose, CA 95192-0028.

[Haworth co-indexing entry note]: "Customer Service: Implications for Reference Practice." Whitlatch, Jo Bell. Co-published simultaneously in *The Reference Librarian* (The Haworth Press, Inc.) No. 49/50, 1995, pp. 5-24; and: *Library Users and Reference Services* (ed: Jo Bell Whitlatch) The Haworth Press, Inc., 1995, pp. 5-24. Multiple copies of this article/chapter may be purchased from The Haworth Document Delivery Center [1-800-3-HAWORTH; 9:00 a.m. - 5:00 p.m. (EST)].

5

term for people who seek material in libraries! The inevitable conclusion of these debates is that no term appears to be entirely satisfactory. As we move into an era where electronic information becomes more dominant, the lack of agreement on terminology for clientele may reflect our uncertain relationships with people we assist.

To many librarians, *patron,* with its origins in wealthy nobility who founded and supported private libraries, and *reader,* which implies users of printed materials but not multimedia, reflect the past. *Patrons* and *readers* were more appropriate when libraries were used exclusively by a highly educated elite and composed almost exclusively of printed materials. The terms, *consumers* and *customers,* lack appeal to many librarians as these terms are seen as appropriate for people who are *purchasing* services or products, whereas information access without fees is an important service principle for many public and academic librarians.

Many librarians may be particularly reluctant to apply the term, *customer,* to our clientele because libraries in the public sector have a particularly complex relationship with their various constituents. Unlike private industry, their services are only indirectly tied to revenues–the public decision makers who have to be convinced of the value of library services are generally not the consumers of the library's services.[1] The consumers may have very little influence over funding of library services. As consumers' demands increase, funding may not follow.

However, the use of the term, *customer,* might imply the establishment of a more positive relationship with citizens. *Customers* are not viewed as passive recipients of uniform services who have very little influence, but rather people actively involved in the process of deciding what would be provided, when, and how.[2] In contrast, *clients* generally have been seen as people in a less involved, less active role, who are heavily dependent upon the professional expertise of the staff.

Customer might be the most appropriate term for future library clientele. In an information age, when information is increasingly viewed as a valuable commodity, libraries may be competing directly with private information services for business. Typical of those with whom libraries may expect to compete in the future is

Ameritech. The Ameritech annual report states, "Customers are at the center of everything we do and at the heart of every decision we make."[3]

In an age where libraries might no longer survive simply because they are an important public good, the profession can learn much from the customer service movement in the business community. Through discussion of service encounter and Total Quality Management concepts, this paper will highlight customer service research and practices in business and explore the implications of these movements for reference services.

THE SERVICE ENCOUNTER

The term, service encounter, is now widely used to describe the moment of interaction between the customer and the service organization. In service encounters both customers and service providers, such as reference librarians, have roles to enact.[4] Unlike manufactured goods, a service product is usually produced with customer involvement. The customer often serves as the co-producer of the final service product. In a library setting, the customer will work with the library staff and the library system to produce a final product which is generally enhancement of knowledge, skills, or enjoyment of leisure activities.

Service encounters are of great interest in the business world because the bottom line is a fundamental belief that service behaviors are ultimately tied to valued outcomes, such as sales and customer satisfaction.[5] Research on customer service encounters can be found in a variety of disciplines, psychology, sociology, communication, and business, particularly in retailing, marketing, and management.

Context

Ford and Etienne discuss the importance of context variables such as busyness, products and services matching customer needs, customers' willingness to spend sufficient time with providers, non-monetary (e.g., effort, convenience) factors in customer decisions, and support received from co-workers.[6] These variables sound both familiar and relevant to reference librarians who interact with customers. Bunge and Murfin have even identified a syndrome of factors generally associated with reference service in libraries reporting lower rates of customer success–some of these factors include context variables summarized by Ford and Etienne.[7]

Behavior

Ford and Etienne also discuss the importance of behaviors in the customer interaction. They classify behaviors used by service providers into three broad categories: (1) courteous service, such as positive emotions, friendliness, immediacy, sociability, attentativeness, touching, or smiling; (2) personalized service directed at determining and meeting the customer's unique needs; and (3) manipulative behaviors relying on deception or control over customer behaviors. Bunge and Murfin, Durrance, and Dyson identify courteous and personalized service behaviors associated with important service outcomes.[8] Ford and Etienne's third category–manipulative behaviors–may on first thought appear more relevant to a sales situation where providers wish to persuade customers to purchase products or services rather than a library situation where service is generally provided without fees. However, all reference librarians can certainly identify interactions where they have worked with customers and persuaded them to change their needs to match what the reference librarian can easily and quickly obtain from the library system. In these instances have we fully informed our customers of the main alternatives that exist beyond the library system? When librarians encourage customers to accept what is readily available in the system, how often do customers feel their needs were met? Examining memorable critical incidents would be useful in exploring instances in which library system constraints rather than customer needs appear to dominate the service interaction.[9]

Customer behaviors and demographics may also influence provider behaviors: research indicates that providers may be influenced by customer gender, dress or status, race and weight, and how demanding, sociable, aggressive or involved customers are in their service encounters. One of the most interesting findings reported is that successful salespersons were those who appeared to be adapting to, and reflecting the sociability of the individual customer; as customers became more aggressive, providers were less likely to perceive their requests as legitimate and less likely to honor their requests.[10] Customers can be beneficial to organizations by recommending the organization to others, replacing materials knocked off shelves and reporting unsafe conditions to employees. Or customer discretionary behaviors can be harmful, such as stealing materials from organizations.[11] Customer discretionary behavior would be an interesting service outcome to employ as well as other measures: customer satisfaction success, finding needed materials, and willingness to return. The impact of customer behavior on reference service has not been systematically explored. Our strongly held philosophical beliefs in equity of reference service to all people (sometimes interpreted as uniform service to all) may make this a difficult area to explore.

TOTAL QUALITY MANAGEMENT

Total Quality Management (TQM) is best viewed as a management philosophy which combines the teachings of W. Edwards Deming and J.M. Juran on statistical process control and group solving processes with Japanese values concerned with quality and continuous improvement. TQM has become increasingly popular in the United States and Europe during the 1980s, most likely as a result of the success of Japanese firms in a number of global markets.[12]

A major underlying impetus for adopting TQM processes in the private sector has been competition and survival. Yet, in the public sector, it is hard to appreciate the notion of competition, because we typically see government entities as being the sole provider of unique services. However, changes in technology have made it possible for private information vendors to compete in significant ways with libraries.[13]

Although there is no universal set of TQM principles, Bowen and Lawler have provided a typical listing: (1) Focus on the Customer; (2) Quality Work the First Time; (3) Strategic Holistic Approach to Improvement; (4) Continuous Improvement as a Way of Life; and (5) Mutual Respect and Teamwork.[14] These broad principles provide a good framework for discussing the TQM movement and its implications for libraries.

Focus on the Customer

In TQM the customer is the ultimate determiner of quality. In other words, customer reactions are regarded as the best measure of quality.[15] An organization puts the customer at the center of its quality strategy; all systems and staff must be organized to serve internal and external customers.[16] In fact, if the organization creates and produces the product or service perfectly according to organizational standards, but it didn't deliver what the customer wanted, it is a failure! One of the most common forms of customer dissatisfaction is the failure of the service/product to provide the expected benefit.[17]

To the customer, value is the benefits received for the burdens endured, such as price, an inconvenient location, unfriendly employees, or an unattractive service facility. Quality service helps an organization maximize benefits and minimize burdens for its customers.[18] Thus, critical to an effective quality process are: (1) thorough identification of customers; (2) their principal service expectations; and (3) a detailed analysis of key work processes that deliver the services.[19]

James Swiss has identified two factors which may make the TQM focus on customers difficult for libraries operating in a public non-profit environment. First, in the public sector the conflict between the program's direct customers (immediate users) and its ultimate customers (general public; taxpayers) can be acute: General taxpayers may prefer to minimize costs while direct customers may expect a level of quality found only at a very high cost.[20]

Second, the focus on customer needs and wants may be less effective in the rapidly changing high technology environment of library reference services. The conventional TQM wisdom that companies should find out what their customers want and use that information to deliver superior quality may work best in situations where customers have stable and well formed preferences. In rapidly changing situations with unstable and uncertain customer preferences, giving customers what they want may not be an effective strategy. Instead, organizations should invest more effort in gaining understanding of various factors influencing actual customer decisions, such as alternatives under consideration, and the manner in which alternatives are evaluated.[21] Understanding how customers make choices in meeting their information needs will assist reference librarians in designing future services of interest to their customers.

Quality Work the First Time

Pursuing quality through TQM requires eliminating or reducing mistakes in the processes organizations use to deliver service.[22] TQM has its roots in statistical control. A key feature is the identification, collection, and use of reliable data for decision making.[23] Data is used as feedback to measure progress towards continuous improvement. The purpose of analyzing data is to identify where variation exits in a process and what causes it. A process "in control" is stable and predictable. Traditional statistical tools for quality improvement are: cause-and-effect diagrams, checklists, Pareto charts, control charts, flow charts, histograms, and scatter diagrams.[24] These TQM tools are useful in displaying data and identifying trends regarding internal library operations. For libraries, the traditional TQM tools may be most useful in analyzing and improving automated reference systems which are an increasingly important component of reference service.

In analyzing the processes involved in the service encounter, traditional TQM statistical tools do not appear to be as useful as other methods. TQM is very much a product of statistical quality control and industrial engineering. Early applications of TQM were for assembly line work and other routine processes. With services, controlling variation and producing services with predictable outcomes is often more difficult.[25] For example, Hebert found that there was a wide range of responses in the way staff dealt with interlibrary loan requests, creating great variability in service which is difficult to control.[26] Customers are also a source of uncontrollable variation which may limit the usefulness of traditional TQM tools. Olzak notes that reference librarians instinctively minimize reference transaction times because customer arrival rates are unpredictable; devoting too much time to one patron shortchanges others and/or shifts the burden of providing reference services to other departmental members.[27]

Services are normally delivering benefits to customers by a system during a process that involves the customer as a co-producer.[28] However, the typical quality program places considerable effort on improving internal processes of the organization. In using TQM statistical process tools, the organization may lose sight of benefits to the customer as the primary goal. The link between customer perceived quality and internal process quality may be weak if quality programs do not start by identifying customer needs and wants–Are we doing the right thing in the eyes of the customer?[29] For example our internal processes may be wonderfully efficient in interlibrary loan, but may not address customer needs.[30]

In analyzing the reference service encounter, traditional TQM tools may only be useful after data has been collected that goes far beyond traditional reference statistics. Aluri fails to provide a customer focus when he suggests using traditional TQM tools to analyze transaction data collected only by reference librarians.[31] Relying solely on staff data tends to focus on information which is often more important to librarians than to customers. A method of data collection which is more focused on customers would be to ask both customers and librarians to identify areas where transactions could be improved; then, as a second step, use traditional TQM tools to analyze the results.

In initial efforts to survey customers, organizations ought to capture all aspects of quality service which customers think are important. Therefore, using exploratory techniques first–open ended interviews, focus groups–is essential. Rating scales are appropriate only as a second step.[32] Berry, Parasuraman and Zeithaml suggest the following methods for building a quality information system: (1) soliciting customer complaints to identify the most common categories of service failure; (2) post transaction surveys–to obtain feedback while the experience is still fresh; (3) customer focus group interviews–to provide a forum for customers to suggest improvements; (4) mystery shopping of service providers–to identify systematic strengths and weaknesses in customer contact service; (5) employee surveys–to identify employee perceived obstacles to improved service; and (5) total market service quality surveys–to identify service improvement priorities.[33]

Once levels of customer perceived quality are known, the information must be used to manage internal processes; if questions asked on a survey do not link back to specific organizational processes being managed, the data collection effort is not worthwhile. For example, an effort that is not useful in managing organizational processes is collecting customer perspectives on "How friendly are library personnel?" The results cannot be linked to any library process and will not be helpful. No one will take ownership of the results. Who should become more friendly? Is it the reference librarians? Student shelvers? Staff at the directions desk? Circulation desk? Or all of the above?

Burns suggests four steps necessary for researching customer service: (1) Find out what the customer wants; (2) Help set performance indicators; (3) Monitor performance in relationship to those indicators; and (4) Provide information that will help implement change.[34] Pulse provides an exceptionally detailed list on setting up a customer focus program which includes five stages: (1) Survey current internal and external customer perceptions through carefully worded questionnaires, carefully structured interviews and focus groups; (2) Set standards in both technical and behavioral terms (e.g., 90% accuracy; ask–did you find what you needed?); (3) Provide prolonged and consistent training and development (e.g., peer coaching); (4) Oversee putting program into practice permanently with goals to incremental improve; and (5) Consolidate by listening and responding to customers' views.[35]

Benchmarking has become identified as a key process used in TQM efforts. Benchmarking establishes an external standard to which organizational operations can be compared. Benchmarking focuses on the means as much as it does the projected end state.[36] To successfully apply TQM methods to the reference process libraries will have to develop data useful in benchmarking, that is, the search for the profession's best practices that lead to superior performance.[37] The first step in benchmarking is identifying process factors useful in validating customer requirements. Benchmarking requires data that are relevant and reliable. As Shaughnessy notes, for libraries, the problem of data collection itself is an enormous challenge. Libraries have never had good information–statistics are largely based on input (e.g., volumes added to the reference collection) or output measures that are simple transaction counts (e.g. number of reference questions answered).

Although developing data on a nationwide scale may be challenging, at least two instruments–SERVQUAL and RTAI–already provide opportunities for the collection of reference process factors. Parasuraman, Zeithaml and Berry have devised an instrument, SERVQUAL, to measure service quality from the customer perspective.[38] They suggest that service quality from the customer perspective can be defined as the judgment that results when the performance of an actual service is compared to expectations of how such a service should perform. SERVQUAL is a multiple 22 item scale which measures expectations and perceptions of service quality. Quality is measured by comparing the difference between ratings assigned to the 22 paired expectations/perceptions statements. The SERVQUAL in its present form, is intended to ascertain customers' global perceptions of an organizations's service quality.

In analyzing findings from SERVQUAL which has been used largely in for profit organizations, Berry, Parasuraman and Zeithaml have concluded that the most important dimensions on which customers judge quality are: (1) reliability–the ability to perform the desired service dependably, accurately, and consistently; (2) responsiveness–the willingness to provide prompt service and help customers; (3) assurance–employees' knowledge, courtesy, and ability to convey trust and confidence; (4) empathy–the provision of caring, individualized attention to customers; and (5) tangibles–the physical facilities, equipment, and appearance of personnel.[39]

Hebert evaluated the service quality of interlibrary loan by utilizing SERVQUAL as the customer evaluation of service and comparing the results with an objective efficiency measure set by library staff.[40] She found a lack of congruence between library and customer measures of interlibrary loan performance. Her results suggest that internal library measures of success should not be substituted for customer evaluation. She concluded that a major deficiency in current measures such as fill rate, which measures the proportion of actual requests that are met, is that it does not measure the extent to which customers' needs are met. A major challenge for libraries and other organizations is to invent appropriate internal measures and rewards that correspond strongly to external customer measures.[41]

Hebert found that the same dimensions which were important in for profit industries were important to interlibrary loan customers: The single most important customer dimension of service, reliability, had the most negative performance score. Likewise responsiveness, which ranked as the second highest dimension for measuring quality, ranked second lowest in performance. The greatest gaps between customer expectations and perceptions of actual service were in staff trying to understand customer needs and the library getting the right book the first time.[42]

Although SERVQUAL is the most widely used method of measuring service quality, the five underlying dimensions vary across service industries.[43] In his study of public sector organizations, Myers identified an additional dimension of service quality–equity, defined by customers as "treating customers as equals, providing service fairly and impartially to all customers."[44] Browne and Edwards contrast SERVQUAL with the Reference Satisfaction measure[45] and call for more exploration of which dimensions are the most important features to consider when customers are making judgments about information services.[46] Despite these limitations, SERVQUAL can be used to obtain useful customer perspectives on the reference process, following the methods employed by Hebert for interlibrary loan.[47]

While SERVQUAL is designed to measure global perceptions of service quality, the Reference Transaction Assessment Instrument (RTAI) can be used to measure service quality at the level of the individual reference transaction. The RTAI, also known as the Wisconsin-Ohio Reference Evaluation Program, allows each library to compare its survey results with those of libraries of similar size and type for average and top scoring libraries. Process factors, such as busyness and time spent can be correlated with patron success. Patron success is defined as finding exactly what was wanted and being completely satisfied. Because the RTAI is valid and reliable and provides comparable data which can be used to identify libraries with high customer success, for reference services the RTAI can be regarded as valuable in establishing external data for benchmarking, a key process in TQM. Janet Brown used the RTAI, a reference area problem log and a suggestion box to collect customer perceptions on service quality.[48] Her report provides excellent detail on how the RTAI can be used as part of a program to assess the quality of reference service.

Measures which focus both on process and outcomes can provide data necessary to improve the reference process and, by improving the process, provide quality reference assistance more frequently, the first time a customer interacts with the library system.

Strategic Holistic Approach to Improvement

TQM is an organizational strategy that drives an ongoing continuous process, one that requires radical changes in organizational design and day-to-day operations. TQM requires a systems orientation with a view of the whole that includes horizontal relationships between processes.[49] TQM organizations require flat structured designs so that everyone can be close to the customers, constantly gathering information about customers' current and future needs.

A strength of TQM is that it is designed to promote improvement as part of a comprehensive systems approach. In contrast, Library efforts have often been piecemeal and not tied to assessment of customer needs. Few libraries regularly survey their customers, and of those that do, a majority fail to initiate action in response to survey results.[50]

In improving reference service, TQM will require a system approach and evaluation of the process as part of the library system. The reference process is part of a broader system, including the physical environment, communication, reference sources, reference librarians, totality of demands on reference librarians' time, library technology, technical services, staffing resources, management's expectations, parent institution's management policies and practices, and conflicting philosophies and practices of reference services.[51] Any product or service has four distinct aspects: a physical product, the service product, the service environment, and the service delivery.[52] In reference service, the physical product is generally the tangible information, or recorded knowledge provided; the service product is staff skills and knowledge applied to the query; the service environment is the reference desk, reference automated systems, printed reference sources; the service delivery is the inter-action of librarian with the customer. Customer perspectives on each of these aspects must be sought to obtain the TQM holistic view.

Continuous Improvement as a Way of Life

A set of standards should be established for all services. Once the organization has reached these minimal standards, the goal should be continuous improvement. In contrast to goal setting, which mea-sures the degree to which goals are met and creates after the fact measurement, in TQM measurement of improvement is a continual process; the aim is to provide continual feedback which can be used to measure progress toward improving a process.[53] In the process of continuous improvement, technology can be an enormous advan-tage for doing things faster and with fewer errors. At Ford, the process of continuous improvement has been institutionalized by routinely surveying customers and talking to them in focus groups. Ford checks with their customers regularly regarding their likes and dislikes, problems and complaints, and how other organizations are serving them better.[54]

Ewell notes the similarities between assessment of instruction and TQM; the most effective assessment techniques provide feed-back about process effectiveness and can be used to correct detected deficiencies before the process is over.[55] He discusses the "minute paper" which is administered to students at the end of every class period. The most common version asks two questions: (1) What is the most important thing you learned today? and (2) What is the single thing that after today is still most unclear to you? The minute paper promotes continuous customer (student) feedback which can be used by the instructor in preparing the next class. A similar practice can be promoted in the reference process to obtain feed-back; two verbal questions might be: (1) Did you find what you needed today? (2) After you have an opportunity to look at the information, will you let me know if you need anything else?

Mutual Respect and Teamwork

Quality improvement requires strong worker participation and total organizational commitment. In TQM training of staff is not a fringe benefit: the continuous staff training requirements associated with TQM are great. Managers should focus on developing skills and abilities necessary to support collective responsibility.[56] Team members will need training in customer satisfaction feedback systems, including skills in developing questionnaires, focus group techniques, mail surveys, listening, and conducting surveys.[57] Training must reach far beyond specific job skills, cover problem solving technologies, problem analysis, statistical process control and quality measurement. International analysis of training costs show that United States corporations spend less on training than do their Japanese and European counterparts.[58] And libraries spend very little of their budget on staff training.

Training does not appear to be a high priority for library organizations. In a recent survey, the recruitment and hiring of qualified personnel topped the list of priorities. Viewed as less important were the issues of compensation, training, and retention.[59] In a view representative of many library managers, Stephen Zink suggests that the responsibility for acquiring knowledge of information technology is largely a personal one: part of the responsibility for being a professional is to keep current in one's field. He notes that library schools need to make a more concerted effort to provide continuing education for librarians already in the field. Although he observes that administrators must lead by example, he does not suggest that the library organization should have a major fiscal responsibility for continuous training and education of staff.[60]

Staff empowerment throughout the service process is viewed as an important method of improving service quality. Staff empowerment involves letting people use their judgment more.[61] The TQM premise is that reference quality can be best monitored and improved by the people who are most intimately involved in and affected by the process working together as a team.[62]

Establishing trust is also important and for this reason Peterson and Hillkirk believe "mystery shoppers" should be avoided because the practice fosters fear and distrust in employees.[63] TQM promotes trust in employees through a fundamental premise that the operational processes of an organization are more often to blame for low quality service than the workers.[64] Some library managers place blame for reference failures on the librarians rather than the system processes.[65] Use of mystery shoppers or other unobtrusive customers in evaluating reference services may promote distrust and fear, particularly if managers have access to information on the performance of individual reference staff.

Teamwork is important in implementing TQM. Reference librarians should spend time in cataloging as well as catalogers spending time at the reference desk. This will reduce barriers to effective teamwork, such as competition, lack of communication, and different priorities.[66]

IMPLICATIONS FOR REFERENCE PRACTICE

In 1994 American Library Association President Hardy Franklin said, "Service is the heart of our profession . . . Our customers–whether they be students, faculty, or members of the general public–are why libraries exist . . . We must market our services in a way that assures our libraries are addressing real needs and that our customers–current and potential–are aware of the benefits available to them."[67]

Will reference services truly place customer perspectives at the heart of our services? Ameritech not only developed a strategy putting customers at the center but went directly to customer groups and asked how they could best address their needs. Ameritech interviews confirmed that, more than ever before, different categories of customers have different requirements–not only in the products and services they want, but in the way they want to do business.[68] In a similar manner, when planning reference services for special populations, libraries will benefit from interviewing different customer groups on a regular basis. Information from research on the service encounter and Total Quality Management will also assist the profession in the development of reference services more strongly focused on customer perspectives and designed to meet the needs of different groups in our population.

Many librarians are reviewing traditional desk arrangements and exploring different methods of providing assistance which might increase the quality of reference service. Context variables such as busyness, services matching customer needs, customer time and effort, and convenience requirements and their links with customer reports of success must be included in evaluations of innovations in reference assistance.

Provider behaviors clearly play an important role in the quality of service. Behaviors related to courtesy and the constellation of behaviors which recognize the importance of the customer's individual query are associated with successful reference service. Using research findings and professional expertise, the Reference and Adult Services Division has developed *Behavioral Guidelines for Reference and Information Services*. These *Guidelines* should be thoroughly tested by exploring the associations between each behavior and customer judgments of quality, including Durrance's measure of willingness to return, and the success measures used by Murfin, Bunge and Gugelchuk.[69] Some of these behaviors will probably be much more significantly linked to customer judgments of satisfaction, success, and willingness to return than others. The most important behaviors could then be the focus of library training programs for all reference employees and included in core courses in library education programs.

The principles of the Total Quality Management movement provide us with insights useful in thinking about quality reference service. The TQM focus on customer service can be a strong challenge to organizations where there is a heritage of the customer having no alternative source of supply, a culture of professional experience and always knowing best, and being always relatively well thought of by the public and thus believing all is well.[70] TQM is not a comfortable fit with the traditional methods of providing reference assistance in libraries. Devising alternative patterns of reference service with a focus on the customer, quality work the first time, a strategic view of the whole library system, continuous improvement, and in an atmosphere of mutual respect and teamwork will be very challenging. But use of TQM concepts has the potential to reap rich rewards for the profession and truly improve the quality of service in the eyes of our customers.

REFERENCES

1. Nancy A. Van House and Thomas A. Childers, "The Use of Public Library Roles for Effectiveness Evaluation," *Library & Information Science Research* 16 (1994): 41-58.

2. J. Stewart and M. Clarke, "The Public Service Orientation: Issues and Dilemmas," *Public Administration* 65 (Summer 1987): 161-177.

3. Ameritech Corporation. *Annual Report* (Chicago, IL: Ameritech, 1993).

4. Mary Jo Bitner, Bernard H. Booms, and Mary Stanfield Tetreault, "The Service Encounter: Diagnosing Favorable and Unfavorable Incidents," *Journal of Marketing* 54 (January 1990): 71-84.

5. Wendy S. Zabara Ford and Christina Nathan Etienne, "Can I Help You? A Framework for Interdisciplinary Customer Service Encounters," *Management Communications Quarterly* 7 (May 1994): 413-441.

6. Ford and Etienne, "Can I Help You?" 413-441.

7. Charles A. Bunge and Marjorie E. Murfin, "Reference Questions–Data from the Field," *RQ* 27 (1987): 15-18.

Factors associated with less successful reference service are: significantly more directing rather than actually helping users with searches, significantly more transactions of two minutes or less, significantly more one-source transactions, significantly more reports from users that they did not receive enough time or help, significantly more communication difficulties with librarians reported by users, and significantly less agreement on patron success by librarians and users.

8. Bunge and Murfin, "Reference Questions," 15-18; Joan C. Durrance, "Factors That Influence Reference Success: What Makes Questioners Willing to Return?" *The Reference Librarian* (published in this volume); Lillie Seward Dyson, "Improving Reference Services: A Maryland Training Program Brings Positive Results," *Public Libraries* (September/October 1992): 284-289.

Finds that the six most important behaviors in providing correct answers (this is an objective measure not a customer success measure) are: (1) verifying specific questions (paraphrase to be certain of the customer's precise question); (2) asking follow-up questions (e.g., does this completely answer your question); (3) using open probes; (4) finding the answer in the first source; (5) clarifying the customer's words to ensure understanding; and (6) giving the customer full attention.

9. Bitner, Booms, and Tetreault, "The Service Encounter," 71-84. An incident should meet four criteria: (1) involving a customer-provider interaction; (2) very satisfying or dissatisfying from the customer's point of view; (3) being a discrete episode; and (4) having sufficient detail to be visualized by the interviewer.

10. Ford and Etienne, "Can I Help You?" 413-441.

11. Ford and Etienne, "Can I Help You?" 413-441.

12. Edward E. Lawler III, "Total Quality Management and Employee Involvement: Are They Compatible?" *Academy of Management Executive* 8 (1994): 68-76.

13. Tim Loney and Arnie Bellefontaine, "TQM Training: The Library Service Challenge," *Journal of Library Administration* 18 (1993): 85-95.

14. David E. Bowen and Edward E. Lawler III, "Total Quality-Oriented Human Resources Management," *Organizational Dynamics* 20 (Spring 1992): 29-41.

15. Lawler, "Total Quality Management and Employee Involvement," 68-76.

22   LIBRARY USERS AND REFERENCE SERVICES

16. Richard M. Hodgetts, Fred Luthans, and Sang M. Lee, "New Paradigm Organizations: From Total Quality to Learning World Class," *Organizational Dynamics* 22 (Winter 1994): 5-19.

17. Clay Carr, "Total Quality Training," *Training* 27 (November 1990): 59-65.

18. Leonard L. Berry, A. Parasuraman, and Valerie A. Zeithaml, "Improving Service Quality in America: Lessons Learned," *Academy of Management Executive* 8 (1994): 32-52.

19. Loney and Bellefontaine, "TQM Training," 85-95.

20. James E. Swiss, "Adapting Total Quality Management (TQM) to Government," *Public Administration Review* 52 (July/August 1992): 356-362.

21. Swiss, "Adapting Total Quality Management (TQM) to Government," 356-362.

22. G. Gregory Lozier and Deborah J. Teeter, "Six Foundations of Total Quality Management," *New Directions for Institutional Research* 78 (Summer 1993): 5-11.

23. Thomas W. Shaughnessy, "Benchmarking, Total Quality Management, and Libraries," *Library Administration & Management* 7 (Winter 1993): 7-12.

24. Lozier and Teeter, "Six Foundations of Total Quality Management," 5-11.

25. Swiss, "Adapting Total Quality Management (TQM) to Government," 356-362.

26. Francoise Hebert, "Service Quality: An Unobtrusive Investigation of Interlibrary Loan in Large Public Libraries in Canada," *Library & Information Studies Research* 16 (1994): 3-21.

27. Lydia Olzak, "Mistakes and Failures at the Reference Desk," *RQ* 31 (Fall 1991): 39-49.

28. Jan Mattson, "Improving Service Quality in Person-to-Person Encounters: Integrating Findings from a Multi-disciplinary Review," *The Services Industries Journal* 14 (January 1994): 45-61.

29. Raymond E. Kordupleski, Roland T. Rust, and Anthony J. Zahorik, "Why Improving Quality Doesn't Improve Quality or Whatever Happened to Marketing?" *California Management Review 35* (Spring 1993): 82-95

30. Hebert, "Service Quality," 3-21.

31. Rao Aluri, "Improving Reference Service: The Case for Using a Continuous Quality Improvement Method," *RQ* 33 (Winter 1993): 220-236.

32. Kordupleski, Rust, and Zahorik, "Why Improving Quality Doesn't Improve Quality," 82-95.

33. Berry, Parasuraman, and Zeithaml, "Improving Service Quality in America," 32-52.

34. Tim Burns, "Researching Customer Service in the Public Sector," *Journal of the Market Research Society* 34 (1992): 53-60.

35. John Pulse, "Customer Focus: The Salvation of Service Organizations," *Public Library Journal* 6 (1991): 1-5.

36. Susan Jurow, "Tools for Measuring and Improving Performance," *Journal of Library Administration* 18 (1993): 113-126.

37. Shaughnessy, "Benchmarking, Total Quality Management, and Libraries," 7-12.

38. A. Parasuraman, Valerie A. Zeithaml, and Leonard L. Berry, "Reassessment of Expectations as a Comparison Standard in Measuring Service Quality: Implications for Further Research," *Journal of Marketing* 58 (January 1994): 111-124.

39. Leonard L Berry, A. Parasuraman, and Valerie A Zeithaml, "The Service Quality Puzzle," *Business Horizons* (September-October 1988): 35-43.

40. Hebert, "Service Quality," 3-21.

41. Kordupleski, Rust, and Zahorik, "Why Improving Quality Doesn't Improve Quality," 82-95.

42. Hebert, "Service Quality," 3-21.

43. Mattson, "Improving Service Quality in Person-to-Person Encounters," 45-61; J. Joseph Cronin, Jr. and Steven A. Taylor, "SERVPERF Versus SERVQUAL: Reconciling Performance-Based and Perceptions-Minus-Expectations Measurement of Service Quality," *Journal of Marketing* 58 (January 1994): 125-131.

44. Thomas A. Myers, *An Analysis of Perceived Customer Contact Service Quality in the Public Sector* (D.P.A. dissertation, Virginia Commonwealth University, School of Community and Public Affairs, 1990).

45. Nancy A. Van House, Beth T. Weil, and Charles R. McClure, *Academic Library Performance: A Practical Approach* (Chicago: American Library Association, 1990).
The Reference Satisfaction measures ask the customer to evaluate the following aspects: relevance of information, appropriateness of amount of information provided, completeness of information provided, helpfulness of staff, and overall feeling of satisfaction.

46. Mairead Browne and Susan Edwards, "How Users Assess the Quality of an Information Service," in Peter Clayton and Russell McCaskie, eds., *Priorities for the Future* (Deakin, Australia: Australian Library and Information Association, 1992).

47. Hebert, "Service Quality," 3-21.

48. Janet Dagnenais Brown, "Using Quality Concepts to Improve Reference Services," *College & Research Libraries* (May 1994): 211-219.

49. Bowen and Lawler, "Total Quality-Oriented Human Resources Management," 29-41.

50. Loney and Bellefontaine, "TQM Training," 85-95.

51. Aluri, "Improving Reference Service," 220-236.

52. Kordupleski, Rust, and Zahorik, "Why Improving Quality Doesn't Improve Quality," 82-95.

53. Jurow, "Tools for Measuring and Improving Performance," 113-126.

54. Donald E. Peterson and John Hillkirk, *A Better Idea: Refining the Way Americans Work* (Boston: Houghton Mifflin, 1991).

55. Peter T. Ewell, "Assessment and TQM: In Search of Convergence," *New Directions for Institutional Research* 71 (Fall 1991): 39-52.

56. Bowen and Lawler, "Total Quality-Oriented Human Resources Management," 29-41.

57. Loney and Bellefontaine, "TQM Training," 85-95.

58. Bowen and Lawler, "Total Quality-Oriented Human Resources Management," 29-41.

59. "Staffing–The Number One Personnel Issue for Libraries," *Library Personnel News* (Spring 1990): 18.

60. Stephen D. Zink, "Will Librarians Have a Place in the Information Society?" *Reference Services Review* (Spring 1991): 76-77.

61. Peterson and Hillkirk, *A Better Idea.*

62. Aluri, "Improving Reference Service," 220-236.

63. Peterson and Hillkirk, *A Better Idea.*

64. Jurow, "Tools for Measuring and Improving Performance," 113-126.

65. Aluri, "Improving Reference Service," 220-236.

66. Terry Mackey and Kitty Mackey, "Think Quality: The Deming Approach Does Work in Libraries," *Library Journal* 117 (May 15, 1992): 57-61.

67. Hardy R. Franklin, "Customer Service: The Heart of a Library," *College & Research Libraries News* 55 (February 1994): 63.

68. Ameritech Corporation. *Annual Report.*

69. Marjorie E. Murfin and Gary Gugelchuk, "Development and Testing of a Reference Transaction Assessment Instrument," *College & Research Libraries* 48 (July 1987): 314-338; Durrance, "Factors That Influence Reference Success."

70. Pulse, "Customer Focus," 1-5.

On the Economics of Reference Service: Toward a Heuristic Model for an Uncertain World

James R. Kuhlman

SUMMARY. A draft, econometric model of reference service suggested as a stimulus to discussion, for revision, and, undoubtedly, for improvement. This greatly simplified representation of a complex system is offered as a heuristic, conceptual aid. Concludes with an illustratative application of the model emphasizing the consideration of patron cost.

Reference service seems an inevitable part of libraries. Inseparable. Inherent. It was there when we visited our first public library. It accompanied our struggles through college. It was part and parcel of our days in library school. As for many an "institution," familiarity may have led the library profession to take it for granted, assume its benefits, and unquestioningly accept its costs. For some practitioners of the reference art, interest in the "dismal science" of economics and reference service intersect only at the point of arguments for increases to the reference budget. But, of course, this isn't the whole story. It's not even accurate as far as it goes.

James R. Kuhlman is Associate Dean of Libraries for Collections and Information Services, The University of Alabama.

[Haworth co-indexing entry note]: "On the Economics of Reference Service: Toward a Heuristic Model for an Uncertain World." Kuhlman, James R. Co-published simultaneously in *The Reference Librarian* (The Haworth Press, Inc.) No. 49/50, 1995, pp. 25-43; and: *Library Users and Reference Services* (ed: Jo Bell Whitlatch) The Haworth Press, Inc., 1995, pp. 25-43. Multiple copies of this article/chapter may be purchased from The Haworth Document Delivery Center [1-800-3-HAWORTH; 9:00 a.m. - 5:00 p.m. (EST)].

WHY AN ECONOMICS OF REFERENCE SERVICE?

Libraries have always been, and remain, extremely expensive. This may seem counter-intuitive to readers fresh from repairs to dilapidated equipment, expert at conjuring a few dollars to purchase just one more book, bloody from slashing serials subscriptions, or lusting hopelessly after the newest computer or communications technology. From the inside our libraries and media centers seem anything but "high priced," especially in view of the benefits we provide. But, from the perspective of our parent institutions and taxpayers we appear decidedly "high-maintenance." For example, in fiscal year 1992-93 alone it cost just under $8 million to operate ONE of the nation's smallest, least opulent research libraries (The University of Alabama).[1] In 1991, the total operating income of public libraries in the United States was $4,654,000,000.[2] And in academic year 1984-85, operating expenditures for U.S. public school libraries and media centers totaled $1,182,280,000.[3] And to make matters worse, the quantity of information proliferates even as the lure of costly, new media combines with inflationary pressures to push each of our libraries further behind.

Each of us is all too well aware that resources have failed to keep pace. Communities find it more and more difficult to support public libraries adequately in the face of competing, often critical needs. The boom years enjoyed by academic and research libraries are of the past–a temporary anomaly not expected to recur.[4] With needs expanding and becoming more expensive while increases in resources stall, libraries of all types and in all regions face a gravely challenging future. Warren Haas has observed that " . . . coping with growth has, in a very few years, been replaced by a need to make fundamental changes in the very definition of what a library is and to recast operations and services in a dramatically different mold . . . under real economic restraints."[5]

From Washington to Main Street tax-payers and consumers continue to demand greater accountability from public agencies and, especially, education. Legislatures and governing boards must respond. In recent years, regional accrediting agencies have adopted new standards requiring colleges and universities to assess and evaluate programs to verify achievement of educational outcomes.[6] As long ago as 1979 Drake and Olsen recognized for academic libraries that:

> Changing economic conditions and pressure for greater pro-
> ductivity from the public sector will be the major factors stim-
> ulating innovation in libraries. It is clear that institutions of
> higher education can no longer afford traditional libraries and
> comprehensive collections. Increasing wage rates and changes
> in consumer demand will force reallocation of library resources
> to provide funds for capital investment, more efficient opera-
> tions and more responsive services.[7]

Somewhat more recently, Cummings extended this theme with the warning that "Tolerance for the view that libraries are intrinsically valuable is changing as a result of financial constraints . . . ," and that " . . . the need to justify the high costs of libraries requires that some effort be made to measure costs, benefits, and cost-effective-ness of various important functions."[8]

Reference services, although their costs are frequently buried in library-wide aggregates for personnel, materials acquisitions, etc., are very "high-maintenance." In a 1983 report on the application of econometric models to the costs associated with units within col-lege and university libraries, Kantor found that the median cost of a " . . . reference query dealt with . . ." was $14.00, and that reference functions consumed 20 percent of total budgets.[9] Simplistically and, no doubt inaccurately, applying that percentage to the 1992-93 expenditures of the small research library alluded to above indicates that reference services cost some $1,600,000.

To the extent that Cummings is correct in concluding that our several constituencies no longer find libraries "intrinsically valu-able" and that expense must be justified by benefits, reference librarians will be well-served by familiarity with the tools of the economist. As Kantor suggests, reference service is expensive and represents a substantial portion of libraries' expenditures. At the same time, the effectiveness of that service appears less than self-evident. After surveying evaluations of reference services covering the period 1967-91 (n = 17), Lancaster observed at least one com-monality:

... they show that the user of a library faces a surprisingly low probability that his factual question will be answered correctly. Overall, the studies tend to support a probability in the range of 50 to 60% ... [10]

TWO FUNDAMENTAL CONCEPTS

Other sources provide clearer, more authoritative introductions to the economist's artistry than this author should attempt.[11] But, a shared understanding of two fundamental principles is necessary to our discussion.

Library budgets, at least in any given fiscal year, can be thought of as modified "zero-sum games," exchanges where " ... the sum of the winnings is always zero, with one player winning what the other loses."[12] If we think of the various library activities, units, or functions as "players," then the library's budget becomes a "game" with "winning" and "losing" measured in dollars. Assuming no overall budget increase (an all too familiar situation), if support of reference service is to increase, then the portion of the budget, and the real dollars, going to one, several, or all other areas and functions must decrease by an equal amount. A "zero-sum game."

An additional reference librarian will result in that amount of salary and benefits not being available to pay for a cataloger, student assistants, travel expenses, books, or serials. A subscription to a new machine-readable index will result in the funds equalling the cost of that subscription (i.e., license fee, equipment, maintenance) not being available to pay for subscriptions to periodicals indexed by the new index and not available for on-demand purchase of individual articles from a commercial vendor, or any other purpose.

Even if the budget increases, "zero-sum" logic applies. With enough budget increase, the addition of a reference librarian or index subscription will not require an actual decrease in funds for other areas in the library. Nevertheless, any increase (proportion of the budget) that reference receives denies other areas or functions that specific potential increase, thus diminishing the potential for increased output in those areas.

Another important and useful concept, closely related to the "zero-sum game," is "opportunity cost"–"What one has to give up or forego in order to do something else."[13] This formulation can be applied very usefully to the "zero-sum" library budget illustration above, but will prove absolutely critical to incorporating library patrons into our heuristic, economic model of reference service. And critical, perhaps, to the survival of reference services scrutinized by unforgiving cost-benefit analyses.

To illustrate, a student preparing a research paper confronts a variety of choices. One involves the library, collecting information, and the allocation, or expenditure, of time. The student knows that she must have information to support her thesis, and recognizes that the quality and quantity of that information will materially affect her desired outcome–a high grade as well as a quality paper. Among other factors, the student also recognizes that the time spent in sorting relevant information once collected, thinking, organizing, careful writing, editing, and attention to the physical presentation will also influence her grade.

In this example, time is the medium of exchange. Our student has a finite supply. She knows that time spent searching for and recording information in the library cannot also be used for the other activities needed to produce her paper. Nor can she use it for the other essential, or non-essential but valuable, activities in her life. She must decide how to allocate her time. At the point she determines that time spent on the thinking-writing-production component of her task has become more valuable than time spent on the information collection component, she will redirect her activities in order to "maximize her welfare."

Opportunity cost will also determine our student's choice of research methodology and sources. Braunstein suggests that "The cost to the user depends on the value of his time (the opportunity cost), the convenience and efficiency of the library, and his efficiency in using the library's collection or in making his needs known to the librarian."[14] Even if she knows that searching *Psychological Abstracts* will lead to more sophisticated research and more complete coverage of her topic our student will consider how much more time and effort that search will consume, the likely benefit of that search, and then compare her estimates (if only intuitively) to the cost and likely benefit of a quicker, easier, if admittedly less elegant, search in *Social Sciences Index* or *Expanded Academic Index.*

COST-EFFICIENCY AND COST-BENEFIT ANALYSES

In view of the high cost of reference services, the zero-sum nature of library budgets, consumer choice, and the growing demand for accountability in the expenditure of public funds, Braunstein has argued that " . . . it is important to examine the costs and benefits associated with each of the feasible alternatives so that one might understand how choices are made."[15] This brings us to two of the policy analyst's and economist's favorite tools: cost-efficiency analysis and cost-benefit analysis.[16]

Cost-efficiency studies seek to determine the least costly (i.e., most efficient) method of achieving a desired outcome, or to determine which of two or more organizations achieve an acceptable outcome at the least cost. In reference services, such analyses might be applied to determine the most efficient means of answering reference questions. They may address the level of personnel used to answer questions or the methodology, for example manually searching an index as compared to the costs, speed, and results of a computerized search.[17] Reports on studies of this type appear in the literature with considerable frequency and can be very useful in problem solving.[18]

While cost-efficiency studies employ relatively straightforward methodology and are far more feasible than cost-benefit studies, they still pose significant obstacles. For example, what exactly are the costs involved in answering a reference question? They clearly include the wages of the librarian or staff member, but are those wages only for the time during which the question is addressed? What about the "dead" time between questions? Shouldn't that be charged as a "cost" in answering questions? But, then how do we account for the reference librarian awaiting questions at the desk at the same time she is also doing general book selection, preparing a book talk for the branch's Wednesday reading group, or writing an article for publication? Surely these activities should not be charged as part of the cost of answering the next reference question. And then there are all those books, periodical indexes, CD-ROMs. How much of the cost of an encyclopedia should be charged to "answering reference questions?" The librarian will certainly use it to provide a direct answer. But, patrons would also use the same encyclopedia independently and quite satisfactorily without the assistance of a librarian.

It is readily apparent that the previous paragraph isn't going anywhere. The next part of that argument probably has something to do with the number of angels that can dance on the head of a pin. That is, in fact, the point. Determining exactly what costs to attribute to which function is extremely complex and almost always arguable. That choice, and how those costs are calculated, will radically affect the outcome of the study. Murfin provides a thorough review of this issue and offers valuable insights into "The most accurate, fair and sensible method of arriving at unit costs for the reference question. . . ."[19]

Even when costs are calculated consistently in comparing processes or institutions, it is difficult to draw conclusions from research conducted in libraries other than one's own–generalizations are limited. Cummings notes that in his study of college libraries for the Council on Library Resources, Kantor found considerable variation in costs associated with monographs acquisitions.

> Selection costs ranged from less than $1.00 per item considered to $4.00. Search costs were as low as $0.25 per item and as high as $3.50. Ordering costs ranged from below $1.00 to more than $5.00 per item.[20]

With only a single investigator, it is very likely that Kantor's methodology remained consistent across the various libraries even if one might want to argue with how he assigned costs. Observing such variability in the findings, it is difficult to conclude what might be appropriate selection, search, and ordering costs. In his efficiency analysis of answering reference questions using paper sources vs. on-line, Anderson gave voice to the frequent frustration encountered by readers of cost-efficiency studies:

> Accurate dollar values in this area are extremely difficult to obtain. Surveying the literature leads one to conclude that the

only way to be certain of your own processing and storage costs is to do your own study–a time-consuming and expensive technique.[21]

If cost-efficiency studies, relatively abundant in the literature, leave methodological doubts and often lack generalizability, then cost-benefit studies prove even more problematic. Cost-effeciency studies at least assume the desirability of the outcomes. To investigate whether searching for the answer to a reference question electronically is more cost-efficient than consulting paper sources implicitly accepts that the outcome, finding the answer to the reference question, is "worth it." It is only the method which is at issue.

Cost-benefit analysis, on the other hand, attempts to determine whether the outcome of the process is, in fact, worth the cost. A researcher's determination that it is more cost-effective to answer reference questions using electronic tools rather than paper equivalents (e.g., $12 per question electronically vs. $14 per question using paper tools) should lead to greater use of the electronic media. On the other hand, a finding that the "value" to patrons of a correctly answered reference question is only $10, might, rationally, cause the organization to consider reallocating resources now spent answering reference questions in order to better serve patrons. Recall both opportunity cost and the zero-sum nature of library budgets.

The cost-benefit approach to the evaluation of library services is a logical response to the demands of accrediting bodies that colleges and universities assess outcomes of the educational process. It could also prove an effective tool in responding to citizen calls for greater accountability in the expenditure of government funds. Unfortunately, all the issues making the results of cost-efficiency studies ambivalent and expensive work their same, inhibiting magic on cost-benefit studies.

In addition, cost-benefit analysis is made even more daunting by the extreme difficulty of accurately identifying and valuating the benefit derived from library services. That public, school, special, and academic libraries are beneficial individually and collectively to society seems, at the very least, self-evident. At least to us. We can certainly name and describe some of the benefits. But, can we define them with enough specificity and concreteness to measure them? Can we approximate the benefit a patron derives from correct answers to reference questions? How might we measure the benefit of reference service? If it is difficult to accurately and consistently ascribe the cost of library services to its various components, how much more difficult must it be to define the benefits? Lancaster recently offered one answer in commenting that "Cost-benefit analyses are very difficult to perform in the information service environment and perhaps no study of this kind has ever been fully credible."[22]

We seem trapped. We've acknowledged that libraries and their reference services are expensive. There seems to be ample evidence that parent institutions, taxpayers, and society in general expect greater accountability for the expenditure of public funds, and that librarians need to better apply the tools of economics to analyzing our operations. At the same time, the use of those tools presents a steep, long, and, as a result, expensive learning curve while the results we can expect from the application of sophisticated techniques such as cost-efficiency analysis and cost-benefit analysis appear ambivalent. One solution, though certainly incomplete and lacking in absolute answers, may be found in the heuristic application of economic thinking to our understanding of reference services.

Models

Many systems and processes at work in the world are either too large or too complex to understand directly. To clarify our grasp of the whole, social scientists and economists frequently construct simplified, theoretical representations–or models–of social processes. Models have been used to illustrate communications within organizations, how people make decisions, and to forecast the weather. Econometric models provide mathematical formulas which assist economists in predicting future business trends and the condition of the economy on the basis of selective data currently available.

Social and econometric models are, after all, just models. As scaled-down representations of far more complex realities their predictive and explanatory powers are severely limited, equally "scaled-down." Relationships presented in models can only approximate reality, some factors are invariably overlooked or the relationships misunderstood. In addition, the accuracy and quality of data determine and limit the predictions and explanations provided by "modeling." No matter how accurately a model of business cycles might express cause and effect, inaccurate factory inventory data will produce faulty predictions for future business cycles. Garbage in, garbage out. In spite of these limitations, models can prove extremely useful.

Toward a Heuristic Model of the Economics of Reference Service

This paper offers a "draft" econometric model of reference service. "Draft" in that the author suggests it as a stimulus to discussion, for revision, and, undoubtedly, for improvement. A "model" in that it is a greatly simplified representation of the economics of the reference system, and, as such, subject to all the limitations and inaccuracies implied above. It is "heuristic" in the sense that it is intended as an aid to thinking about improving reference service rather than as a calculator of definitive answers.

To construct and apply aspects of the model, we will first assemble and define the building blocks called variables. Even though we have little expectation of giving accurate values to these variables we can still use them heuristically, to help us think.

To calculate the benefit of reference services to a single client we must first identify the benefits derived from answered reference questions, the reference collections (both print and electronic), results of online searches, and all other reference activities. The total benefit of reference services to a single patron then equals the sum of benefits derived from answered questions, the reference collections, online searches, and all other reference activities including the final, or "nth," activity. This can be represented in econometric shorthand by the following formula as constructed in Exhibit I:

$$B_R = B_{RQ} + B_{RC} + B_{RO} + \ldots B_{RN}.$$

EXHIBIT I. Calculation of the Benefit of Reference Services to a Single Client

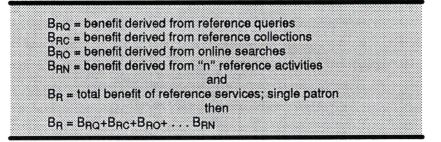

B_{RQ} = benefit derived from reference queries
B_{RC} = benefit derived from reference collections
B_{RO} = benefit derived from online searches
B_{RN} = benefit derived from "n" reference activities
and
B_R = total benefit of reference services; single patron
then
$$B_R = B_{RQ}+B_{RC}+B_{RO}+ \ldots B_{RN}$$

The benefit received by all library patrons is calculated by summing the benefits derived by patron one, patron two, patron three, through the nth patron, and may be expressed as:

$$B_{SUMR} = B_{R1}+B_{R2}+B_{R3}+ \ldots B_{RN}.$$

In similar fashion, to calculate the benefit to a single patron derived from a library's general collections we must identify benefits derived from books, serials, recordings, manuscripts, and all other materials. The total benefit derived from the collections by a single patron then equals the sum of benefits derived separately from books, serials, recordings, manuscripts, and all other formats including the final, or nth, format. This is represented by the formula constructed in Exhibit II:

$$B_C = B_{CB}+B_{CS}+B_{CR}+B_{CM}+ \ldots B_{CN}.$$

Following the example above, the benefit received by all patrons may be expressed as:

$$B_{SUMC} = B_{C1}+B_{C2}+B_{C3}+ \ldots B_{CN}.$$

For the sake of brevity, let us acknowledge that the total benefit to all library patrons derived from other library services would be constructed in the same way and would be represented as:

EXHIBIT II. Calculation of the Benefit of the Collections to a Single Client

B_{CB} = benefit derived from books
B_{CS} = benefit derived from serials
B_{CR} = benefit derived from recordings
B_{CM} = benefit derived from manuscripts
B_{CN} = benefit from the "nth" part of the collection
and
B_C = total benefit from collections; single client
then
$B_C = B_{CB} + B_{CS} + B_{CR} + B_{CM} + \ldots B_{CN}$

B_{SUMILL} = total benefit from ILL derived by all patrons
B_{SUMN} = total benefit from the "nth" library service derived
by all patrons

On the cost side, the total cost of reference services equals the sum of the library's cost for personnel, materials, vendor charges, and all other components contributing to providing reference services. As discussed above, summing all library expenses associated with reference service is extremely complex, detailed, and subject to wide variation in execution. Conceptually, however, it can be represented simply as $E_R = E_{RP} + E_{RM} + E_{RV} + \ldots E_{RN}$ as derived in Exhibit III.

The structure of the formula representing cost of reference services applies to all other library services and functions. For example, in the model we will let E_C represent library expenses for collections so that $E_C = E_{CP} + E_{CM} + E_{CV} + \ldots E_{CN}$. The total expense of additional library functions is represented as:

E_P = library cost of purchased services
E_N = library cost of "n" activities,

and total library costs as:

$E_{SUM} = E_R + E_C + E_P + \ldots E_N.$

The cost incurred by an individual patron for any use of reference services is the sum of monetary expenses, such as photocopies,

EXHIBIT III. Calculation of Library Expenses for Reference Services

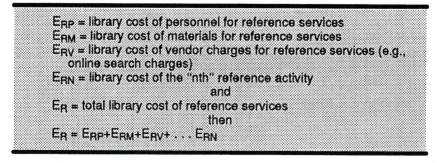

E_{RP} = library cost of personnel for reference services
E_{RM} = library cost of materials for reference services
E_{RV} = library cost of vendor charges for reference services (e.g., online search charges)
E_{RN} = library cost of the "nth" reference activity
and
E_R = total library cost of reference services
then
$E_R = E_{RP} + E_{RM} + E_{RV} + \ldots E_{RN}$

online search fees, or transportation, and opportunity cost. As calculated in Exhibit IV, this may be represented as:

$$C_R = C_{MR} + C_{OR} + \ldots C_{NR}.$$

The total cost incurred by all patrons using reference services is then $C_{SUMR} = C_{R1} + C_{R2} + C_{R3} + C_{R4} + \ldots C_{RN}$.

Cost-benefit may be calculated as the ratio benefit divided by cost. It can be seen that the value of the fraction increases directly as the value of benefit increases relative to cost. This occurs if benefit (B) increases and cost (C) remains at least constant, or if benefit (B) remains constant and cost (C) decreases.

The cost-benefit of reference service for a single patron as calculated in Exhibit V may be represented as $B_R/(E_R+C_R)$. It is important to recall that B_R and C_R actually represent summations of costs as derived in Exhibits I and III, respectively, and E_R the summation of all aspects of library expense through factor E_{RN} (Exhibit III). The cost-benefit of collections is $B_C/(E_C+C_C)$; online searches, $B_O/(E_O+C_O)$; and the nth library function, $B_N/(E_N+C_N)$.

These formulations can represent the calculation and comparison of any two or more cost-benefits. Once calculated (far easier said than done), we simply compare for the best possible ratios. For example, we might find that calculations based on values for all variables result in:

EXHIBIT IV. Calculation of the Cost of Reference Services Incurred by a Single Client

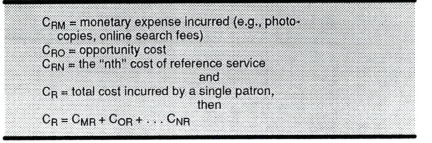

C_{RM} = monetary expense incurred (e.g., photo-copies, online search fees)
C_{RO} = opportunity cost
C_{RN} = the "nth" cost of reference service
and
C_R = total cost incurred by a single patron,
then

$$C_R = C_{MR} + C_{OR} + \ldots C_{NR}$$

EXHIBIT V. Calculation of the Cost-Benefit of Reference Service

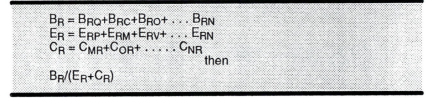

$$B_R = B_{RQ} + B_{RC} + B_{RO} + \ldots B_{RN}$$
$$E_R = E_{RP} + E_{RM} + E_{RV} + \ldots E_{RN}$$
$$C_R = C_{MR} + C_{OR} + \ldots \ldots C_{NR}$$
then

$$B_R/(E_R + C_R)$$

$$((B_C/(E_C + C_C)) > ((B_R/(E_R + C_R)) > ((B_O/(E_O + C_O)).$$

In an ideal world, we would then be able to increase benefits to patrons and reduce costs in such a way as to maximize benefits at the least possible cost. This is implicit in the zero-sum nature of library budgets, and would result in the maximization of the expression $(B_{SUM}/(E_{SUM} + C_{SUM}))$ where:

B_{SUM} = benefits from all library services derived by all patrons
E_{SUM} = library expenses for all services

and

C_{SUM} = cost for all library services incurred by all patrons.

We can also use the same formula structures to construct cost-efficiency analyses designed to identify the most effective method of accomplishing a library process. For example, let E_R represent library expenses required to answer reference questions. Let Q_T represent the total number of questions asked and Q_W the number of unsatisfactory answers. Again we let C_{SUMR} represent the sum of costs incurred by all patrons in using reference services. The methods to be tested might include a desk staffed by a professional (1), a desk staffed by support staff (2), and a totally self-service reference collection (3). The following represents the number of correct responses as a function of the cost incurred by both library and patrons in each method:

$$(Q_T\text{-}Q_W)/(E_R+C_{SUMR})$$

The result of long, painstaking, and detailed cost-efficiency analyses might produce:

$$(Q_T\text{-}Q_W)_3/(E_R+C_{SUMR})_3 > (Q_T\text{-}Q_W)_2/(E_R+C_{SUMR})_2 > (Q_T\text{-}Q_W)_1/(E_R+C_{SUMR})_1$$

indicating the greatest cost-efficiency in self-service reference, the least in a professionally staffed desk. Recall, however, that our cost-efficiency model makes no attempt to consider patron benefit.

How might such a cold, economic look at reference service ever prove useful? This paper already made the case that finding meaningful values for the model variables is costly and time-consuming; more than likely inaccurate and arguable, as well. In fact, though, it has already proven useful–heuristically, that is.

The very act of model building led the author to identify components of patron benefit, patron cost, and library expense. Most readers will have questioned each of those choices, rejected some, added several the author inexplicably overlooked. Most readers have speculated as to how the values of the several variables could be determined. Questioned their usefulness. Challenged the suggested relationships.

One important effect of this "draft" model is to formally implant the library service consumer into our consideration of cost. The model makes a very clear statement: the summation of all patron costs, including opportunity costs, is weighted as heavily as library expenses. Consideration of patron cost infrequently informs discussions of library budget allocation, but should in all cases. Braunstein found that " . . . it can tentatively be concluded that the major costs of using a library are borne by the user. . . . "[23]

A Case Study

In order to illustrate an application of our model with some emphasis on the impact of the consideration of patron cost, let us examine a recent decision involving reference services, costs, and economic thinking at Hypothetical University Library. Like most mid-sized academic libraries, Hypothetical University's reference collection included many expensive subscriptions to indexes, abstracts, and other reference serials (E_{RS}), CD-ROMs (E_{RE}), and a good, though not outstanding, selection of reference monographs (E_{RB}). There were, of course, salary and benefits for professional, support staff, and student assistants (E_{RP}), online search charges (E_{RO}), and some, although indeterminate, expense for overhead (E_{RX}). Hypothetical University Library's expenditures for then existing reference services would then be:

$$E_{R1} = E_{RS}+E_{RB}+E_{RP}+E_{RO}+E_{RX}+ \ldots E_{RN}$$

Several years ago, library staff decided that the next major step beyond paper indexes, accessing online databases via remote vendors, and stand-alone CD-ROM indexes would be the installation of other bibliographic files on the mainframe-based online catalog (OPAC)(E_{RDATA}). Knowing that license fees for this environment would be very expensive and that new, costly software would be required, the library canceled all expendable paper subscriptions and reduced services and staffing to the minimum. This resulted in a new projected cost of reference:

$$E_{R2} = E_{R1}-(E_{RS1}+E_{RP1}+E_{RO1})+E_{RDATA}.$$

Unfortunately, even after expense reductions, the cost of reference including OPAC mounted bibliographic files exceeded the existing cost of reference services ($E_{R2}>E_{R1}$). The library staff scrutinized other library cost centers and reduced those expenses to the least tenable amount resulting in E_{SUM2}. Unfortunately, E_{SUM2} was still greater than both E_{SUM1} and the library's budget. Unable to reallocate funds from any other function, and subject to the logic of zero-sum budgets, the library had no alternative but to forego adding other bibliographic files to the OPAC.

Essentially, planners at Hypothetical University Library assumed online indexes and abstracts on the OPAC would be preferable to the then available formats, executed a series of rough cost-efficiency studies, adjusted inputs and variables, and concluded that something approximating the "old way" (E_{SUM1}) remained more cost-effective (and within budget) than adding indexes to the OPAC (E_{SUM2}). The fact was, however, that Hypothetical University Library had *always* had enough money in its several million dollar budget to add the files to the OPAC. It just couldn't find the will to liberate sufficient funds from pre-existing commitments such as E_{R1}, E_C, etc.

Note that this relatively typical approach to decision-making made use of cost-effectiveness techniques. As such, library planners accepted at face value that patrons derived maximum benefit in the most desired proportion from the various library collections and services resulting in the necessity of continuing resource allocation to maintain existing outputs.

Analysis of resource allocation at Hypothetical University Library by means of a heuristic, cost-benefit model might lead to markedly different conclusions. For example, let ($B_{SUMR1}/(E_{R1}+C_{SUMR1})$) represent the cost-benefit of reference services as they exist and ($B_{SUMR2}/(E_{R2}+C_{SUMR2})$) the cost-benefit of reference services augmented by indexes integrated into the OPAC. As part of the analysis, reference staff found that patrons perceived the use of indexes on the OPAC as reducing the time it took to locate the call numbers of cited journals by 60% (the result of linking article citations to the bibliographic and holdings records of owned periodicals), a significant reduction in opportunity cost.[24] In addition, time savings accrued from the ability to access indexes and abstracts remotely without physically coming to the library. In this illustration, the resulting increase in benefits enjoyed by patrons combined with reductions in patron cost more than compensated for the increase in library expenses caused by the implementation of databases on the OPAC, or ($B_{SUMR2}/(E_{R2}+C_{SUMR2})$) > ($B_{SUMR1}/E_{R1}+C_{SUMR1}$)). By re-examining the relative cost-benefits of all library services, library staff at Hypothetical University may discover that $(B_{SUMR2}/(E_{R2}+C_{SUMR2})) > (B_{SUMC}/(E_C+C_{SUMC})) \geq (B_{SUMILL}/E_{ILL}+C_{SUMILL})) \geq (B_{SUMN}/(E_N+C_{SUMN}))$. This would occur largely as the result of factoring patron benefit and cost into library considerations.

In fact, Hypothetical University Library staff may find that the assumed benefits of some of its collections or services were not as valuable to patrons as always believed. They may also discover that more accurate consideration of both patron benefit and cost leads to adjustments in inputs (i.e., personnel, funds) which increase real benefit to patrons while keeping the library's expenditures within its zero-sum budget.

NOTES

1. *ARL Statistics, 1992-93,* (Washington, D.C.: Association of Research Libraries, 1994), Table 9, "Total Operating Expenditures," p. 59.

2. U.S. Department of Education, Office of Educational Research and Improvement, National Center for Education Statistics, *Digest of Education Statistics, 1993,* (Washington, D.C.: Government Printing Office, 1993), Table 408, p. 432.

3. *Digest of Education Statistics, 1993,* Table 403, p. 427. The most recent, comprehensive data available.

4. Anthony M. Cummings, *University Libraries and Scholarly Communication: A Study Prepared for the Andrew W. Mellon Foundation,* (Washington, D.C.: The Association of Research Libraries for The Andrew W. Mellon Foundation, 1992), pp. xvi-xviii.

5. Martin Cummings, *The Economics of Research Libraries,* (Washington, D.C.: Council on Library Resources, Inc., 1986), p. 7.

6. See, for example, Southern Association of Colleges and Schools, Commission on Colleges, *Criteria for Accreditation,* 1992-1993 ed. (Decatur, Georgia: Southern Association of Colleges and Schools, 1992), pp. 15-17.

7. Miriam A. Drake and Harold A. Olsen, "The Economics of Library Innovation," *Library Trends* 28 (Summer 1979): 102.

8. Martin Cummings, *The Economics of Research Libraries,* p. 77.

9. Kantor summed unit costs over 32 libraries and found " . . . that 50% of the total budget eventuates in service as in-house use of library materials." It is important to note that Kantor assumed that "This is presumably not true at public libraries." Paul B. Kantor, "Cost and Productivity in Library Operations," in *Productivity in the Information Age: Proceedings of the 46th ASIS Annual Meeting,* vol. 20, (Washington, D.C.: American Society for Information Science, 1983), p. 298.

10. F.W. Lancaster, *If you want to evaluate your library . . .* , 2nd ed., (Champaign, Illinois: Graduate School of Library and Information Science, University of Illinois, 1993), p. 159.

11. See, for example, Richard B. McKenzie, "The Economist's Paradigm," *Library Trends* 28 (Summer 1979): 7-29. Note in particular his discussion of marginal cost and marginal benefit, pp. 12-14.

12. William Safire, *Safire's Political Dictionary*, (New York: Random House, 1978), p. 808. The concept was popularized and expanded in Lester C. Thurow's *The Zero-Sum Society: Distribution and the Possibilities for Economic Change*, (New York: Basic Books, 1980).

13. W. Paul Vogt, *Dictionary of Statistics and Methodology: A Nontechnical Guide for the Social Sciences*, (Newbury Park: Sage Publications, 1993), p. 160. For more in-depth discussion of "opportunity cost" from an economist's perspective see McKenzie, "The Economist's Paradigm," p. 10.

14. Yale M. Braunstein, "Costs and Benefits of Library Information: The User Point of View," *Library Trends* 29 (Summer 1979): 80.

15. Ibid.

16. For a thorough discussion, including extensive literature reviews, of cost-efficiency and cost-benefit studies of reference services see Marjorie E. Murfin, "Cost Analysis of Library Reference Services," in *Advances in Library Administration and Organization*, vol. 11, ed. Gerard B. McCabe and Bernard Kreissman (Greenwich, CT: JAI Press, 1993), pp. 1-36. See also Martin Cummings, *The Economics of Research Libraries*, pp. 76-80.

17. For a particularly intriguing investigation of the cost-efficiency of using support staff or professionals in responding to reference questions, see Murfin, "Cost Analysis of Library Reference Services," pp. 21-23.

18. See for example, Tina Roose, "Online or Print: Comparing Costs," *Library Journal* 110 (September 15, 1985): 54-55; Charles R. Anderson, "Budgeting for Reference Services in an On-Line Age," *The Reference Librarian* No. 19 (1988): 179-194; Nancy L. Eaton and Nancy B. Crane, "Integrating Electronic Information Systems into the Reference Services Budget," *The Reference Librarian* No. 19 (1988): 161-171.

19. Murfin, "Cost Analysis of Library Reference Services," pp. 1-14. See also, Anderson, "Budgeting for Reference Services in an On-Line Age," pp. 185-186.

20. Martin Cummings, *The Economics of Research Libraries*, p. 25.

21. Anderson, "Budgeting for Reference Services in an On-Line Age," p. 185.

22. Lancaster, *If you want to evaluate your library . . .* , p. 304.

23. Braunstein, "Costs and Benefits of Library Information," p. 81.

24. Although an estimate, this is the figure identified by students in a management information systems course at The University of Alabama during the spring of 1993.

Marketing Reference Services

O. Gene Norman

SUMMARY. In this article, the marketing concept is related to reference services. Following a review of the literature, an overview of marketing is explored, including research, the marketing mix, the strategic plan, the marketing plan, and the marketing audit. The application of marketing to reference services is made through the marketing mix elements of product, price, place, and promotion.

Marketing reference services can make a difference. For more than two decades, librarians have been using the marketing concept to market library and information services. Most writers have discussed the topic positively and have concluded that marketing can be especially beneficial for a library. It can help to improve the material and services offered by a library, including reference services. It also can assist in delivering these materials and services more effectively to the library users. In other words, it can provide needed information to the client at a time, place and cost that is desirable.

Many definitions can be found for marketing. This dictionary definition gets to the heart of the matter: "In a general sense, everything that is done to get the product to the customer, but more specifically not just selling a product, but discovering and then furnishing the customer's wants and needs."[1] More simply put,

O. Gene Norman is Head of the Reference Department at Indiana State University Libraries, Terre Haute, IN 47809.

[Haworth co-indexing entry note]: "Marketing Reference Services." Norman, O. Gene. Co-published simultaneously in *The Reference Librarian* (The Haworth Press, Inc.) No. 49/50, 1995, pp. 45-60; and: *Library Users and Reference Services* (ed: Jo Bell Whitlatch) The Haworth Press, Inc., 1995, pp. 45-60. Multiple copies of this article/chapter may be purchased from The Haworth Document Delivery Center [1-800-3-HAWORTH; 9:00 a.m. - 5:00 p.m. (EST)].

" . . . marketing means satisfying human needs."[2] The idea of marketing is to allow every person to be his own authority regarding his own personal needs instead of prescribing a client's needs through an authority figure such as a librarian.

In the business world, the marketing concept developed gradually through a series of stages. The production era, which emphasized the production and distribution of products, came first after the Industrial Revolution. In the 1920s, the sales era, which emphasized the use of personal selling and advertising to sell products, followed the production era. Both the sales and the production eras overlooked customers' needs and frequently left them dissatisfied.

Finally, in the 1950s, many businesses began to realize that sales could not be assured by merely producing a product and promoting it. They recognized the importance of determining customers' needs through an information system which we now refer to as research. When businesses began to view the identification of customers' needs as the *starting point*, they moved into the marketing era.

LITERATURE REVIEW

A 1982 survey identified 94 publications related to marketing libraries and information services.[3] In 1989, a follow-up survey listed a 114-item bibliography on recent trends and developments in marketing libraries and information services.[4] A voluminous amount of literature has been written about marketing libraries in general, but only a few publications appear to be limited to marketing reference services specifically.

In 1989, Bickford completed a paper in which he assessed the marketing of reference services to the business community by three public libraries.[5] He found that each library used different types and levels of marketing, but they all felt their efforts were successful.

Two years later, Rothlisberg reported on his use of bibliographic instruction to market reference services to a culturally diverse population at Northland Pioneer College at Holbrook, Arizona.[6] He found that students who took instruction benefitted by being more comfortable in using the center. In 1986, the Library Instruction Conference also published *Marketing Instructional Services. . . .* [7] It includes papers on the 1984 Conference which discusses a variety of ways to promote bibliographic instruction.

Several authors have written on marketing areas frequently related to reference services. These areas include government publications, microforms and electronic information services. Heisser wrote an article in 1986 on marketing government publications in New England through the use of a marketing survey, a workshop, advertising and public relations.[8] In 1987, Lyle surveyed twelve academic libraries and reported on techniques they used to publicize government documents collections.[9]

Pitch,[10] Whitmore,[11] McIntosh,[12] and Raikes[13] have written about numerous ways to market microforms. Pitch, an academic librarian, emphasized public relations, special events, and publicity. Whitmore conducted an experimental study in microform use instruction using a slide-tape presentation and a handout. McIntosh discussed many practical suggestions for promoting microforms from using mobiles to guided tours. After Princeton University's Microforms Division was reorganized and relocated, Raikes described the various ways it was promoted.

Several publications have reported on marketing electronic information services. Markee presented a discussion about marketing online services through the use of a marketing plan in 1982.[14] Eight years later, Tenopir described how several online database vendors market their services, frequently to be used with the end user, directly to the corporate information professional.[15] Embry and Neely reported on an aggressive marketing campaign to market CD-ROMs at the University of Louisville during 1989.[16] In 1990, Dennis wrote about an intriguing three-day information fair which was presented by librarians and faculty to promote a course at Salem State College in Massachusetts on a variety of computer technologies.[17] More recently, Jackson portrayed an extensive marketing program at Texas Woman's University Libraries at Denton, Texas to promote CARL Uncover2 and OCLC's FirstSearch, along with the Libraries' online catalog.[18]

Two books, which cover marketing of libraries in general in depth, also should be helpful in marketing reference services. Wood combines marketing libraries with strategic planning and includes sample plans and useful illustrations.[19] Weingand integrates marketing and planning in a similar manner and discusses and illustrates the various elements in detail.[20]

Kotler and Andreasen's book on marketing nonprofit organizations remains the standard for such institutions, including libraries.[21] This third edition of the book has placed an increased emphasis on combining strategic planning and marketing. Part II of this latest edition, which contains seven chapters, deals with "Strategic Planning and Organization."

OVERVIEW OF MARKETING

Marketing requires a number of activities in order to satisfy the needs of the client. These activities involve: conducting research to discover needs; preparing a program around the marketing mix of product, price, place, and promotion; designing a strategic plan to set general goals, objectives, and strategies; preparing a marketing plan to determine marketing goals, objectives, and strategies; and performing a marketing review and audit, after a period of time, to evaluate the marketing program. Ideally, this program should encompass the entire library, but it could be limited to reference services.

Research

One of the most effective ways to determine the needs of library users is through research, and it doesn't have to be made difficult or mysterious. Some information may be available from in-house reports, suggestion box files, or observation. To determine specific needs, the reference staff may need to conduct surveys through a brief paper questionnaire or by telephoning selected clientele. An even better technique may be to use a focus group of selected library users to give you an immediate opinion regarding matters of interest to the reference department. Persons interested in focus groups may benefit from reading Scharf and Ward[22] or Widdows, Hensler and Wuncott[23] on the topic.

If your library is located near an academic institution with a business program, marketing instructors may be willing to have their class assist the library with conducting marketing research. Librarians doing marketing research on their own may wish to consult a number of authors who have written extensively about the subject. They include Kim and Little, Butler and Gratch, and Kotler and Andreasen.[24]

Marketing Mix

After conducting research, the next step for the reference department is to design a marketing program around the marketing mix of product, price, place or distribution, and promotion. In the reference department, products usually consist of materials and services, but Kotler and Andreasen state that: "A product is anything that can be offered to satisfy a need."[25] Materials and services should be designed to serve the client. A product goes through a life cycle during which time it develops, matures, and finally declines in utility. Due to this phenomenon, reference librarians must constantly evaluate their materials and services to decide if they need to be changed, continued, or withdrawn. The librarian also should be alert to opportunities for developing new products as additional needs arise. Weingand emphasizes the importance of the product in the marketing mix by saying that: "The success of all other marketing efforts hinge directly upon the quality and excellence of the products which are designed."[26]

The element of price may seem repulsive to many reference services readers. A number of reference librarians who work in the trenches feel that most services should be free. In contrast, recent research indicates that 18 of 20 libraries surveyed charged for one, or more, of fourteen items.[27] Library and reference services administrators need to review the objectives of the institution and the department to determine what fees, if any, are necessary. Perhaps Drake's forecast of ten years ago has become even more timely today when she said that: "The economics of the new technologies will make it difficult, if not impossible, for many public libraries to offer services at no charge."[28]

Keep in mind that nonmonetary costs such as psychological, time, and location impediments can also take their toll. For example, if the reference desk is located in an inconvenient spot or if it is closed during times of high demand, these barriers may cost reference services a high number of clients.

The place aspect of the marketing mix is concerned with such areas as location, storage of products, and distribution of materials and services. As far back as 1976, Drucker summarized the importance of the place element in libraries when he said that: "A really functional library is one where people can better circulate, find what they want, and get people in, but get them out again, satisfied."[29]

In reference services today, one must not only be concerned with getting clients into and out of the library building, but the librarian must be aware of how to assist a library user, by telephone or E-Mail, who is attempting to access the online catalog or an array of other electronic information services. Many materials, once stored conveniently on library shelves, now are more conveniently accessed through a computer. Numerous patrons who formerly were satisfied with coming to the library building for their information now expect those materials and informational data to be delivered directly to their dormitories, offices, and homes.

The promotion part of the marketing mix involves personal selling, publicity, advertising in various media, sales promotion, and packaging.[30] It is a way to communicate to potential library users about your materials and services, and it frequently is the element most closely associated with marketing by librarians due to its relationship to "selling" a product. Personal selling usually includes persuasive conversation and consists of individual contact with library user. Consequently, it can be one of the most effective, as well as the most labor intensive, methods of promotion.

Publicity, one of the most frequently used forms of promotion, usually is thought of as free communications. It, generally, can be found as a news story in a newspaper or magazine, but it also can be heard as a public service announcement on radio or television. Roberts and Blandy discuss and illustrate news releases and public service announcements and may be useful to reference librarians who have been assigned to prepare these kinds of promotion.[31]

Advertising in newspapers, radio, and television is costly, and as a result, many reference services areas cannot afford it. Although it is expensive, this type of promotion has the potential of reaching large numbers of people quickly. Libraries which can afford it may wish to use it for important events and special occasions. Another form of advertising which libraries should not overlook is direct mail. It often can be more focused and cost less per contact. Kotler and Andreasen list seven advantages of using direct mail for non-profit groups, and they identify seven steps to use in establishing a direct mail program.[32]

The sales promotion aspect of promotion has been defined as: "Short term incentives to encourage purchase or sales of a product or service or the performance of a behavior."[33] It may consist of the use of coupons, contests, or small samples of the product or service.

Packaging is used to make materials and services more appealing to a client. Pride and Ferrell note that: "Packaging involves the development of a container and a graphic design for a product."[34] This form of promotion uses color, size, shape, and design to sell a product or service.

Public relations also is related to promotion. Passarelli describes it as " . . . a communications function, a conscious effort to influence other people and groups through communication processes."[35] PR is much broader in its relationships than publicity and may involve directing and receiving communications not only from customers but to other publics such as government officials. Roberts and Bland discuss various types of communications used in public relations and how PR can be planned, implemented, and evaluated.[36]

In the process of promoting materials and services, the reference librarian may wish to direct these promotional efforts to specific audiences; e.g., to faculty in an academic institution or perhaps one-parent families in a public library setting. Directing promotional efforts to specific groups is called segmentation. The advantage of segmentation is that it allows the library to send information to persons most likely to benefit from it.

Strategic Plan

Kotler and Andreasen,[37] Wood,[38] and Weingand[39] have written of the importance of integrating strategic planning in with marketing. A strategic plan is needed before developing a market plan. Wood defines strategic planning as " . . . a method of planning that matches an organization's resources with its best opportunities."[40]

She states that: "It starts with a vision of an ideal future and focuses on present conditions and actions needed to prepare and position the library for that future."[41]

Riggs has continued further to identify the areas which one should consider in developing a strategic plan. These areas are: " . . . a mission statement, goals, objectives, strategies, alternatives and contingencies, policies and resource allocations, and their implementation and evaluation."[42] If the library already has a strategic plan, the reference department should use it to help determine reference services goals, objectives and strategies.

The Marketing Plan

When the strategic plan has been completed, the marketing plan should be prepared. Wood has defined a marketing plan as " . . . a product-specific or target-market-specific plan, setting forth marketing objectives in quantitative terms and outlining strategies for achieving those objectives. . . . "[43] The types of marketing plans may vary somewhat, but Kotler and Andreasen say that: "A marketing plan should contain the following sections: executive summary, situation analysis, objectives and goals, marketing strategy, action programs, budgets, and controls."[44]

Persons having difficulty in developing a marketing plan may wish to consult Thompson's *Marketing Plan Workbook for Nonprofit Organizations.*[45] Thompson, a marketing professor specializing in the nonprofit area, has designed the book to include market planning categories, and blank lines are left for the reader's response. Wood also provides sample marketing plans which may be helpful.[46]

At this point, there is a need to identify the detailed activities, or action programs, of the marketing plan in order to implement it. Specific librarians should be made responsible for such things as requesting any needed materials. Other persons can be assigned the task of writing publicity for the media, if needed. Due dates should be established for completing all activities. Budgets may need to be established, or identified, to purchase materials.

Controls need to be established to see what progress has been made in implementing the plan. The person implementing the plan needs to check goals and objectives periodically, perhaps monthly or quarterly, to see if they are being met. Additional actions may need to be implemented with due dates to meet certain goals. Finally, a complete review of the marketing plan should be made.

The Marketing Audit

To systematically examine its audiences, services, and materials, the reference department needs to conduct a marketing audit every three to five years. Kotler and Andreasen define the marketing audit as " . . . a comprehensive, independent and periodic examination of an organization's marketing environment, objectives, strategies, and activities with a view of determining problem areas and opportunities and recommending a plan of action to improve the organization's strategic marketing performance."[47] The marketing audit is an important means of control which Wood says should be "comprehensive," performed according to an orderly "systems orientation," done independently by an outside consultant, and conducted regularly, not just when a crisis develops.[48] Wood acknowledges, however, that in actual practice a marketing audit may be ignored or only be done when a crisis arises.

APPLICATIONS TO REFERENCE SERVICES

In determining marketing techniques which are applicable to reference services, let us go back and examine them according to the elements of the marketing mix of product, price, place or distribution, and promotion. It is important to examine the current situation, what other libraries are doing, and the opportunities which are available to reference departments.

Product

If the quality of the product is critical to the success of the marketing effort as Weingand has stated, reference librarians need to produce and maintain effective products. In a recent survey, this writer identified thirty-five products offered by twenty Midwestern libraries.[49] These products included the familiar books, periodicals, microforms, reference and information services, bibliographic instruction, online searches, online catalogs, and CD-ROMs. A couple of less common products also surfaced such as a public library providing businesses sets of Roladex cards with pertinent questions and answers regarding library services and a university library delivering library materials to students, faculty, and administrators in their dormitories or offices. Because of increased expectations and demands upon library staff, one public library chose to "demarket," or discontinue, the distribution of Internal Revenue Service tax forms.

Due to the life cycle of a product, the reference librarian must constantly re-evaluate the need for a product. Some materials or services may need to be modified or discontinued. A few years ago, the Indiana State University Libraries' Reference Department retired an aging notched card file collection of abstracts on alcoholism which was purchased several years earlier with grant money.

Perhaps more importantly, reference librarians must identify and locate new services which fill current needs. A public computer terminal which can access the Internet would immediately allow client access to an astounding number of documents, statistics, online library catalogs and other sources of information. A patron could: telnet to another computer site on the Internet; access and download entire documents through ftp (file transfer protocol); and contact gopher sites around the world for weather information, job lists, recent U. S. Supreme Court decisions, and local telephone directories of educational institutions.

Indiana State University Libraries has established its own gopher, and the Reference Department is in the process of indexing information found on the Internet through the use of "bookmarks" which can be called up for quick access to a variety of documents and data. In addition, locally produced bibliographies and pathfinders are being put on the gopher for the use of faculty, staff, students, and the world. Through the use of research, creativity, and technology, it is possible for reference librarians to identify new, or different, client needs which can result in additional new products.

Price

Which reference materials and services justify a charge? This is not an easy question, but a recent survey indicated that almost 66%

of twenty libraries charge for photocopying, lost materials, and overdue materials, and forty percent had a fee for online database searching.[50] Only twenty percent asked patrons to pay for interlibrary loan service. More recently, some libraries have been known to charge for computer disks to download material found on CD-ROM databases, and selected libraries have put coin boxes on computer printers. In some instances, academic and public library reference departments have arranged to charge outside agencies, such as a business, an increased fee for special reference and information services rendered.

Pricing policies need to be established with the library administration for reference and information services, along with other fees charged by the library. The library needs to review its mission and objectives and compare them with budgetary considerations to determine any need for cost recovery or other priorities. The reference staff also should make every effort to eliminate any psychological and access barriers by being aware of how to put clients at ease during the reference interview and arranging materials and services so they are immediately available.

Place

The library building and the reference desk area should be designed with colors and texture to be attractive and pleasant, and the areas should be well maintained. This helps to provide what Kotler and Andreasen call "atmospherics . . . the conscious designing of space to create or reinforce specific effects on buyers, such as feelings of well-being, safety, and intimacy, or awe."[51] Some buildings also are divided into multiple sections which prevent immediate access to needed information. Splitting collections into strange arrangements also prevent efficient distribution of information. A good sign system, as described in Van Allen,[52] can assist patrons in getting through the library and the reference collection.

There are other ways of distributing reference services information. They include: interlibrary loan, telefacsimile transmission, telephone calls, and electronic mail. A recent trend in CD-ROM and online databases is to provide full-text documents in electronic format. After a search has been completed, entire articles, and other documents, can be printed off or downloaded to a computer disk.

With the availability of the Internet, reference services librarians now can search the globe to retrieve desired data.

Promotion

During a recent survey, twenty librarians were asked a series of questions relating to promotion. Eleven, of the twenty librarians, thought that reference services and reference collections needed the most promotion.[53] Ten, of the twenty librarians, also felt that the new technology services should be given a priority for promotion. All of the twenty libraries surveyed were involved with personal selling, and forty-five percent preferred this labor-intensive approach to promotion which can be used with individuals or groups.

Free publicity also is a popular promotional device for libraries. Reference librarians, possibly assisted by a PR staff member, can write news releases about new materials to be sent to the local newspaper, radio, and television stations. Briefer public service announcements also can be written about some important aspect of reference services and mailed to radio and television stations to be read on the air. Other means of publicity which may be useful in reference include: one-page letters and memos; posters; flyers; brochures; photography sessions; talk shows; press conferences; and book reviews. It is important that someone in the library maintain contacts with the various types of media in the community. Roberts and Blandy describe, and often illustrate, these methods of publicizing reference services.[54]

Direct mail is frequently used by libraries to publicize materials, services, and events. It is relatively inexpensive and can be targeted to specific groups. For the past several years, the Reference Department at Indiana State University Libraries has received a good response from faculty and staff to mailed checklists of bibliographies, pathfinders, and CD-ROM handouts which are available upon request. This year the bibliographies and pathfinders are being put on the library gopher for easier access.

Paid advertising in newspapers and on radio and television is expensive. Usually, only larger libraries can afford this form of promotion, but it does have the advantage of reaching a larger audience. One large public library has used drive-time radio for a brief ad to reach a large segment of the commuting public.

Sales promotion has been used by some libraries. When online searching began, several libraries gave patrons coupons to use for free searches. On special occasions, libraries also have held contests to attract patrons. The advantage of using sales promotion is in getting the patron's attention which leads to providing an immediate incentive.

Another way for reference services librarians to promote their materials and services is to use packaging. One should use a consistent logo on stationery, bibliographies, and other handouts. A specific color, size, shape and/or design may be used effectively with other publications. For some reason, we usually get a better response from yellow checklists of bibliographies than with blue or green. One library also promoted database searches by putting the searcher's name on the completed search.

CONCLUSION

Marketing reference services is a management tool which enables a reference librarian: to determine the needs of clients; to prepare a strategic plan for identifying goals, objectives, and strategies; to design a marketing plan to determine marketing goals, objectives and strategies; and to evaluate the marketing program through periodic reviews and a marketing audit. In recent years, there has been an increased emphasis on integrating strategic planning in marketing which helps to strengthen the marketing program.

There are tremendous changes taking place today in institutions and businesses across the country as they attempt to redefine themselves. In 1993, two institutes were held on rethinking reference at the University of California, Berkeley and at Duke University. A third institute was held in 1994 at the University of Iowa. Much of the redefinition which is being done is due to access to information and technology.

Writing in a recent issue of *Online,* the President of Muir & Associates clearly articulates the situation. He says that:

> A physicist may take eight years to formulate, and a biochemist one day to replicate, but a librarian can do ten years of research

in an hour–that's powerful. But before all the librarians and online searchers of the world rush out and demand a raise (and appropriate recognition), stand back and think about the need for marketing–think about the need to create an awareness of your potential contribution. No longer should the library feel like a distant professional cousin to the arts, science and engineering disciplines. But does anyone out there *know*?[55]

Today a reference librarian must be an access engineer, a teacher, an information specialist, a computer specialist, and a consultant, as well as a librarian. One way in which reference librarians can let their clients, administrators and colleagues know about their expertise, materials, services, and potential is through the use of marketing techniques outlined above. If we are to be effective, Muir reminds us that marketing takes time, and its success should not be based upon one project completed or one problem solved. Instead, successful marketing tends to result from a combination of successful efforts, staying the course, and persistence.[56]

REFERENCES

1. Rachel S. Epstein and Nina Liebman, *Biz Speak* (New York: Franklin Watts, 1986), 138.

2. Elizabeth J. Wood, *Strategic Marketing for Libraries: A Handbook*. (New York: Green Press, 1988), 3.

3. O. Gene Norman, "Marketing Libraries and Information Services: An Annotated Guide to the Literature," *Reference Services Review* 10(Spring 1982): 69-80.

4. O. Gene Norman, "Marketing Library and Information Services: An Annotated Guide to Recent Trends and Developments," *Reference Services Review* 17(Spring 1989): 43-64.

5. David L. Bickford, "An Assessment of the Marketing of Public Library Reference Services to the Business Community" (Master's paper, University of North Carolina at Chapel Hill, 1989).

6. Allen P. Rothlisberg, *Marketing Reference Services through Bibliographic Instruction at Northland Pioneer College* (Alexandria, VA: ERIC Document Reproduction Service, 1991) ED 332 706.

7. Carolyn A. Kirkendall, ed., *Marketing Instructional Services: Applying Private Sector Techniques to Plan and Promote Bibliographic Instruction: Papers Presented at the Thirteenth Library Instruction Conference Held at Eastern Michigan University, May 3 & 4, 1984* (Ann Arbor, MI: Pierian Press, 1986).

8. David C. R. Heisser, "Marketing U. S. Government Depository Libraries; Preliminary Report on a Public Awareness Campaign in New England," *Government Publications Review* 13(January-February 1986): 55-65.

9. Jack W. Lyle, *An Investigation and Description of Certain Actions Taken to Publicize the Documents Collection of Selected Academic United States Government Documents Depository Libraries in Illinois, Indiana, Kentucky, Michigan, and Ohio* (Alexandria, VA: ERIC Document Reproduction Service, 1987) ED 281 555.

10. Judi Pitch, "Microform Awareness through a Public Relations Campaign," *Microform Review* 15(Winter 1986): 28-30.

11. Marilyn P. Whitmore, "An Innovative Approach to User Acceptance of Microform," *Journal of Academic Librarianship* 9(May 1983): 75-79.

12. Melinda McIntosh, "Promoting Microform Collections in the Library," *Microform Review* 11(Summer 1982): 172-75.

13. Deborah A. Raikes, "Microforms at Princeton," *Microform Review* 11(Spring 1982): 93-105.

14. Kathleen M. Markee, "Online Services–Marketing," in *National Online Meeting; Proceedings–1982, New York March 31-April 1, 1982 Sponsored by Online Review,* comp. Martha E. Williams and Thomas H. Hogan (Medford, NJ: Learned Information, 1982), 329-34.

15. Carol Tenopir, "Librarians as an Online Sales Force," *Library Journal* 115(December 1990): 94, 96, 98.

16. Carmen Embry and Glenda S. Neely, "To Market, To Market: Academic Reference Departments and the Promotion of CD-ROMs in 1989," *The Southeastern Librarian* 39(Winter 1989): 143-44.

17. Nancy Dennis, "'New Technologies for Libraries and Classrooms': An Information Fair," *Research Strategies* 8(Winter 1990): 37-39.

18. Patricia A. Jackson, "Introducing CARL Uncover2 and FirstSearch: One University's Experience," *Texas Library Journal* 69(Summer 1993): 62-64.

19. Elizabeth J. Wood, *Strategic Marketing for Libraries: A Handbook* (New York: Greenwood Press, 1988).

20. Darlene E. Wingand, *Marketing/Planning Library and Information Services* (Littleton, CO: Libraries Unlimited, 1987).

21. Philip Kotler and Alan R. Andreasen, *Strategic Marketing for Nonprofit Organizations,* 3d ed., (Englewood Cliffs, NJ: Prentice-Hall, 1987).

22. M. Koch Scharf and J. Ward, "A Library Research Application of Focus Group Interviews," in *Energies for Transition: Proceedings of the Fourth National Conference of the Association of College and Research Libraries, Baltimore, Maryland, April 9-12, 1986,* ed. D. A. Nitecki (Chicago: Association of College and Research Libraries, 1986), 191-93.

23. Richard Widdows, Tia A. Hensler, and Marlaya H. Wyncott, "The Focus Group Interview: A Method for Assessing Users' Evaluation of Library Services," *College & Research Libraries* 52(July 1991): 352-59.

24. Choong Han Kim and Robert David Little, *Public Library Users and Uses: A Market Research Handbook* (Metuchen, NJ: Scarecrow Press, 1987); Meredith Butler and Bonnie Gratch, "Planning A User Study–The Process Defined," *College & Research Libraries* 43(July 1982): 320-30; and Kotler, *Strategic Marketing for Nonprofit Organizations,* 200-34.

25. Kotler, 423.

26. Weingand, 56.

27. Norman, "Marketing Library and Information Services: An Annotated Guide to Recent Trends and Developments," 46.

28. Miriam Drake, "User Fees: Aid or Obstacle to Access?" *Wilson Library Bulletin* 59(May 1984): 634.

29. Peter F. Drucker, "Managing the Public Service Institution," *College & Research Libraries* 37(January 1976): 7.

30. William M. Pride and O. C. Ferrell, *Marketing: Basic Concepts and Decisions*, 3d ed. (Boston: Houghton Mifflin Co., 1983), 323.

31. A. F. Roberts and S. G. Blandy, *Public Relations for Librarians* (Englewood, CO: Libraries Unlimited, 1989).

32. Kotler, 556-59.

33. Kotler, 543.

34. Pride, 158.

35. Anne B. Passarelli, *Public Relations in Business, Government and Society: A Bibliographic Guide* (Englewood, CO: Libraries Unlimited, 1989), xi.

36. Roberts, 7, 24-30.

37. Kotler, 156-99.

38. Wood, 99-153.

39. Weingand, xiii-xiv.

40. Wood, 100.

41. Ibid.

42. Donald E. Riggs, *Strategic Planning for Library Managers* (Phoenix, AZ: Oryx Press, 1984.

43. Wood, 105.

44. Kotler, 265.

45. Robert E. Thompson, *The Marketing Plan Workbook for Nonprofit Organizations* (Terre Haute, IN: Graphic Edition, 1987).

46. Wood, 144-48, 171-85.

47. Kotler, 638.

48. Wood, 112-13.

49. Norman, "Marketing Library and Information Services: An Annotated Guide to Recent Trends and Developments," 46.

50. Ibid.

51. Kotler, 477.

52. Peter R./Van Allen, "A Good Library Sign System: Is It Possible?" *Reference Services Review* 12(Summer 1984): 102-06.

53. Norman, "Marketing Library and Information Services: An Annotated Guide to Recent Trends and Developments," 48.

54. Roberts, 31-51.

55. Robert F. Muir, "Marketing Your Library or Information Service to Business," *Online* 17(July 1993): 41.

56. Ibid., 46.

A Brave New World: User Studies in the Humanities Enter the Electronic Age

Judy Reynolds

SUMMARY. An important part of reference services is the quality of the print and electronic resources. With the growth of electronic information in the field, it is essential to consider the information needs and behaviors of all humanists as we begin to design tools for the humanities. This article reviews the studies of the research habits of humanists. It discusses their work habits, their use of the library, the design of access and indexing systems, and electronic resources.

Humanists have long been considered to be major users of libraries; library resources are thought to be the source of primary

---

Judy Reynolds is Literature Librarian at San Jose State University, Library, 1 Washington Square, San Jose, CA 95192.

[Haworth co-indexing entry note]: "A Brave New World: User Studies in the Humanities Enter the Electronic Age." Reynolds, Judy. Co-published simultaneously in *The Reference Librarian* (The Haworth Press, Inc.) No. 49/50, 1995, pp. 61-81; and: *Library Users and Reference Services* (ed: Jo Bell Whitlatch) The Haworth Press, Inc., 1995, pp. 61-81. Multiple copies of this article/chapter may be purchased from The Haworth Document Delivery Center [1-800-3-HAWORTH; 9:00 a.m. - 5:00 p.m. (EST)].

material–the laboratory for the creation of scholarly and creative work in the field. As catalogs evolved from the very work-intensive hand written shelflist, to typed cards based on L.C. Union Lists, to L.C.-supplied cards, to the current automated databases with MARC records, we have seen librarians increasingly interested in studying how patrons use the systems and in redesigning them to increase effectiveness.

Although it may seem that most studies of patron information-seeking have focused primarily on scientists and secondarily on social scientists, there is actually a substantial body of literature on research methods and tools for humanists. In 1945, Swank studied the relative utility of the library catalog versus subject bibliographies.[1] He found that the subject headings used by libraries were too broad to retrieve pertinent materials. Is it any wonder that many subsequent user studies often reveal that scholars have tended to discount library catalogs and librarians as a sources of scholarly information?

Despite knowing many of the shortcomings of library catalogs, for many years the economics of information provision allowed for little modification of library records. Instead, libraries created in-house guides and published bibliographies to fill in the gaps. Automated systems now provide opportunities to enrich records and provide additional access points without each institution making the investment of original cataloging.

What do we know of the information needs and behaviors of those persons in the fields of art, music, literature, philosophy, religion, theatre and history? The first part of the paper reviews the literature concerning work habits, library use, and the design of access and indexing systems for the humanities, including issues related to cataloging/indexing, precision of subject terms, enhanced controlled vocabulary, and the importance of primary sources. The second section discusses the role of electronic sources in the humanities, the role of libraries and librarians in an electronic age, and the potential for enhancing access to humanities sources through electronic systems.

WORK HABITS

What do we know about the populations of humanists that we have studied up to now? They work alone, do not delegate research, sometimes rely on browsing, use books and older material, use mainly monographs, rely heavily on their own personal collections, value libraries, use a wide variety of material rather than a well-defined core of material, cite unique items located in special collections and often do not like using microforms.[2] Stamm describes the research process for artists as "private," "contemplative" and "intuitive."[3]

They tend to use information that is delivered to them such as book reviews and publishers' notices as well as that which they come across in their work–in bibliographies or from informal discussions with colleagues at work and conferences.[4] A new trend is the burgeoning interest in recent books and journal articles.[5] Previous studies indicated that humanists were largely interested in retrospective materials. It appears that more powerful print and online indexes are beginning to reshape the humanists options. Is locating current material, a process that was very time-consuming and not very productive (or even impossible) given the available indexing, now recognized as a viable option by scholars?

Gould, in a report prepared for the Research Libraries Group, describes the transition of humanities scholarship into the electronic age.

> Conversations with scholars make it clear that many prefer the familiar and unsystematic methods of consulting footnotes and colleagues, and that they consider on-line bibliographies both difficult and expensive to use. But as the volume of scholarship increases, informal strategies for identifying secondary literature may become less effective. Moreover, reliance on the 'invisible college' presupposes membership in a network. Although established scholars at leading research institutions may have easy access to information on recent work in the discipline, younger scholars and those at institutions outside the inner circle may be less fortunate. Timely and comprehensive access to information on current scholarship is vital to all scholars; automated research tools are capable of delivering it.[6]

The one thing that is clear in reviewing the literature is that the most studied population is the college and university faculty (and occasionally students) who are publishing or writing papers. As the study of the humanities in higher education will doubtless continue, these patrons will remain with us. However, future studies of information needs should focus more broadly on the artist, artisans and general public beyond academia and their use of information in these fields.

With the advent of electronic resources librarians may need to broaden their definition and design services and future studies to encompass a broader population. On the Internet, we have seen an opening up of communication without much regard for the status of the writer and people becoming more critical of the authority of the author of electronic messages. The new technology and its multi-media presentation are attracting increased attention and we may be working with a broader spectrum of humanists with more varied interests.

Economic forces, such as the costs in time and money weighed against the utility of the return, are factors in determining research behavior. Mooer's Law says that an information system will not be used when it's more trouble than it's worth.[7] Crawford says a scholar looks at a new systems and asks, "How much time must we invest in order to learn them? Will they really make our work better or more efficient?"[8] One author writes of the frustration of searching in preparing a paper on indexing: "The thesis of this paper was supported in the process of its preparation–it took five times as long to retrieve the references to document the ideas that the author recalled having heard or read as it did to write the paper. Presumably, a search to determine whether any of the ideas believed to be new in this paper had ever been expressed before in the literature would take many years, requiring a sequential reading of the library-information science literature, rather than the consultation of indexes."[9]

Many of the habits of humanists (such as dependence on proper names, titles and geographical names) with automation may be expanded to include more search options as the new generation of humanists discovers new ways to manipulate catalogs and indexes. If the new indexes are well designed, the economic rewards of effort expended will gain the support of these new scholars. Humanists especially stand to benefit in the hard-to-search areas where automation can provide free text searching. This new option will enable humanists to search for common terms such as the themes, genre terms and interdisciplinary topics that are so central to the humanities.

LIBRARY USE

Libraries are important to humanists, who have tended to be concerned primarily about their collections. "Faculty concern for libraries, as the National Enquiry on Scholarly Communication discovered, is for their repository function. The organization of knowledge does not worry them; they are not concerned about its complexities, its problems, or its promise."[10] Except for situations where collections and their arrangement are unique, librarians are not often consulted, the exception being that researchers report they rely on staff at special collections.[11]

When humanists do use the catalog, who is doing the searching? A study showed that older researchers make heaviest use of the library.[12] One study showed that the higher the level of education, the less frequent the use of subject searching.[13] Yet another study found that faculty with the highest rank perform subject searches and that humanists made relatively high use of keyword searching.[14] Possibly new scholars focus more on following up on footnotes and rely more heavily on the work of known scholars prominent in the invisible college, whereas established scholars, secure in their positions, can afford the luxury of searching more broadly. Studies differ on the utility of catalog use to scholars; because humanists and their needs are so varied, the differences may tell us that, rather than prescribing a limited design appropriate for a specific population, a range of options is necessary to satisfy the needs of all manner of patrons.

Another economic aspect of research is the decision to go to a remote location. Just as it is very convenient to receive notice of new publications at home or in the office, busy faculty find it easier to use their campus library. A survey of faculty by Broadbent indicated that faculty would prefer more in-depth coverage of the local library rather than access to other library catalogs.[15] Humanists weigh the economic factors of the cost in their time and money against the return in useful information when they are evaluating the value and resources. Libraries have not been regarded as having provided much added value to their collections or as having been players in the invisible college of the humanities.

Electronic document delivery may entice faculty to use the Internet to search without geographical barriers. The Internet and its global links may act as an incentive to investigate and visit other libraries, especially their special collections. Perhaps exclusive access to special collections will, at least in large part, disappear as quality images of collections, such as the Dead Sea Scrolls, become available via the Internet. Monies formerly spent on visiting collections in remote locations could be re-directed toward connecting the humanist and digitized version of manuscripts, art objects, etc. Libraries should support this access for everyone, opening up the collections for universal access without fearing that rare materials will be damaged by members of the general public. Making digitized copies of archived materials may actually help to preserve the originals, sparing them the damage of repeated exposures to the heat and light of photocopying.

DESIGN OF ACCESS AND INDEXING SYSTEMS

Cataloging/Indexing

Who are we cataloging for? Does everyone want or need the same level of cataloging? Can we provide catalogs/indexes designed to provide for the needs of researchers, artists, students and the general public? Wilson and Farid believe that patrons, including scholars, often only need a "nodding" familiarity with the research on a topic and would benefit by more evaluative works. They call for "more reviews, more authoritative critical surveys, more compendious works of reference, more works of *haute vulgarization,* more works of synthesis."[16] Stone suggests that, "effective reviews are more useful than abstracts because they provide a framework within which the likely quality and relevance of an item can be judged."[17] Although humanists would benefit if abstracts were available, their work is extremely difficult to abstract or classify.[18]

Gould feels that, because general bibliographies are not heavily used by scholars and because there is increased need for interdisciplinary material, that "the greatest promise for bibliographic projects may lie in offering access to existing bibliographies in ways that make them more useful for interdisciplinary research and encourage scholars to take advantage of what are now under utilized resources."[19] She urges development of humanities databases that would provide access to trade catalogs, research in progress and to information beyond that of traditional Western civilization: Also, machine-readable catalogs should be developed in order to support the new research that explores beyond the traditional limits of the accepted canon and crosses over into other disciplines. Her recommendations support Walker's findings that humanists need a range of databases.[20] Gould lists four categories of primary source needs that should be developed: visual material; archival material; machine-readable data files; and older printed material, much of it published in Europe.[21]

Precision of Subject Terms

In many cases, especially in the arts, the works themselves are expressed in a nonverbal language that defy translation into verbal language. Bates, Wilde and Siegfried conclude from their study of scholars using online databases, that the need of humanists "to combine terms from a wide variety of distinct categories suggests that searching in the humanities may be inherently more complex than in the sciences."[22] And Mandel and Herschman found that patrons searching online tended not to use the help that was available in the form of thesauri.[23]

Hurych found that humanities researchers expressed their requests in clear terms, but that the indexing and abstracting services were not as sophisticated as those in other fields and the researchers were not as familiar with the indexing structure of the discipline.[24] "One of the worst enemies of reliability is the tendency of the user to approach the catalog on a different level of specificity from that of the subject cataloger or the existing literature," writes McCarthy.[25] Wiberley feels that authority work to link variant forms of proper terms and/or names is essential to support research in the humanities.[26]

A study of entry terms in leading humanities encyclopedias partially confirms that subject access in the humanities is difficult. Though the assumption that the vocabulary is often imprecise is correct, in many cases it is also often quite straightforward, using names of persons or single creative works.[27] The humanities may have a dynamic, personal, and somewhat gossamer quality that defies our ability to outline clearly their characteristics. Stone states that the "fuzziness" of the humanities will increase with the use of computing and that even the traditional divisions between areas of study are not clearly defined. She points to Langridge's work which "distinguishes two distinct groups of disciplines within humanities; those such as art and religion which are characterized by creativeness and symbolic expression, and those represented by history and philosophy, which are characterized by intellectual analysis and literal expression."[28]

In contrast, a study of indexing in the humanities by Wiberley came to a different conclusion. His work indicates that there are two distinctive branches of the humanities and suggests that their needs be considered when designing retrieval systems. Philosophy and religion constitute one branch and they make heavy use of common terms such as "epistemology," "religious experience," "painting," and "tuba," which "designate any one of a class of things or the class itself." The other branch, which includes music, art, and literature, use more singular proper terms such as Charles Dickens, *All the King's Men,* which "are the names of people and creative works whose existence in space and time has been ascertained."[29] Historians, too, encounter much the same problems when their searches extend beyond proper terms. "Historians tend to employ an imprecise vocabulary in the classification of their periods–using designations such as medieval, 19th-century, 1817-25, and early modern."[30]

Walker studied the sheer number of terms used and success with subject headings, rather than the use of proper terms. In comparing the use of terms in representative major humanities indexes, she found that art had the greatest and history the narrowest spread of subject terms. The duplication among the indexes in the various disciplines was minimal and controlled vocabulary searching averaged a significantly higher retrieval rate than did use of titles. Natural language was most successful in history and religion, but controlled language retrieved more items.[31] We need to keep in mind that novice users may perform best with only a single search using one search protocol.[32] Walker says that, "the challenge to designers of future systems lies in the provision of the most effective combination of explicit and transparent features, and the simplification of vocabulary transfer between databases."[33]

Traditional research, including the study of specific artists, works of art and geographical locations, is fairly well served by subject terms but would be improved with additional support for authority control. Bates, Wilde and Siegfried suggest that key areas for improving search options are geographical, chronological and discipline terms.[34] While proper term searching may predominate, we should be cautious in concluding that systems should be designed around just this approach. Searching styles and index terms may have evolved more because they were all that was available and the limited avenues of approach determined scholars' habits. Interviews with humanists found that scholars had learned to work with the existing information structure and had few suggestions for its improvement.[35] The *MLA International Bibliography* was published for sixty years before it began providing the option to search for themes in literature. As Pankake notes, the future holds exciting new options for established scholars. "We can ask different questions now of literature and art and history than people were able to ask before." "We do it because it is what we can do, not because it is morally superior to our predecessors' work. Using a computer is part of what is exciting today in the humanities."[36]

At least for newer humanist, unfamiliar with the field, subject headings can be very useful. The growing emphasis on interdisciplinary research and the tendency of humanists to revel in the use of metaphor and poetic language, however, makes it difficult to assign adequate subject headings. Instead, the addition of access to tables of contents and indexes would benefit all levels of humanists. Frost suggests adding abstracts and subject headings for chapters.[37] Ross would "collapse separate authority files for author and subject and give user the option to select all records."[38]

Enhanced Controlled Vocabulary

For sophisticated users, mounting established, evaluative bibliographies would be very useful. Bates, Wilde and Siegfried also propose the introduction of "discipline terms into database indexing and retrieval by providing a special classification that indicated the various special senses in which humanities scholars use them. Discipline terms would thus have more specific meanings and provide more precise retrieval for humanities searchers."[39] Anyone who has tried to limit a search to "literature" can see the merits of this suggestion.

Those new to the field would benefit from enriched vocabulary. Perhaps we should provide cataloging/indexing options for different levels of humanities users and allow them to tailor the search to suit their needs. For example, a scholar might find "Elizabethan" to be quite specific. But I doubt that the uninitiated student looking for one of Shakespeare's plays, who thought the title was "Penguin" or "Pelican," would have any idea how to broaden his search to the appropriate time period or countries. Automated systems with enriched cataloging/indexing might provide the option to go to broader or narrower qualifiers regularly used in the humanities such as nationality, period of time, genre, movement. A patron whose search resulted in too large or small a set could choose to modify the selection. An authority file could link "Elizabethan" to English writers, to writers of the 16th century or even to the genres of drama and poetry. A search for Monet could be broadened to include Impressionists or painters. The search software must make the choice of options obvious to the patron and librarians must point them out in reference and instruction sessions. Scholars, too, would profit from enriched vocabulary. In working on the *Rutgers Inventory of Machine-Readable Text in the Humanities,* Hoogcarspel finds there is a need for more subject terms such as "corpus" or "French novels."[40]

Another possibility is to incorporate established tools, such as the *Genre Terms: a Thesaurus for Use in Rare Book and Special Collections Cataloguing* as well as providing the ability to move up or down in terms of specificity into our cataloging. Stebelman reports that MLA has significantly improved the utility of its index by including searching by genre, broad literary period, location and literary technique.[41] Bates, Wilde and Siegfried advocate basing indexing on specialized thesauri such as Getty *Thesaurus of Art-Historical Place Names* to provide best indexing terms.[42] Novice searchers would have more options for appropriate search terms. Scholars would have the opportunity to search by discipline terms, which are especially useful for searching special collections. Patrons would also benefit from simultaneous online access to works such as the *Fiction Catalog*.

On the other hand, there is evidence that indexing efforts should be limited to areas in which the vocabulary of the humanities is most precise and that unrestricted searching be available for the less well defined topics. Wiberley argues that because vocabulary is so dispersed for terms other than proper names, titles and places, "there should be little effort to employ controlled vocabulary for certain kinds of subject access in the humanities."[43] Walker suggests that the increasing interest in interdisciplinary topics argues for using free text and educating users to construct better search nets.[44]

Primary Sources

Many citations make implicit references to primary sources making it very difficult to quantify the number of times a primary work is referenced.[45] Acknowledging one's intellectual debt when one cannot retrieve the original citation is problematic.[46] And users tend to "formulate their queries according to what they think the system can offer, so the query as presented may differ significantly from the real need."[47] One can only measure what patrons did, not what they could have done.[48]

Stern found that references are subject to an aging process. "The more contemporary the author, the greater is the use made of primary sources by scholars."[49] "As the body of secondary material and the various critical apparatuses and other editorial structures build up around the works of a creative writer, the use of the text itself decreases in favor of other types of research material directly related to the text."[50] She found that the amount of citing increases for more theoretical works. "Literary researchers use more critical material of other researchers when they write about literary theory than when they write about the creative writer and his work."[51] A survey by Guest of humanities researchers supports this, finding that scholars are more likely to consider the library important if their research is theoretical rather than applied.[52]

Several studies conclude that, as primary sources are the raw material of the humanities, we should concentrate available funds on making special collections and archives available, rather than purchasing mainly secondary materials.[53] Jones suggested that "secondary works become obsolescent but primary sources would retain their value over time."[54] As there is no clear and effective way of predicting what materials may be used in the future, libraries should heed Stone's warning of the "need for a sensitive approach to relegation and storage."[55]

ELECTRONIC SOURCES

Saule believes that librarians have an essential but difficult role teaching scholars in the humanities to use electronic resources. She states that "historically, humanists have been skeptical about the value of computers in their research and have been hesitant to try new research techniques. The very structure of humanities disciplines is not conducive to computerization."[56]

Katzen outlined the stages in the use of computers for resources in the humanities. In the first stage, control of computing was centralized and scholars were provided access in order to create indexes and concordances and to do text analysis. In the second phase, the process was decentralized and control of the new computers moved to the scholar's desk where they were used for word processing, automating personal card files and for computer-assisted instruction. Connecting to online databases, online catalogs and local area networks via telecommunications and networks marks the third phase.

Value of Humanities Databases

Katzen asked librarians why the humanities databases were not more heavily used and they attributed it to shortage of staff, charging for searches, inadequacy of database coverage, lack of retro-spective coverage. She notes a key problem for financing any com-puting project in the field is that, "humanities computing often requires much computer storage for long periods."[57] An untapped source with great potential lies in linking the vast numbers of per-sonal databases that humanists have created.[58]

Bibliographic control of electronic texts is still a problematic, unresolved area for scholarly use. Hoogcarspel listed the major challenges that emerged in working on the *Rutgers Inventory of Machine-Readable Text in the Humanities.* Because sources often have no title screen, the bibliographic information can be inconsis-tent and incomplete. Many items make no reference to the original print version. And libraries must catalog without looking at the item, not having either the software or documentation for the soft-ware being cataloged or the hardware on which to run it. She hails the Text Encoding Initiative (TEI), guidelines for scholarly text preparation, and the use of Standard Generalized Markup Language (SGML), as effective steps toward solving these problems. She too calls for enhanced indexing including form, genre fiction subject and archival terms. Copyright questions also makes owners to be afraid to share their valuable databases.[59]

The medium is the message, as McLuhan said, and some aca-demics are slow to warm to innovation that is not done without style. "The appearance of computer jargon shows, to some people, that the message has not really been assimilated and the common ground does not yet exist."[60] Schwartz asks if electronic publishing disrupts the current publish or perish academic rewards system.[61] Many faculty, especially the newer ones, wonder if they can spare the time to work on electronic projects, saying that such projects are not recognized as suitably academic.

Importance of Standards

Currently, specialized indexes are produced by a number of ven-dors and patrons need to use several search protocols if they are to be successful. Even if they succeed in this task, indexing standards are not uniform and differences between the database producer and the index software vendor may not mesh smoothly. For example, the *MLA International Bibliography,* when searched with Silver-

Platter software, does not always produce consistent results when looking for fields such as language. Eileen Mackesy of the Modern Language Association has called for standardization of the bibliographical and other elements of humanities databases.[62] Stone, too, suggests that in the humanities there is a need to work together "for co-ordinated development of secondary services."[63]

As text files in the humanities constitute a large investment, it is important that their entries be standardized if they are to be manipulated for a variety of purposes over time. Crawford explains why librarians should insist on standards for electronic text files. "My inability to read an incompatible database impairs my freedom of inquiry. If we are to succeed in distributing information to humanists electronically, unnecessary inconsistencies must be discouraged."[64] The Standardized General Markup Language (SGML) is designed to accomplish this task. It has proven quite successful with a variety of projects such as the French text database *ARTFUL*, (American and French Research on the Treasury of the French Language), the *Oxford English Dictionary* and the electronic journal *PostModern Culture*.[65] Adhering to standards may not be essential for all text files. Efforts such as Michael Hart's Project Gutenberg, The Online Book Initiative and the Wiretap Online Library have as their goal the distribution of texts, hoping to provide computer users with quality reading material. They are promoting literacy and not especially concerned with entry standards. Scholarly and popular electronic publishing both have their place in electronic publishing, as they do in print.

The Role of Libraries and Librarians

Clearly, people would like to have libraries and library service available to them anywhere, any time with a minimum of effort. Crawford suggests that, "some users would appreciate being able to use modems to consult reference and circulation desks . . . " "Also, the ability of library staff to handle routine exchanges with users during off-peak hours may contribute to using staff more efficiently."[66] Already in some libraries traditional reference service has been replaced or augmented in part by such services as well as electronic directories and prototype expert systems. The role of "libraries without walls" is also being filled by listservs and other electronic services. Krol predicts that "software worms" acting as "Knowbots" will soon function as reference librarians, searching the Internet.[67]

Electronic resources will supplement, not supplant, print. Many who have used e-mail find themselves printing many of the documents from e-mail and electronic journals articles and purchasing manuals on the use of systems. Visual resources face the challenge of providing quality images and finding sufficient computer storage space. Wiberley is not convinced that we can supply the humanists journal needs solely by electronic means. "There is much greater need in the humanities to read the entire document, and this is done more easily when the document is in paper rather than online."[68] Schwartz points out that universities that think they will save money by cutting paper journals are very short sighted. "Libraries or computer centers will foot the bill for all the paper used to download thousands of articles form the Internet, many in multiple copies."[69] And there is also the cost of computer storage space, especially for those universities that provide the scholarly databases.

Lynch contends that it is too early for us to contemplate entrusting the responsibility for the public and private records of human endeavor to electronic sites. "A reasonable number of independently controlled archive sites for certain material are necessary to provide confidence in the continued integrity and accessibility of our scholarly, historical, and cultural record. In cases when key components of the record represent valuable intellectual property that is owned by publishers, however, we have yet to establish and reach consensus on the compacts of responsible behavior necessary to ensure acceptance of a conversion of the print publication base to electronic format."[70]

Librarians have a role in alerting patrons to the critical thinking issues involved in utilizing information. The role of the publisher in validating the accuracy of information resources is in a state of transition. Issues such as qualifications of the author, currency and accuracy of the information, nature and motives of the "publisher," quality of the data, edition, and the like need to be closely scrutinized. The current surge of information is overwhelming. Pankake suggests that, "we should be active as gateways to electronic information, and even provide reference service to scholars at those schools in our locales which lack the full panoply of sophisticated online sources."[71] Librarians can act as boundary spanners, linking scholars to quality materials in specific disciplines in packages that are polished and relatively easy to use. Examples of such efforts are now in process in the development of library gophers and World Wide Web services.

Plum and Smalley caution that just enhancing retrieval is only part of the librarian's task with regard to humanists. They note that, even before the introduction of the Internet, humanists saw the library as infinite. "Rather than *relevance* the humanities scholar is waiting to be convinced of *worth.*" "Meaning is unlocked, indeed created by, the personal engagement the researcher brings to the interaction." They believe that success in the introduction of automated tools depends on focusing some of the decision making back onto the humanists, involving them in the design of systems such as gophers.[72] Stone agrees, stating that, "communication between libraries and faculty takes on increasing importance."[73] She continues and cautions against too narrow a definition of our constituents, "If there is any strength in the view that society needs the outcome of humanities scholarship then this gives support to the view that public libraries have an increasing role to play."[74]

CONCLUSION

In 1982 Stone, reexamining fundamental questions in earlier work on the humanities, asked if use of resources was limited because the research methods options were inadequate leading to heavy use of secondary tools to supplement library catalogs. She asked why there was not more work being done to improve this widely recognized situation.[75]

Today, we are still asking the same questions, but we are developing possible solutions. Past research has provided information about what has worked within the limited confines of available access. Clearly proper term searching is essential and it should be fortified with more options and links to reference resources that will provide both elucidation and evaluation. Discontinuing subject access except for proper terms seems both premature and rash.

Subject access has never been available for works of fiction, art or music. Subject terms, especially with enhanced authority control and links to subject encyclopedias, bibliographies and the like, may prove very useful to scholars and the general public. Keyword searching, which has already proven useful, could exploit the addition of tables of contents, indexes and the like. We need to study the effect of enhanced cataloging, options for levels of searching, and free text searching additional portions of the record. With that information, we could better determine which, if any, portions of the record could be eliminated in the humanities.

With the rush of enthusiasm for new systems and trying new options, librarians can play an important role by insisting on the importance of standards for cataloging, machine readable text files and for authority work. We must be vigilant and articulate about how requiring the MARC record will provide humanists the benefit of a powerful, dependable, and universally applicable retrieval system. While it may be possible to create a new, friendly catalog using World Wide Web, if the product is not transferable and does not contain all the elements of MARC, the patron will be shortchanged.

Many of today's automated systems are as daunting to the uninitiated as were Model T's that needed to be cranked to start. We must articulate the need for "friendly" systems and appropriate cataloging, hypertext links and indexing systems, for, after all, we see more patrons engaging with the systems than do the vendors. We can not only link patrons and works, but also creators of primary works and those who can help them package their works in traditional or new ways. In the electronic age, the edges of the invisible college are in flux. Where faculty formerly collaborated on publications with other faculty, many now need to work with individuals with expertise in computing, multi-media and copyright law, and we can bring them together.

Automation holds potential for opening up vast areas of cooperation and access to special collections in the humanities. Becher describes the isolation in which humanists worked in the past and the price they paid for it.

> Research in the humanities, however, is relatively immune, both because the contribution it is able to make to the wider society is less directly utilitarian, and because–for the reasons

explored in earlier chapters–scholarly enquiry of this kind is neither readily amenable to large-scale collective activity nor for the most part financially demanding. But *ipso facto* its comparative freedom from the fetters of government and commerce is won at the expense of a philistine perception that it is marginal and irrelevant as well as small-scale and trivial.[76]

Automation is attracting the attention of a new group of patrons, many of whom may not have been attracted to the humanities in traditional formats. If we truly believe that the humanities, in its study of the unique views and visions of human experience, is essential to the world, we must articulate the need for funding to support its continuation at every level, from the most scholarly to the popular. There will be economic pressures to focus funding on all-purpose databases. Librarians need to stand up for the development and maintenance of specialized databases so that resources in the humanities can be fully exploited.

We must involve the humanists in the design of their research tools, recognizing them as partners in this endeavor. We rue the lack of consultation with librarians on research projects, but we are often guilty of the same isolation when we develop information systems.

NOTES

1. Swank, Raynard, "The Organization of Library Materials for Research in English Literature," *Library Quarterly* 15 (1945):49-74.

2. Immroth, J. "Information Need for the Humanities," in Debons, A. *Information Science: Search for Identity.* Proceedings of the 1972 Nato Advanced Study Institute of Information Science, New York, 1974, pp. 249-62; Bebout, Donald Davis and Oehlerts, "User Studies in the Humanities: A Survey and a Proposal," *RQ* 15 (Fall 1975):40-44; Soper, M.E., "Characteristics and Use of Personal Collections," *Library Quarterly* 46, no.4 (Oct. 1976):397-415; Heinzkill, Richard, "Characteristics of Reference in Selected Scholarly English Literary Journals," *Library Quarterly* 50 (July 1980):352-365; Steig, Margaret F., "Information Needs of Historians," *College and Research Libraries* 42, no.6 (Nov. 1981):549-560; Stone, Sue, "Progress in Documentation, Humanities Scholars," *Journal of Documentation* 38 (Dec. 1982):292-313; Smalley, Topsey N. and Stephen H. Plum, "Teaching Library Researching in the Humanities and the Sciences: a Contextual Approach," pp.135-170 in Oberman, Cerise and Katina Strauch, eds., *Theories of Bibliographic Education; Designs for Teaching.* R.R.Bowker, New York, 1982.

3. Stamm, Deirdre C., "How Art Historians Look for Information," *Art Documentation* 3 (Winter 1984):117-119.

4. Stern, Madeline, "Characteristics of the Literature of Literary Scholars," *College and Research Libraries* 44, no.4 (July 1983):203; Stoan, Stephen K., "Research and Library Skills: and Analysis and Interpretation," *College and Research Libraries* 45 (March 1984):102-103.

5. Guest, Susan S., "The Use of Bibliographic Tools by Humanities Faculty at State University of New York Albany," *The Reference Librarian* 18 (Summer 1987):167.

6. Gould, Constance, *Information Needs in the Humanities*. RLG, Stanford, CA, 1988,pp.51-2.

7. Mooer, Calvin N., "Mooer's Law, or Why Some Retrieval Systems are Used and Others are Not," *American Documentation* 11, no.3 (July 1960):p.ii.

8. Crawford, David, "Meeting Scholarly Information Needs in an Automated Environment," *College and Research Libraries* 47 (Nov. 1986):570.

9. Weinberg, Bella H., "Why Indexing Fails the Researcher," *Indexer* 16 (April 1988):6.

10. McCarthy, Constance, "The Faculty Problem," *Journal of Academic Librarianship* 11 (July 1985):143.

11. Wiberley, Stephen E. and William G. Jones, "Patterns of Information Seeking in the Humanities," *College and Research Libraries* 50, no.6 (Nov. 1989):638-645.

12. Guest, Susan S., (1987).

13. Markey, Karen. *Subject Searching in Library Catalogs*. OCLC, Dublin, 1984.

14. Frost, Carolyn O., "Faculty Use of Subject Searching in Card and Online Catalogs,"*Journal of Academic Librarianship* 13, no.2 (May 1987):86-92.

15. Broadbent, Elaine, "A Study of Humanities Faculty Library Seeking Behavior," *Catalog and Classification Quarterly* 6 (Spring 1986):23-37.

16. Wilson, Patrick and Mona Farid, "On the Use of the Records of Research," *Library Quarterly* 49, no.2 (April 1979):143.

17. Stone, Sue, (1982):299.

18. Stern, Peter, "Online in the Humanities," *Journal of Academic Librarianship* 14 (July 1988):161-164.

19. Gould, Constance, (1988):51.

20. Walker, Geraldine, "Searching the Humanities: Subject Overlap and Searching Vocabulary," *Database* 13 (Oct. 1990):41.

21. Gould, Constance, (1988):52-3.

22. Bates, Marcia J., Deborah N. Wilde and Susan Siegfried, "An Analysis of Search Terminology Used by Humanities Scholars: the Getty Online Searching Project Report Number 1," *Library Quarterly* 63, no.1 (Jan. 1993):36.

23. Mandel, Carol A. and Judith Herschman, "Online Subject Access-Enhancing the Library Catalog," *Journal of Academic Librarianship* 9 (July 1983): 149.

24. Hurych, Jitka, "After Bath: Scientist, Social Scientists, and Humanists in the Context of Online Searching," *Journal of Academic Librarianship* 12, no.3 (July 1986):158-65.

25. McCarthy, Constance, "The Reliability Factor in Subject Access–Enhancing the Library Catalog," *Journal of Academic Librarianship* 9 (Jan. 1986):54.

26. Wiberley, Stephen E. Jr., "Names in Space and Time," *Library Quarterly* 58 (Jan. 1988):25.

27. Wiberley, Stephen E., "Subject Access in the Humanities," *Library Quarterly* 53, no.4 (Oct. 1983):420-433.

28. Stone, Sue, (1982):306.

29. Wiberley, Stephen, (1988).

30. Falk, Joyce Duncan, "Searching by Historical Period in the History Databases," in *National Online Meeting: Proceedings, 1981*, Williams, Martha E. and Thomas H. Hogan, comps. Learned Information, Medford, NJ, 1981:200.

31. Walker, Geraldine, "Searching the Humanities: Subject Overlap and Searching Vocabulary," *Database* 13, no.5 (Oct. 1990):41.

32. Ward, Sandra and Laura M. Osegueda, "Teaching University Student End-users About Online Searching," *Science and Technology Libraries* 5, no.1 (Fall 1984):17-31.

33. Walker, Geraldine, (1990):45.

34. Bates, Wilde and Siegfried, (1993):36-7.

35. Reynolds, Judy (1983), unpublished paper.

36. Pankake, Marcia, "Humanities Research in the 90s: What Scholars Need; What Librarians Can Do," *Library Hi Tech* 9, no.1 (1991):14.

37. Frost, Carolyn, (1987).

38. Ross, James E., "Artists and Poets Online," *Cataloging and Classification Quarterly* 7 (Spring 1987):97.

39. Bates, Wilde and Siegfried, (1993):35.

40. Hoogcarspel, Annelies, "The *Rutgers Inventory of Machine Readable Text in the Humanities*: Cataloging and Access," *Information Technology and Libraries* 13, no.1 (March 1994):27-34.

41. Stebelman, Scott, "Vocabulary Control and the Humanities: A Case Study of the *MLA International Bibliography*," *The Reference Librarian* 47 (Summer 1994).

42. Bates, Wilde & Siegfried, (1993):34.

43. Wiberley, Stephen, (1988):26.

44. Walker, G., "Online Searching in the Humanities: Implications for End-users and Intermediaries," in *Online Information 88; Proceedings of the 12th International Online Information Meeting*, London, Dec. 6-8, 1988. Learned Information, Oxford 1988:401-412.

45. Garfield, Eugene, "Is Information Retrieval in the Arts and Humanities Inherently Different from that in Science? The Effect that ISI's Citation Index for the Arts and Humanities is Expected to have on Future Scholarship," *Library Quarterly* 50, no.1 (1980):40-57; Heinzkill, Richard, (1980).

46. Kochen, Manfred, "How Well do We Acknowledge Intellectual Debts?" *Journal of Documentation* 43, no.1 (March 1987):54-64.

47. Bates, Wilde and Siegfried, (1993):11-2.

48. Steig, Margaret, (1981).

49. Stern, Madeline, (1983):204.

50. Stern, Madeline, (1983):208.

51. Stern, Madeline, (1983):207.

52. Guest, Susan, (1987):166.

53. Wiberley, Stephen, "Sources for the Humanities: Measuring Use and Meeting Needs," in Stueart, Robert D. and Richard D. Johnson, eds., *New Horizons for Academic Libraries; Paper Presented at the First National Conference of the Association of College and Research Libraries, Boston, Massachusetts, November 8-11, 1978.* K.G.Saur, New York, 1978; Gould, Constance, (1988).

54. Stone, Sue, (1982) reference to Jones, C., Chapman, M. and Carr Woods, P. "The Characteristics of the Literature Used by Historians," *Journal of Librarianship,* 4, (1972):137-56.

55. Stone, Sue, (1982):306.

56. Saule, Mara R., "User Instruction Issues for Databases in the Humanities," *Library Trends* 40, no.4 (Spring 1992):612.

57. Katzen, May, "Application of Computers in the Humanities," *Information Processing and Management* 22 (1986):264.

58. Crawford (1986),p.571.

59. Hoogcarspel (1994),p.33.

60. Crawford, David, (1986):570.

61. Schwartz, Charles A., "Scholarly Communication as a Loosely Coupled System: Reassessing Prospects for Structural Reform," *College and Research Libraries* 55, no.2 (March 1994):108.

62. Mackesy, Eileen M., "Perspective on Secondary Access Services in the Humanities," *Journal of the American Society for Information Science* 33, no.3 (May 1982):151.

63. Stone, Sue, (1982):306.

64. Crawford, David, (1986):572.

65. Price-Wilkins, John and others, "Text Files in Libraries: Present Foundations and Future Directions," *Library Hi Tech* 9, no.3 (1991).

66. Crawford, David, (1986):574.

67. Krol, Ed. *The Whole Internet; User's Guide and Catalog.* O'Reilly & Associates, Inc., Sebastopol, 1994:350.

68. Wiberley, Stephen E. Jr., "Habits of Humanists: Scholarly Behavior and New Information Technologies," *Library Hi Tech* 9 no.1 (1991):19.

69. Schwartz, Charles A., (1994):112.

70. Lynch, Clifford A., "Rethinking the Integrity of the Scholarly Record in the Networked Information Age," *Educom Review* 29, no.2 (March/April 1994):39.

71. Pankake, Marcia, (1991):13.

72. Plum, Terry and Topsy N. Smalley, "Research as Repatriation," *The Reference Librarian* 47 (Summer 1994).

73. Stone, Sue, (1982):304.

74. Stone, Sue, (1982):305.

75. Stone, Sue, (1982):305.

76. Becher, Tony, *Academic Tribes and Territories; Intellectual Enquiry and the Cultures of Disciplines.* The Society for Research into higher Education & Open University Press, Stony Stratford, 1989:138.

Information Seeking Patterns: Social Sciences

Mary B. Folster

SUMMARY. In the last three decades, there have been a number of studies that have explored the information-seeking behavior of social science researchers. Over the years several themes have remained constant. Journals remain the preferred source of information and rank above most every other source. References to relevant materials are identified through following the citations from journals in hand rather than utilizing indexing and abstracting services. Libraries and librarians are not viewed as a primary, or in some cases, even an important source of information. This article will review some of the major studies that have been done in this area and discuss the implications of the findings for the development of services for this group of clientele.

INTRODUCTION

Over the last three decades a considerable body of literature has emerged dealing with the information needs and information seeking patterns of researchers in the social sciences. The impetus for studying users and potential users of libraries and information systems has usually been the desire to improve service by making it more responsive to the clients' needs.[1]

Mary B. Folster is Head of the Social Science Reference Library at the University of Wisconsin-Madison, 8432 Social Science Building, Madison, WI 53706.

[Haworth co-indexing entry note]: "Information Seeking Patterns: Social Sciences." Folster, Mary B. Co-published simultaneously in *The Reference Librarian* (The Haworth Press, Inc.) No. 49/50, 1995, pp. 83-93; and: *Library Users and Reference Services* (ed: Jo Bell Whitlatch) The Haworth Press, Inc., 1995, pp. 83-93. Multiple copies of this article/chapter may be purchased from The Haworth Document Delivery Center [1-800-3-HAWORTH; 9:00 a.m. - 5:00 p.m. (EST)].

Prior to the 1960s, the vast majority of research on the use of information by researchers were reports on the use of scientific and technical information. These were generally questionnaire based user studies that gathered basic demographic data and provided quantitative data on the kinds of materials needed by and used by these groups. Since the early 1960s there has been a concerted effort to determine what type of information is being used and how it is being used by social science researchers.

CITATION PATTERNS AS A MEASURE OF USE

The mid 1960s saw an emergence of studies that looked at information seeking behaviors of social scientists. This was an important addition to the large amount of research that already existed on information gathering behaviors in science and technology. Although there were some user studies conducted, these early studies tended to draw heavily on the research methodologies employed to study literature use in the sciences, primarily citation studies.

The results of the studies of social scientists led researchers to make a number of observations about the type of material used, the date of publication, the language of publication and the discipline or subject area represented by the material. There was a tendency to then compare the findings from the social science studies to the findings from the previous work in the sciences.

An analysis of footnotes and citations from a sample of British periodicals in the social sciences provided data that indicated that, in the social sciences, the volume and relative importance of non-periodical literature was greater than in the natural sciences.[2] A survey of the use of Social Science periodicals carried out at the British National Lending Library in 1965 led researchers to the conclusion that, compared with science and technology, social scientists make relatively little use of abstracting and indexing publications and that they make little use of foreign language materials.[3]

In a follow up study, the results of the National Lending Library study were analyzed to ascertain factors specific to the social sciences rather than in comparison to the sciences. An observation made in the original study was that there was an identifiable core of heavily used materials and that there were relatively few journal titles cited. The subsequent study indicated that periodicals were relatively less cited in the social sciences than in the sciences and technology partly because there were relatively fewer periodicals.[4]

The results of the citation studies of the 1960s tended to indicate that the social sciences fall somewhere between the humanities (which rely heavily on fairly well-established data, such as historical archives, or texts) and the sciences and technology (which depend on newly accumulated facts and data). The social science disciplines, therefore, reflected characteristics of both in terms of the citation patterns which emerged.[5]

The social sciences could be classified by the degree to which they utilized materials which represented the forefront of research, as represented by citations to recently published material, or the extent to which they relied on historical or archival literature. These were referred to, respectively, as 'hard science' and 'soft science.'[6] In a study of the characteristics of the literature used by historians, it was determined that, along the spectrum of hard vs. soft sciences, history would fall into the "soft" realm of the social sciences, since, through a citation analysis it was determined that this discipline made heavy use of archival materials.[7]

USER STUDIES

Researchers soon reached the conclusion that citation studies had certain limitations as a methodology for assessing user needs. While they could serve as an indicator of actual cited use, they did not measure potential use or background information gathering activities that were not cited. Therefore, citation studies were an "indicator" of use but were not a "measure" of use.[8]

The 1960s did produce an interesting user study. A survey of British students at Southampton University revealed that the students did not avail themselves of library services and that they made very little use of reference materials. One of the results of this survey was a recommendation from the researchers that reference staff make an effort to initiate contact with the students.[9] One of the librarians actually registered for one of the seminars, and, as a result, became recognizable to the students. The students were then more likely to approach this person for assistance. In a follow up survey, there was a considerable change in attitude toward the library indicating a break down of the barriers between the staff and the students.[10]

THE INFROSS PROJECT

The 1970s saw increasing attempts to design research that would go beyond the descriptive aspects of materials usage and to develop profiles of the users and their needs. Methodologies were developed that could provide insight into the information needs of groups, their characteristics, and their present information seeking behavior.

Most notable among these were the INFROSS project studies which were designed to assess the information needs of British social scientists.[11] The project, the Investigation into Information Requirements of the Social Sciences, was carried out in the late 1960s and early 1970s. It was unique in that it employed a number of methodologies as a means of lending validity to the findings regarding the information needs of social scientists. The researchers sent mailed questionnaires to a very large sample of British Social Scientists. This was supplemented by interviews conducted with a moderately sized sample. Furthermore, a small sample of respondents was intensively studied over a continuous period of time.

Some of the findings of the INFROSS project were enlightening to the information profession. When asked about methods of locating information, a quarter of the respondents indicated that they had never used abstracts, indexes, or library catalogs, didn't search library shelves or use book reviews as a source of information and nearly half had never consulted librarians. The most useful method of locating information was following up references in books and journals that individuals had already acquired.

The major conclusions of the INFROSS study were that, while social scientists attached a high importance to the locating of references, they relied on citations from journals to identify those resources and did not rely on traditional bibliographic tools. They also depended heavily on colleagues and subject experts in their respective fields and did not consult library catalogs or librarians very much at all.[12]

Other user studies conducted in the 1970s reinforced the findings of the INFROSS project. A study of social science faculty at the University of Illinois concluded that one-half to three-quarters of the respondents relied on citations in journals as their primary source of information.[13] This same study also led the researchers to the conclusion that the majority of faculty surveyed used the library as a supplementary rather than as a primary source of serial information.

SMALL GROUP USER STUDIES

The 1980s saw a move away from the traditional macro approach, that is, studying large groups, to a micro approach involving more intensive study of small, well-defined, discrete groups. The studies from this period also reflect more vigorous statistical analysis of data and an increasing interest in the use of qualitative methods, such as observation and unstructured interview techniques.

A major example of this type of research is the INISS project. The study, the Information Needs in Social Services project, utilized structured observation techniques in a study of social work practitioners and managers. Using structured observations and interviews with social service staff members at all levels, the researchers assessed how information was looked for, obtained and utilized. The results of the investigation led to the conclusion that information officers and librarians had taken a relatively low-key role. The recommendation of the researchers was that, in order to be effective, information officers needed to become more dynamic, to exploit the informal network, to become more familiar with tasks performed by staff, to visit work sites, to attend meetings and discussion groups and to acquire additional skills in organizational communication.[14]

EMERGING ROLES FOR LIBRARIANS

In a survey conducted by the American Council of Learned Societies (ACLS) in November, 1985, it was found that scholars continued to rely heavily on journals, although they indicated that they found it difficult to keep up with the literature in their fields. Scholars ranked libraries lower than their own personal collections in importance as a source of information, reinforcing the findings from previous years. This study did find that scholars were beginning to become much more aware of many of the emerging technological advances in libraries, although only about half of the respondents took advantage of the resources available to them, particularly computerized literature searching and online catalogs.[15]

The authors of the report on the ACLS survey suggest that as the growth of emerging technologies offers an opportunity for scholars to enhance their scholarly communications, the failure of librarians to take on a leadership role in the introduction and promotion of such services could well result in the relinquishing of this important information role to campus automation services. [16] Other reports of research conducted in the 1980s reinforced the concept that librarians needed to reconsider their roles as information providers in a rapidly changing information environment.

A series of interviews of British Social Scientists was conducted as a follow-up study to some of the findings of the INFROSS project. One of the findings of these interviews was that researchers suffered from lack of time to do their work properly, to communicate with colleagues, and to seek information.[17] Studies such as these begin to lay the groundwork for the possible role that information providers could fulfill in the information gathering process.

BEHAVIORAL MODELS

Studies that emerged in the late 1980s and into the 1990s further developed the technique of looking more closely at the information seeking patterns of researchers and the activities associated with each kind of information gathering process.

Several behavioral models were developed to identify the various steps in the information seeking process. These models break the information-seeking process down into identifiable activities.[18]

1. "Starting" is the actual identification of a topic and the commencement of the initial search for information.

2. "Chaining" or "chasing" refers to the activity of following up on references by using one citation as a link to other citations.
3. "Selecting" or "sifting" or "differentiating" involves the decision about which cites to follow up on and which to filter out as unwanted materials.
4. "Locating" is the actual finding of the information.
5. "Monitoring" is the process of maintaining current awareness in a particular area of interest by regularly following particular sources.
6. "Extracting" refers to the process of systematically working through a particular source to locate material of interest. This involves the reading of material to determine which of the material becomes incorporated into the final report.
7. "Assembly and dissemination" is the actual drawing together of material for publication or some other form of dissemination.

IMPLICATIONS

As we look at the behavioral model, and the component parts of it, we can begin to develop a framework through which to see the services that libraries traditionally provide and their place in the research process.

Only one process, that of selecting, is one in which the library plays a significant role. Library services such as cataloging and inter-library loan are clearly important aspects of this stage of the research process. However, these traditional roles do not play an important part in the initial search for relevant sources. Researchers rely more on items in hand to identify appropriate cites rather than relying on library services. As shown in studies to date, the library serves primarily as a source for obtaining previously identified information, but not as a resource to identify relevant information.

The processes of selecting and monitoring are not activities traditionally associated with academic librarians, although many libraries have implemented various services at some levels. This has, however, long been a model for special librarians. Often involved in projects right from their inception, special librarians often become actively involved in decisions about which materials to follow up on and which to forego. They are also actively involved in the monitoring process through current awareness and SDI services.

CONCLUSION

From the studies that have been reviewed here, we are given a general understanding of the overall information seeking behavior of social scientists. Several conclusions are pervasive in studies done over decades: (1) Social scientists place a high amount of importance on journals; (2) Most of their citation identification comes from journals, a practice that has been referred to as "citation tracking";[19] (3) Informal channels, such as consulting colleagues and attending conferences, are an important source of information; and (4) Library resources, such as catalogs, indexes, and librarians, are not very heavily utilized.

Journals are clearly the most important source of information in the research process. Tracking citations is also an essential factor in the acquisition of information. The overwhelming response in favor of journals as a primary source of subsequent citations leads to the conclusion that, if we are to adequately satisfy the information needs of social science researchers, all that is possible must be done to ensure that the primary journals of a field are made available. As shrinking budgets lead to increased cancellation of journal titles, all that can be done to ensure access, such as document delivery services, should be exploited. If this is the most important source of information for social science researchers, then it should be one of the highest priorities in terms of the development of information services.

It has been shown that consulting colleagues and experts in the field is a valued method of information seeking. Most academic library reference positions require a host of library related skills. Many position descriptions do not, however, list subject expertise as a required qualification and many do not list it as a desired qualification. In institutions where bibliographers with subject expertise are fulfilling reference service roles, this may begin to satisfy a need. It is unlikely, however, that faculty and advanced level researchers will perceive these subject librarians as "experts" in the field unless the librarians take a proactive role in the various stages of the research process.

Library resources, such as catalogs, indexes and abstracts are not very heavily used as resources for identifying relevant resources. It has been suggested that printed indexes and abstracts have failed as effective tools for information seeking and have, instead, been chaotic, exasperating, and bewildering experiences.[20] The skill of the reference librarian in using these tools effectively and in identifying empirical research among the many types of reports indexed may well be invaluable to the researcher. Unfortunately large academic libraries usually do not have regular current awareness search services in place. As a customized user service, however, the model that many Special Libraries employ in providing this level of service may well be worth reconsidering in light of the massive amount of evidence that we have regarding the importance of the journal literature and the reluctance on the part of researchers to use indexing services.

Computerized services ranked very low in their importance to the research process in many of the studies reviewed. In a fairly recent study of Ethnic Studies scholars, the respondents indicated that their five most important means of identifying information for their research were citations in other publications, abstracts and indexes, bibliographies, library catalogs, and book reviews. They did indicate, however, that they preferred printed indexes and abstracts, that they did not rely heavily on librarians, and they expressed a reluctance to use databases in electronic formats.[21] It has been suggested that the failure on the part of faculty to utilize existing library services may be due in part to the failure on the part of librarians to teach users about available services.[22]

There has been much debate over the years as to the value of promoting instructional services to faculty. If the researchers already see themselves as well served in their current activity of scanning journals and tracking citations, then they are not likely to attend instructional sessions in the use of library services. They may well be better served by current awareness and document delivery services.

The ACLS survey indicated that librarians are remiss in introducing and promoting emerging technologies and new service.[23] It may well be that the upcoming decade will be spent rethinking which services will be provided, how these services will be provided, at what level reference librarians will get involved in the provision of services, how new services will be promoted, and how new services will be evaluated.

Based on the information that we have gained from three decades of research, it would seem that high on the list of services would be document delivery services, current awareness services, customized search services, and training in new technologies.

REFERENCES

1. Varlejs, Jana, ed. *Information seeking: Basing services on users' behaviors.* Jefferson, NC: McFarland & Company, Inc., 1987, p.67.

2. Guttsman, W. L., "The literature of the social sciences and provision for research in them," *Journal of Documentation* 22 (September 1966):186-194.

3. Wood, David N. and Cathryn A. Bower, "The use of social science periodical literature," *Journal of Documentation* 25 (June 1969):108-122.

4. Earle, Penelope and Brian Vickery, "Social science literature use in the UK as indicated by citations," *Journal of Documentation* 25 (June 1969):123-141.

5. Line, Maurice B., "Information requirements in the social sciences: some preliminary considerations," *Journal of Librarianship* 1 (January 1969) 1-19.

6. de Solla Price, Derek J., "Citation measures of hard sciences, soft sciences, technology, and hard science," In. C.E. Nelson and D. K. Pollak, eds. *Communication among scientists and engineers.* Lexington, MA: Heath, 1970.

7. Jones, Clyve, Michael Chapman and Pamela C. Woods, "The characteristics of the literature used by Historians," *Journal of Librarianship* 4 (July 1972):137-156.

8. Earle and Vickery, 1969.

9. Line, Maurice B., "Student attitudes to the University Library: a survey of Southampton University," *Journal of Documentation* 19 (September 1963):100-117.

10. Line, Maurice B. and Mavis Tidmarsh, "Student attitudes to the university library: a second survey at Southampton University," *Journal of Documentation* 22 (June 1966):123-135.

11. Line, 1969.

12. Line, Maurice B., "The information uses and needs of social scientists: an overview of INFROSS," *Aslib Proceedings* 23 (August 1971): 412-434. Maurice B. Line, J. M. Brittain and F. A. Cramer, *Investigation into information requirements of the social sciences, research report no 1: information requirements of researchers in the social sciences.* Bath University of Technology University Library. (May 1971)

13. Stenstrom, Patricia and Ruth B. McBride, "Serial use by social science faculty: a survey," *College and Research Libraries* 40 (September 1979):426-431.

14. Streatfield, David R. and Thomas D. Wilson, "Information services in English social services departments: Implications of Project INISS," *Behavioral and Social Sciences Librarian* 1 (Spring 1980):189-199.

15. Epp, Ronald H. and JoAn S. Segal, "The ACLS survey and academic library service," *College and Research Libraries. News* 48 (February 1987): 63-69.

16. Epp and Segal, 1987.

17. Slater, Margaret, "Social scientists' information needs in the 1980s" *Journal of Documentation* 44 (September 1988):226-237

18. Ellis, David, "A behavioral approach to information retrieval system design," *Journal of Documentation* 45 (September 1989):171-212. David Ellis, "Modeling the information-seeking patterns of academic researchers: A grounded theory approach," *Library Quarterly* 63 (October 1993):469-486.

19. Folster, Mary B., "A study in the use of information sources by social science researchers," *Journal of Academic Librarianship* 15 (March 1989):7-11.

20. Cohen, David J., "Scholarly communication and role of libraries: Problems and possibilities for accessing journal articles," *The Serials Librarian* 17 no.3-4 (1990):43-48.

21. Buttlar, Lois and Lubomyr R.Wynar, "Cultural pluralism and ethnic diversity: Authors as information users in the field of Ethnic Studies," *Collection Management* 16 no.3 (1992):13-33.

22. Lancaster, F. W., "Assessment of the technical information requirements of users," in Alan Rees. ed. *Contemporary problems in technical library and information center management: A state of the art.* Washington, D.C.: American Society for Information Science, 1974, p.78.

23. Epp and Segal, 1987.

Scientists, Information Seeking, and Reference Services

Marilyn Von Seggern

SUMMARY. Decades of research on the information-seeking behavior of scientists have shown heavy reliance on informal communication and personal collections. Entry into the literature is often gained through references in journal articles and other primary literature. This paper discusses these behaviors and some reasons for their use. Improvements in reference services to the scientific user community must be based on an understanding of scientific communication, information-seeking behavior, and the information needs of the user. Examples of user-oriented reference service are given.

INTRODUCTION

The voluminous literature on information users, information needs, and information seeking, much of it based on studies of scientists and engineers, has been accumulating rapidly since the 1940's.[1] Though many questions about information users' behavior have yet to be addressed and study of rapidly advancing technology on this behavior is in progress, certain patterns and characteristics have been established. To examine, rethink, and redesign our reference/information services to the scientific community, we must understand these information needs and information-seeking

Marilyn Von Seggern is Head of Reference, Owen Science & Engineering Library, Washington State University, Pullman, WA 99164-3200.

[Haworth co-indexing entry note]: "Scientists, Information Seeking, and Reference Services." Seggern, Marilyn Von. Co-published simultaneously in *The Reference Librarian* (The Haworth Press, Inc.) No. 49/50, 1995, pp. 95-104; and: *Library Users and Reference Services* (ed: Jo Bell Whitlatch) The Haworth Press, Inc., 1995, pp. 95-104. Multiple copies of this article/chapter may be purchased from The Haworth Document Delivery Center [1-800-3-HAWORTH; 9:00 a.m. - 5:00 p.m. (EST)].

behaviors. This article discusses the implications for restructuring services suggested by the accumulation of knowledge in this area.

This discussion excludes engineers and the research and development environment. The work setting, goals, training, processes, and output of scientists and engineers are different enough that they cannot be lumped together in discussions of communication channels, information needs, and information-seeking behavior. Library services to the engineering community also must be distinctive and tailored to meet their needs. Pinelli has summarized the research studies which differentiate the two groups.[2]

Studies have shown that there are likewise relevant distinctions among scientific disciplines, but it is accurate to say that, in general, to fill their information needs scientists rely heavily on informal channels of communication, personal collections of journals, books, and copies of articles, and the interconnectedness of the literature in finding and referencing related work. The formal secondary literature, either print or automated is consulted less frequently. Many researchers do not rely on library collections or on librarians to assist them in satisfying information needs or negotiating the complex collections and organizing principles of libraries.

In one of the many studies establishing these principles, Grefsheim reported three major information sources for biotechnology researchers: the scientists' own experiments, personal communication with other scientists, and textual material, most often personal journal subscriptions.[3] Only a few came to the department's library on a regular basis.

This study also found that personal computers were affecting information seeking and use. All those surveyed used automated bibliographic search results, and 35% said they were most likely to do the searching themselves. Thus, as computer skills become more prevalent, systems more intelligent, and as physical access to such systems and other specialized information databases is improved, some aspects of information seeking may be changing, though at varying rates among disciplines. A report of geoscientists from the same time period found that whereas 44% request a database search at least once a year, none were end-user searchers.[4]

SCIENTIFIC COMMUNICATION

To understand the way in which information is sought and used, it is essential to understand the scientific communication system which serves scientists as contributors as well as users. The system exists to share information in such a way as to determine scientific priority and intellectual property rights. To individuals this confers recognition from peers and opportunities for enhancing the institution's status, continuing research activities through competitive grants, and achieving economic and job security.[5]

Key characteristics of this system are peer-review of submitted work to maintain high quality standards, and the public aspect of the scientific record which ensures equal access to contributors as well as users of the system. Refereed journal articles continue to be "the established medium of record and dissemination"[6] in the sciences because this medium meets the criteria of establishing priority while providing for a relatively fast dissemination of results.[7] Subramanyam provides a good description of the structure of scientific literature and progression from research to publication.[8]

The rapidity with which many subfields are developing has meant exponential growth of the literature in the past few decades, more specialization and interdisciplinarity, increasing collaboration, and reduced ability for the researcher to effectively monitor and track discoveries in fields and subfields other than her or his own.[9]

INFORMAL COMMUNICATION

Numerous studies have shown that most information needs of scientists are met through informal communication, including verbal and written personal communication, informal sharing of research results, and discussions at seminars and professional meetings.[10] The give-and-take of informal communication allows researchers to dispense as well as absorb new information, connect with experts in their field, and float ideas and hypotheses. The multi-month to multi-year process of submission, peer-review, acceptance, publication, and abstracting of new knowledge is far too delayed to be useful for keeping abreast in a competitive environment. Even before the advent of electronic mail, discussion lists, preprint systems and journals, research results were informally distributed long before the article appeared in a reputable journal. Though secondary literature sources may be consulted more in other phases of problem-solving such as initiation of a new research project, non-reliance on and non-use of indexing/abstracting media and search services for staying current on a research front is not surprising.

The "invisible college" concept[11] describes the communication network that forms in research areas of rapid growth. It was shown by Crane to contribute substantially toward the growth of knowledge.[12] In one study, research areas characterized by high interpersonal interaction were compared with fields of low interaction. Two specialized areas with a high degree of interpersonal communication activity demonstrated a period of exponential growth of numbers of publications and authors publishing for the first time. Observations of two fields of low communication showed a linear cumulative growth of publications and the failure of knowledge to cumulate.[13] Invisible college characteristics–the network of collaboration, recruitment of students and other researchers, and generation and exchange of new ideas–appears to be critical to productivity. Since the advent of electronic mail and discussion lists, the detrimental effects of being outside the crucial loop of these tightly formed networks may be lessening.[14]

ACCESSIBILITY AND CREATIVITY

Physical accessibility appears to be an important factor in the determination of what is read and cited by researchers. One of the most accessible and frequently used sources is the personal collection. Soper's dissertation study of authors in the sciences, social sciences, and humanities investigated the relationship between works referred to in their papers and personal collections, finding that a majority of citations (59%) were in fact located in their own collections.[15] One-fourth of the works cited had been found in departmental or institutional libraries while libraries outside the institution were consulted for twelve percent of the citations, including only 0.7% received from interlibrary loan.

Soper discovered that scientists found nearly 74% of their citations in their personal collections; this is the highest noted though that of social scientists follows closely. The lack of adequate institutional library collections was not the reason for the high use of personal collections since only 8% of the citations found in personal collections were not also in the institutional library. When researchers were interviewed about reasons for personal collections, convenience was mentioned most frequently. They also preferred their own classification systems, their own environments for use of their collections, and the lack of barriers (e.g., temporary unavailability because of binding and use by others) experienced in the library system. Predictably, scientists' personal collections consisted heavily of journal articles, including preprints, reprints, and photocopies.

This tendency to bypass the library and the formal literature search process has been explained in several ways. For example, research may be too highly creative and individualistic to follow structured search procedures.[16] Researchers pick up bits and pieces of information from hundreds of sources, all with the potential of contributing in some way to a research project. Footnotes and references lead to many citations on the same or related topics because "to an extraordinary degree the primary literature indexes itself, and does so with greater comprehensiveness, better analytics, and greater precision than does the secondary literature."[17]

Another explanation is the very limited time constraints within which a variety of needs must be fulfilled. Orr listed two categories of "input needs": regular needs which include current awareness, everyday reference, and "personal" (stimulation and feedback), and episodic needs consisting of retrospective search, instruction, and consultation (the latter applying more to engineers and applied scientists).[18] Researchers logically batch these needs; the preference for informal channels or other information gathering methods allow multiple needs to be met at once, for instance stimulation and feedback while gaining current awareness in discussion with a colleague. Information sources are chosen for their return on the investment of the limited time and energy the researcher has available. Orr suggests that scientists' "estimates of both cost and likelihood of success may be poor because of incomplete knowledge, or biased by atypical experiences," but the choices are rational.[19]

HOLISTIC RESEARCH, USER-CENTERED SERVICES

Wilson,[20] Orr,[21] Stoan,[22] Durrance[23] and others have written critically of narrowly-focused user studies which have looked at fragmented parts of literature and library use rather than the information user and the context of information seeking with particular needs in mind. Attempting to understand information use by studying to what extent abstracting/indexing resources are used in a scientific field, for example, is a one-dimensional approach to investigating the complex information gathering systems of scientists. A holistic approach considers the psycho-social context of the information-seeking situation so that the "problem environment"[24] can be understood. The focus is not on answering the question asked but considering the problem which caused the information need.

Redesigning our reference/information services to incorporate this view, to become "user-centered,"[25] is the imperative of our time. Special libraries with well-defined, limited user populations have tended to provide more specialized service; many others have more recently begun the transition. Rather than waiting at the reference desk for users to ask (or not ask) their questions, the information specialist becomes familiar with the information needs of researchers, may spend time in the information user's environment and participate in problem-solving activities to understand the context of the problem, and offers specialized services in response to this. Information technology facilitates such transitions to user-oriented service by allowing the full range of resources to become available in the networked environment at library or user workstations.

Numerous examples can already be found in the literature. Four research groups in microbiology in an academic institution received the services of an information scientist team member for a ten-month trial period.[26] Services included consultation on and processing of information problems and delivery of copies of selected references from database searches. Changes in the scientists' information habits were that less time was spent in discussion with others in the lab but informal communication external to the lab increased significantly. Less time was also spent in reading and scanning the literature but there was more in-depth reading of articles. Through comparison with a control group it was deduced that the information scientist affected the information-seeking patterns of the researchers by providing enough relevant literature so that more time could be spent in other, potentially more productive, information-gathering activities.

Orr termed this phenomenon the "global competition for scientists' communication time."[27] He cited an earlier study showing that the more accessible the literature, the more time a group of chemists spent reading but the total time devoted to scientific communication did not increase. To make significant contributions at appropriate points in the research process, information specialists must be positioned for proactive service to their users.

In another example, the Oncology Department at The Johns Hopkins University renegotiated for a full-time "knowledge worker" to replace more traditional library services in their satellite library.[28] This librarian provides education for students, faculty, and staff in finding and managing information, assembles technologies for use in scientific communication, and assists with solving specific information problems. Similar positions, titled Personal Information Management Specialists, have been developed at the Welch Library at the same institution and the University of California, San Francisco Library.[29]

Such projects demonstrate not only restructuring of document delivery, user education, and reference services but also the design of products and services to meet the needs of users. Florance and Matheson state that "in the environment of scientific communication, those needs revolve around the retrieval, creation, manipulation, management, and dissemination of new knowledge."[30] The Welch Library has demonstrated new roles in knowledge organization and management by using librarians' expertise to assist in producing and managing scientific databases, coordinating integrated access to the institution's information resources, and developing workstations for which the focal point is the scientist's knowledge work in accordance with the university's mission of creating and disseminating new knowledge.

CONCLUSION

If librarians are determined to play an integral role in managing and delivering information, a solid understanding of scientific communication and how scientists use this system is essential. User studies must focus on the holistic view of the user, the problem prompting the question, and the context of the problem. Our responses must then address the mission and goals which we determine will serve user needs. Durrance summarizes what lies ahead: "The challenge facing the field is not only to learn how to identify information needs, but also to create new services and reshape existing service delivery patterns around these extraordinarily diverse needs–and to do it without shutting down existing library services. That challenge has continued over decades and, given the complexity of the problem, is likely to continue for many more."[31] Informed, continuing discussion, the sharing of ideas, projects, and research findings, and full implementation of information technology will assist in redefining and redesigning reference/information services to more fully address our users' needs.

REFERENCES

1. Melvin J. Voigt, *Scientists' Approaches to Information* (Chicago: American Library Association, 1961), 1-2.

2. Thomas E. Pinelli, "The Information-Seeking Habits and Practices of Engineers," in *Information Seeking and Communicating Behavior of Scientists and Engineers,* ed. Cynthia Steinke (New York: The Haworth Press, Inc. 1991), 5-25.

3. Suzanne Grefsheim, Jon Franklin, and Dianna Cunningham, "Biotechnology Awareness Study, Part I: Where Scientists Get Their Information," *Bulletin of the Medical Library Association* 79 (January 1991):36-44.

4. Julie Bichteler and Dederick Ward, "Information-Seeking Behavior of Geoscientists," *Special Libraries* 80 (Summer 1989):169-178.

5. Philip Doty, "Electronic Networks and Social Change in Science," in *Proceedings of the 55th Annual Meeting of the American Society for Information Science Annual Meeting,* ed. Debora Shaw (Medford, NJ: Learned Information, 1992), 185-192.

6. Maurice B. Line, "The Publication and Availability of Scientific and Technical Papers: An Analysis of Requirements and the Suitability of Different Means of Meeting Them," *Journal of Documentation* 48 (June 1992): 201-219.

7. A.J. Meadows, *Communication in Science* (London: Butterworths, 1974), 55.

8. Krishna Subramanyam, *Scientific and Technical Information Resources* (New York: M. Dekker, 1981), 4-10.

9. William D. Garvey, *Communication: the Essence of Science* (Oxford, UK: Pergamon Press, 1979), 8.

10. Among many sources: Bentley Glass and Sharon H. Norwood, "How Scientists Actually Learn of Work Important to Them," in *Proceedings of the International Conference on Scientific Information* (Washington, D.C.: National Academy of Sciences-National Research Council, 1959), 1:195-197; Belver C. Griffith and A. James Miller, "Networks of Informal Communication Among Scientifically Productive Scientists," in *Communication Among Scientists and Engineers,* ed. Carnot E. Nelson and Donald K. Pollock (Lexington, MA: Heath & Co., 1970), 125-140; Susan Crawford, "Informal Communication Among Scientists in Sleep Research," *Journal of the American Society for Information Science* 22 (September-October 1971): 301-10.

11. Derek de Solla Price, *Science Since Babylon* (New Haven: Yale, 1961).

12. Diana Crane, *Invisible Colleges: Diffusion of Knowledge in Scientific Communities* (Chicago: University of Chicago Press, 1972).

13. Ibid, 24-26.

14. Philip Doty, Ann P. Bishop, and Charles R. McClure, "Scientific Norms and the Use of Electronic Research Networks," in *Proceedings of the 54th American Society for Information Science Annual Meeting,* ed. Jose Marie Griffiths (Medford, NJ: Learned Information, 1991), 24-38.

15. Mary Ellen Soper, "Characteristics and Use of Personal Collections," *Library Quarterly* 46 (October 1976): 397-415.

16. Stephen K. Stoan, "Research and Library Skills: An Analysis and Interpretation," *College & Research Libraries* 45 (March 1984): 99-109.

17. Ibid, 103.

18. Richard H. Orr, "The Scientist as an Information Processor: A Conceptual Model Illustrated with Data on Variables Related to Library Utilization," in *Communication Among Scientists and Engineers,* ed. Carnot E. Nelson and Donald K. Pollock (Lexington, MA: Heath & Co., 1970), 143-189.

19. Ibid., 146.

20. T.D. Wilson, "On User Studies and Information Needs," *Journal of Documentation* 37 (March 1981): 3-15.

21. Orr, "Scientist as an Information Processor."

22. Stephen K. Stoan, "Research and Information Retrieval Among Academic Researchers: Implications for Library Instruction," *Library Trends* 39 (Winter 1991): 238-57.

23. Joan C. Durrance, "Information Needs: Old Song, New Tune," in *Rethinking the Library in the Information Age,* United States Department of Education (Washington, D.C.: U.S. Dept. of Education, 1989), 159-177.

24. S.E. MacMullin and R.S. Taylor, "Problem Dimensions and Information Traits," *The Information Society* 3 (1984): 91-111.

25. A definition of "user-centered" is in Ruth C.T. Morris, "Toward a User-Centered Information Service," *Journal of the American Society for Information Science* 45 (January 1994):20-30, which defines it as "a focused approach to thinking about information services and systems: one that regards information as something in part constructed by users, that recognizes common traits which humans share in processing information, and that views the contexts in which information needs arise (and the contexts in which they are pursued) as significant factors in the design of user-centered information systems and services."

26. Julie M. Neway, *Information Specialist as Team Player in the Research Process* (Westport, CT: Greenwood Press, 1985), 57-81.

27. Orr, "Scientist as an Information Processor," 166.

28. Valerie Florance and Nina W. Matheson, "The Health Sciences Librarian as Knowledge Worker," *Library Trends* 42 (Summer 1993): 196-219.

29. Ibid, 196-197.

30. Ibid, 211.

31. Durrance, "Information Needs," 159-160.

INFORMATION SEEKING PATTERNS: DIVERSE POPULATIONS

Library Services for Persons with Disabilities

Jill Mendle

SUMMARY. The Americans with Disabilities Act of 1990 (ADA) prohibits discrimination with respect to the disabled in public entities and in "public accommodations and services operated by private entities." Passage of the ADA has prompted libraries all over the country to evaluate services to these users and has generated a vast number of resources on the ADA and on services to disabled patrons. This article examines the burgeoning literature and presents a case study of The University of Alabama Libraries' efforts to meet these users' needs. The case study focuses on the establishment of an adaptive technologies lab to serve the needs of blind, visually impaired and learning disabled students, and upon the continual efforts to heighten staff awareness.

Jill Mendle is Reference Librarian and Coordinator of Services for Users with Disabilities at The University of Alabama Libraries, Tuscaloosa, AL 35487-0266.

[Haworth co-indexing entry note]: "Library Services for Persons with Disabilities." Mendle, Jill. Co-published simultaneously in *The Reference Librarian* (The Haworth Press, Inc.) No. 49/50, 1995, pp. 105-121; and: *Library Users and Reference Services* (ed: Jo Bell Whitlatch) The Haworth Press, Inc., 1995, pp. 105-121. Multiple copies of this article/chapter may be purchased from The Haworth Document Delivery Center [1-800-3-HAWORTH; 9:00 a.m. - 5:00 p.m. (EST)].

INTRODUCTION

Recently an academically able student at the University of Alabama checked out a book. He did it in the usual way, using the online catalog to locate the call number and a printer to record the location. Yet when the transaction was completed, book in hand, the student broke into a broad smile and announced to nearby patrons and library staff that this was the first time in his life that he had checked out library material on his own. The student is totally blind. He had used adaptive equipment to read the catalog and a Braille printer to print the location and call number; his independence was the result of a year's work on the part of library staff and students with disabilities, and a highpoint in an exhilarating, though occasionally discouraging and frustrating, journey.

In a sense, the student's smile is a direct consequence of the Americans With Disabilities Act of 1990 (ADA). Among its findings, ADA stated that "census data, national polls, and other studies have documented that people with disabilities, as a group, occupy an inferior status in our society, and are severely disadvantaged socially, vocationally, economically, and educationally." The purpose of the act is "to provide a clear and comprehensive national mandate for the elimination of discrimination against individuals with disabilities," to provide "enforceable standards against this discrimination," to "ensure that the Federal Government plays a central role in enforcing the standards established in this Act," and "to invoke the sweep of congressional authority . . . in order to address the major areas of discrimination faced day-to-day by people with disabilities." Since the ADA prohibits discrimination in public entities and in "public accommodations and services operated by private entities," it relates directly to public and private libraries.[1]

Passage of the ADA and an increasing awareness of the needs of persons with disabilities has prompted libraries all over the country to look more carefully at their disabled populations and at the services offered to them. This article will explore the burgeoning body of resources on library services for users with disabilities and then turn to a case study of how one institution, The University of Alabama Libraries, has addressed the mandate of the ADA.

THE LITERATURE: A SELECTIVE REVIEW

Inevitably the passage of the ADA created an accompanying literature, intended to guide libraries through the maze of ADA implementation and to provide an understanding of the library needs of persons with disabilities. For the most part, these sources fit into four categories: general information on the ADA, information on library compliance with the ADA, library services for special populations, and information on adaptive technologies. The two latter categories, of course, had been discussed before, and were in a sense a part of the pressure for the ADA. Two general sources, *Complying With the Americans With Disabilities Act: A Guidebook for Management and People With Disabilities* by Don Fersh and Peter W. Thomas and *Implementing the Americans With Disabilities Act* by Lawrence O. Gostin and Henry A. Beyer, provide a good basic understanding of the ADA. Both cover the history of the act and earlier disability legislation and offer a thorough explanation of the act's titles and terminology, an important inclusion since a new, often confusing, ADA language now exists. Useful also is Gostin and Beyer's section on implications of the ADA for persons with psychiatric, mental, and developmental disabilities, an increasingly prominent group of library users.[2]

Library compliance with the ADA is thoroughly covered in *How Libraries Must Comply with the Americans With Disabilities Act (ADA)*, edited by Donald D. Foos and Nancy C. Pack. Of particular note are the chapters by Michael Gunde, which explains how the act's titles relate to libraries, and by Ruth O'Donnell, which provides a six-step ADA planning model.[3] *Surveying Public Libraries for the ADA*, a guide to compliance prepared for the Pinellas Public Library Cooperative, combines general information with a self-evaluation inventory; belying its title, the survey is helpful to other kinds of libraries as well.[4] Readers may also want to consult a recent ALA preconference publication, *The Americans with Disabilities Act: Its Impact on Libraries The Library's Responses in "Doable" Steps.*[5] More condensed guides to library compliance can be found in Foos and Pack, "Library Compliance with the Americans With Disabilities Act" and Gunde, "Working with the Americans With Disabilities Act" and "Working with the Americans with

Disabilities Act Part II."[6] And in another clear, concise overview of library compliance, "The Americans with Disabilities Act and its Effect on Public Libraries," Christopher Lewis explains the titles, compliance, enforcement, and deadlines, paying careful attention to physical barriers, equal access to programs, and weaknesses of the ADA (the vague terminology, for example).[7]

The literature on library services for persons with disabilities consists of general guides and how-to manuals, descriptive accounts of library programs, and discussions of the library needs of users with specific disabilities. Ruth Velleman's exceptional overview, *Meeting the Needs of People with Disabilities: a Guide for Librarians, Educators, and Other Service Professionals* includes information on almost every aspect of services to persons with disabilities. Of particular interest are Velleman's discussions of highly specialized library programs for the disabled and her careful and sensitive treatments of a broad range of disabilities.[8]

Serving the Disabled, by Keith C. Wright and Judith F. Davie, is a manual offering general information, resource lists, and work-sheets on adult and youth programs, reference services, collection development, and new technologies.[9] The April 1990 issue of Illinois Libraries, edited by H. Neil Kelley, stands out as a valuable comprehensive study of library services for persons with disabilities. It includes articles on the varied services coordinated by Illinet, extending from talking book and television services to story hours for deaf and visually impaired children and programs for senior citizens.[10] In a similar vein, *Libraries Serving Underserved Populations*, an issue of *Library Trends*, is devoted to meeting the library needs of the deaf. Chapters cover communication with the deaf, collection development for deaf populations, and literature for deaf children.[11] Melanie Norton's chapter, "Effective Bibliographic instruction for Deaf and Hearing-Impaired College Students" offers techniques for group and individualized bibliographic instruction and suggestions for appropriate handouts.[12]

Meeting the library needs of persons with developmental, learning, or mental disabilities is an especially vexed issue. Darlene Weingand, "The Invisible Client," discusses materials and services for the learning disabled at the Westchester, New York Public Library and offers guidelines for other libraries to evaluate their services to this group. Fay Zipkowitz, " 'No One Wants to See Them': Meeting the Reference Needs of the Deinstitutionalized," describes the efforts of the Rhode Island Department of State Library Services to bring library service to newly mainstreamed users, while Sally Reed, "Breaking Through: Effective Reference Mediation for Nontraditional Public Library Users," treats the attitude of the library staff toward users with mental illness, a crucial and sensitive topic.[13]

Since new products appear constantly, information on adaptive technologies will undoubtedly increase in the next few years. Barbara Mates' *Library Technology for Visually and Physically Impaired Patrons* identifies available technologies and their use in a library setting. Although some newer technologies are not included, Mates' thorough product descriptions, her glossaries and bibliographies, and her extensive lists of vendors and resources make this a highly useful source for those new to the field.[14] John Jax, "Library Services for Students With Disabilities at the University of Wisconsin-Stout," describes adaptive equipment used for blind, visually impaired and learning disabled students as well as the adaptations made to physical access and furnishings.[15] Grant and Jones provide a nuts-and-bolts overview of the daunting technology of a voice catalog in "The Three T's for a Talking Online Catalog: Technology, Teamwork, Teaching."[16]

Developing a program for users with disabilities is a work-in-progress that needs continual refinement as services are expanded or revised; sometimes information is needed more rapidly than printed publication characteristically permits. Fortunately guidance is available from national and regional library associations and through the Internet. Through the LITA Adaptive Technologies Interest Group and The Association of Specialized and Cooperative Library Agencies (both groups of ALA), librarians have access to conference programs, informal discussion groups, and handouts. National and regional conference exhibits also offer the opportunity for hands-on demonstrations of the latest adaptive equipment. Electronically, a growing number of e-mail lists accessed through the Internet or BITNET allow subscribers to share information on particular disabilities, ADA compliance issues, and adaptive technologies.[17] In addition, an online workshop and an electronic journal are offered through EASI (Equal Access to Software and Information), an organization that operates under the aegis of the American Association of Higher Education.[18] Information about services and resources of The National Library Service for the Blind and Physically Handicapped of the Library of Congress is available through the Library of Congress gopher, LC Marvel.

CASE STUDY: THE UNIVERSITY OF ALABAMA LIBRARIES

The University of Alabama Libraries serve a large campus community, students and faculty from other local colleges, and the town population. Some users are persons with disabilities. Of course, the University had attempted to meet the needs of the disabled before 1992, the ADA's target year for implementation. The Rehabilitation Act of 1974, the precursor to ADA, prohibited discrimination in programs or activities receiving Federal financial assistance.[19] Well before ADA, consequently, the University had developed an awareness of its responsibility to the disabled. Much of what might have been supposed to be the University's direct responsibility, however, was borne by the state of Alabama: most disabled students were assisted by the on-campus presence of a state agency, the Office of Disabled-Student Services. The Office hired teaching assistants to serve as readers (for the blind) and interpreters (for the deaf), to retrieve books from library stacks, and otherwise to provide academic assistance. In the years before the passage of the ADA, the Libraries installed Braille lettering on elevators and purchased a Kurzweil reader. Except for the Kurzweil, adaptive equipment was not available. Many students came to campus with their own equipment; some simply depended on family or friends for library help. Disabled-Student Services did such a thorough job of handling the library needs of the visually impaired that the Kurzweil was rarely used.

Passage of the ADA created an increased awareness of the needs of disabled persons, in part the result of greater assertiveness of the disabled community. With ADA, the University (hence the Libraries) also assumed a new and direct legal responsibility for meeting the needs of the disabled. While the Office of Disabled-

Student Services continues to be present on campus, it no longer has primary responsibility for the provision of academic support services. The University and Libraries responded to the new situation with new policies and institutional structures. The hub of the Libraries' efforts was, and remains, the University Libraries Committee on Specialized Access, with responsibility to develop, coordinate and evaluate library services for users with disabilities. Conceived of partly as an advocacy group, the committee included library staff members, faculty and students with disabilities, and representatives from various related campus offices. The committee also served initially as a planning body. Through subcommittees, committee members began work on projects related to physical accessibility, staff awareness, public relations, and electronic access. The chair of the University Libraries Committee on Specialized Access also served as part of a campus-wide network of liaisons for the disabled; the Libraries Planning Officer was made part of the University ADA Task Force, an oversight group.

The primary focus of the Libraries' efforts in the first two years has been the establishment of an adaptive technologies laboratory for blind, visually impaired, and learning disabled students. Made possible through a generous donation, the laboratory is housed in the recently-constructed Eric and Sarah Rodgers Science and Engineering Library, about two blocks from the main library building. As presently equipped, the lab consists of two workstations. One workstation is designed for those with limited vision—that is, for those who need material (text or graphics) enlarged. Through Telesensory cards and software, the workstation links a personal computer to a large-screen VGA monitor as well as to a Closed Circuit Display (CCD) camera and a separate video/TV monitor. Access routes are also available to a laser printer and a Telesensory Everest Braille Embosser. It is also possible to use Vert Pro, a text-to-voice synthesizer. Most important of all, users are able to access AMELIA (the Libraries' online catalog) and the Internet and have information enlarged or "read" to them. In certain instances, two users can work simultaneously at the workstation, one using the CCD system and the other the online catalog or a word processor.

The second workstation is for use primarily by persons who are unable to read at all. It is equipped with a personal computer and super VGA monitor, the Vert speech recognition system, and the OsCar optical character recognition system. The OsCar enables text to be scanned and projected on to the monitor and either read by the voice synthesizer or stored for later use. The material can be converted to a word processing program and edited, or printed on a laser printer or the Everest Braille Embosser. This workstation also allows access to AMELIA and the Internet as well to the other options available on the Rodgers Library LAN.[20]

Installation of and initial training for the adaptive equipment was provided by representatives from Telesensory, the primary vendor. After this phase, the chair of the electronic access subcommittee of the University Libraries Committee on Specialized Access (a library staff member with computer expertise) assumed responsibility for equipment and training. It was expected that committee members (including the blind and visually impaired students who were the lab's first users) would train the next generation. The opening of the lab was accompanied by a massive public relations campaign, including press and television coverage and a series of demonstrations for alumni and townspeople as well as the traditional student population. These quickly developed a user clientele. Yet more important than sheer hours of use is quality of use. Within months, several users were working independently in the lab who previously would have required readers and constant direct assistance.

But marvelous as adaptive equipment is, there are a surprising number of library transactions that must be handled the old-fashioned way–through direct personal assistance. Users with visual impairments still need research and reference assistance with print sources that are too cumbersome to transport to the adaptive lab or too difficult to use without help; even the use of an index can be excruciatingly complex for the visually disabled. They also need help with electronic sources that are not available in adaptive formats (CD-ROMs on stand-alone stations for example). Standard reference procedures need to be rethought, and sometimes become as complex and time-consuming to the librarian as to the patron. A user cannot be told to browse the southern history collection for the perfect source on the civil war or that the encyclopedias are "by the window." Once a source has been found, a user without sight may be unable to photocopy the needed pages to be used on adaptive equipment or given to readers. And assistance is particularly needed if a user finds a citation in an index to a source available only in microform. Beyond reference, the standard bibliographic instruction program of a tour with handouts may be impossible.

In the early stages of the Libraries' work with the visually impaired, most library assistance to disabled users was handled through the reference unit, a result of the circumstance that the chair of the Libraries Committee on Specialized Access (who soon became the Coordinator for Services to Library Users with Disabilities) was a reference librarian. Other reference staff members and student workers assisted with all library needs–paging and photocopying as well as research. The burden soon became more than the reference staff alone could handle; gradually the users were weaned from the reference unit and encouraged to take their needs directly to other appropriate departments. This was not always easily done. Like others, disabled patrons were comfortable working with staff members who had helped them successfully in the past. Today, new users are asked to contact departments directly for routine assistance, and the entire library staff is encouraged to handle all but the most complex requests. A policy statement prepared by committee members provides guidance to staff. Users are encouraged to plan ahead to allow the staff time to provide special assistance.

Meeting the needs of individuals with other disabilities has been easier and more straightforward. Persons with hearing impairments conduct most business at the Libraries without difficulty (although emergency evacuation for the hearing impaired remains a pressing concern). To enable the hearing impaired to receive telephone reference assistance and to conduct other library transactions by telephone, the Libraries have acquired a TDD (telecommunications device for the deaf). The TDD enables the Libraries' staff to receive and send typed messages over telephone lines to a hearing impaired person with another TDD. The Libraries also participate in the Alabama Relay Network, itself part of a national network service of intermediaries that transact telephone business for the hearing impaired. A recent and representative transaction consisted of a TDD patron keyboarding a request for a book to a TDD operator at the network, who called the reference desk to check if the Libraries held the book in question. The Libraries did not–it was a cookbook– and the reply was returned in TDD form via the network operator. At present, no user has requested a signer or bibliographic instruction tour with an interpreter; the Libraries would enlist the services of the Disabled-Student Services if one became necessary. Libraries offering adult and children's programs or video collections probably will find it useful to train a staff member to sign and provide equipment with closed-caption decoding capabilities; by law most television sets currently on the market have built-in closed caption capability.

Persons with mobility impairments constitute a large portion of the disabled user population. The Libraries have found that most are able to take care of their own library needs. All buildings in the system are wheelchair-accessible, have specially designated parking spaces and curb cuts, and are equipped with wheelchair-accessible AMELIA and CD-ROM terminals. Elevators are presently being fitted with protruding buttons for users with poor hand coordination. At present, the main concerns of library users with motor impairments are navigating the stacks and retrieving items from high shelves or hard-to-access areas–a retired stack collection housed in the basement, for example. However, the expanded use of very large, motorized carts and wheelchairs has increased rather than decreased mobility problems in tight or confined spaces–individuals using these devices have considerable difficulty entering elevators and using photocopying, microform, and terminal equipment. Like users with visual impairments, these users are encouraged to let the staff in each department know what they need and, if possible, to give advance notice.

The Libraries' renewed commitment to provide full services for persons with disabilities has led to the development of staff awareness and publicity programs. The staff awareness program is designed to introduce the staff to the library needs of users with disabilities and to reinforce the Libraries' commitment to these users. The program is also a sensitivity awareness program for, as Zipkowitz points out, some staff members are not eager to serve all populations.[21] In one instance at the Libraries, a staff member was unwilling to assist a person who was not visibly disabled–in this case an arthritic person. Particularly difficult situations arise with users whose disabilities make their behavior unusual or difficult, as is sometimes the case with some kinds of mental and learning disabilities, or with disfigured users. The staff awareness program addresses these very hard issues. The Libraries have had to train student workers, for example, to work with a user who, for reasons of physical disability, virtually screams.

A central part of the staff awareness program is a manual prepared by the staff awareness subcommittee, sent to every staff member for personal use and used in a disability awareness segment of the Libraries' new staff orientation program. The manual offers suggestions for assisting users with visual, hearing, mobility, developmental and learning disabilities. In addition, it contains a list of persons on campus who work with the disabled, and some general information on the ADA. Student workers, often the first staff members library users encounter, also will be trained in serving the disabled through a segment conducted by the Coordinator during the yearly student worker orientation workshops.

A strong public relations campaign has brought the Libraries' efforts to the attention of the campus and the local community. An effective part of the campaign has been demonstrations of the adaptive equipment by blind and visually impaired students for alumni, University administration, and interested community and campus groups. A highpoint of the public relations effort was the inauguration of the adaptive lab, during which guests from around the state and the local media had a chance to view the equipment and to talk to students about their use of the lab and their other library needs. As a result of the publicity generated by the inauguration, the School of Communications at the University prepared a short program on the adaptive lab, which was aired on Alabama Public Television. Recently, a local television network filmed a graduate student who has cerebral palsy using the wheelchair-accessible AMELIA and CD-ROM terminals, and being helped at the circulation desk. The film was shown on the local United Cerebral Palsy Telethon and is being considered for the 1995 national telethon.

PROBLEMS

The Libraries began to develop the program for services to users with disabilities with a great deal of enthusiasm, confident that the problems that invariably arise with any new endeavor would be easily worked through. Yet the Libraries were working with a new group of users with complex and very individual needs as well as with new technologies and new and extremely vague legislation. Launching the program proved slower than anticipated; satisfactory solutions to some problems are still being sought, and new problems keep cropping up. Some services, bibliographic instruction for example, have not yet been standardized and are being handled on an individual basis.

Many of the continuing concerns center on the adaptive lab. The installation of equipment was a long and difficult process. An initial specification proved inadequate, and the Libraries were forced to order new equipment, notably a personal computer with a more powerful microprocessor and significantly more RAM. The vendor was repeatedly called upon to provide additional training; considerable assistance was also sought from campus computer experts. Once up and running, both workstations experienced system failures from unknown causes, leaving users and staff frustrated. The training of new users, at first handled by members of the electronic access subcommittee, bogged down as it became apparent that some adaptive equipment was difficult to use and some users had impairments that made training complex; training required anywhere from ten minutes to ten hours, depending on the computer skills and particular needs of the user. Subcommittee members, with regular library jobs or classes to attend, were unable to afford the time proper training required. Clearly too much was asked of the student committee members, who had quite enough to do managing their own affairs.

And as publicity attracted new users, management of the lab became an additional concern. Located in a second floor room of a branch library, access to the lab and equipment was hard to monitor. Yet access had to be controlled: expensive equipment had to be protected from accidents and unintentional abuse as well as from theft. Students also used the lab's equipment for appropriate but originally unanticipated purposes. While the lab was originally designed to meet users' needs for library access, students delighted with the capabilities of the equipment used the lab for a variety of homework needs. The equipment was not always available for AMELIA use or to "read" library materials, and walk-ins sometimes had lengthy waits. The lab's success also created a need for more management and attention than the committee could give. Recently, a decision was made to focus the committee effort more on advocacy and to put the actual management, training, and equipment maintenance in the hands of the staff members of the Rodgers Library, the ADA Coordinator, and a computer consultant. At present, all staff members at the Rodgers Library are being trained to assist users in scanning and enlarging material and accessing AMELIA. Simple user guides are being prepared and will soon be available in Braille and enlarged formats. More extensive training will be handled through the Coordinator with guidance from the consultant and Disabled-Student Services.

Institutional arrangements have also needed refining. Since not only the Libraries are involved in ADA activities, continuing efforts are needed to identify and coordinate adaptive computer services on campus. Library staff members are part of a University committee devoted this task. This group will attempt to determine what adaptive equipment should be available on campus and who should be responsible for training, maintenance, and publicity. Ideally, adaptive equipment will be more widely available in campus computer labs for homework needs, and the library lab will be primarily used for library tasks.

CONCLUSION

The University of Alabama Libraries' effort began in the early days of the ADA and was particularly impelled by the donation that allowed for the establishment of the adaptive lab. Both factors shaped the Libraries' experience. While two members of the Libraries' staff (including the author) attended the June 1992 ADA preconference (cited note 5) and otherwise prepared for the task ahead, unquestionably the Libraries' were on the front end of the learning curve. Some useful literature was available but librarians had yet to develop and shape a body of ADA experience (including a history of false steps and mistaken assumptions) as a guide to others. Hindsight suggests we might have begun a more intensive self-evaluation as recommended by Black and O'Donnell.[22] We would also have emphasized more staff awareness at an earlier stage; technology can never substitute for personal kindness and sensitivity. Many aspects of ADA compliance are not technology-intensive, and although less dramatic than voice catalogs, are no less important to the individuals involved. The literature now available is an excellent place to begin for any group working through the puzzle of the ADA: in addition to producing some in-house expertise, it helps to generate enthusiasm and commitment.

The generous gift that established the lab was a blessing, and so it remains. Because of it, the Libraries had a high-profile, relatively quick "result" to display–a great benefit to its users, a morale-builder for individual staff, an encouragement to other donors. But the lab also put us on the high seas of ADA technology and administration before we had learned to swim, or even had our life vests. Again, had the Libraries the benefit of experience–even other's experience–we would have avoided at least some of our errors. We would not have underestimated training needs and would have understood the wisdom of buying hardware seemingly in excess of current needs.

Of course, not all experience is transferable. As Dalton points out in her "Exemplary Library Programs and Services for Those With Disabilities" in *The Americans with Disabilities Act: Its Impact on Libraries The Library's Responses in "Doable" Steps,* there are many different ways to provide services to the disabled.[23] The committee approach, and the equipment and services chosen by the University of Alabama Libraries may not be appropriate for a different user population, or a library with different funding and staffing arrangements. The University of Alabama Libraries chose adaptive equipment, as the most appropriate choice for a large university library attempting to meet the needs of an academically diverse population ranging from freshman to doctoral candidates. A community library with a different user population may prefer to emphasize a large print, Braille, or talking book collection or to offer a volunteer reader service. A library may find that a delivery program for users unable to leave their homes is a necessary part of its services or that a resource center would best suit the needs of its users. There is no single right way. The needs of a particular community will become apparent with an evaluation of users and current services. Fortunately, the growing literature and electronic resources now ensure that libraries need not work alone in determining a suitable program.

While the Libraries will continue to work on publicity and staff awareness programs and to refine the management of the lab, future efforts will focus more on institutional cooperation, funding for additional labs, and unresolved issues connected with adequate emergency procedures for persons with disabilities. Bolstered by success but slightly more hesitant and certainly wiser because of setbacks, the Libraries face these challenges acutely aware that efforts to meet the needs of the disabled, like the lives of the disabled themselves, will never be a matter entirely of routine. There will be a moment of triumph every time a disabled student checks out a book.

REFERENCES

1. The Americans With Disabilities Act of 1990, Public Law 101-336, 26 July 1990, Sections 2(a)(6), 2(b)(1-4), Title III.

2. Don Fersh and Peter W. Thomas, *Complying with the Americans with Disabilities Act: a Guidebook for Management and People with Disabilities* (Westport: Quorum Books, 1993). Lawrence O. Gostin and Henry A. Beyer, eds., *Implementing the Americans with Disabilities Act: Rights and Responsibilities of all Americans* (Baltimore: P. H. Brookes Pub. Co., 1993).

3. Michael G. Gunde, "Libraries and the Americans with Disabilities Act," pp. 1-31 and Ruth O'Donnell, "Planning to Implement the ADA in the Library," pp. 32-70 in Donald D. Foos and Nancy C. Pack, eds., *How Libraries Must Comply with the Americans with Disabilities Act (ADA)* (Phoenix: Oryx Press, 1992).

4. J. B. Black et al., *Surveying Public Libraries for the ADA.* (Pinellas County, Florida: Pinellas Public Library Cooperative, 1992).

5. Joanne L. Crispin, ed., *The Americans with Disabilities Act: Its Impact on Libraries The Library's Responses in "Doable" Steps,* (Chicago: American Library Association, 1993).

6. Donald D. Foos and Nancy C. Pack, "Library Compliance with the Americans with Disabilities Act," *RQ* 32 (Winter 1992): 255-67. Michael G. Gunde, "Working with the Americans with Disabilities Act," *Library Journal* 116 (December 1991): 91-100, and Gunde, "Working with the Americans with Disabilities Act Part II," *Library Journal* 117 (May 1992): 41-2.

7. Christopher G. Lewis, "The Americans with Disabilities Act and its Effect on Public Libraries," *Public Libraries* 31 (January/February 1992): 23-8.

8. Ruth A. Velleman, *Meeting the Needs of People With Disabilities: a Guide for Librarians, Educators, and Other Service Professionals* (Phoenix: Oryx Press, 1990).

9. Keith C. Wright and Judith F. Davie, *Serving the Disabled* (New York: Neal-Schuman Publishers, 1991).

10. Illinois Libraries 72 (April 1990).

11. *Library Trends* 41 (Summer 1992) [*Libraries Serving an Underserved Population: Deaf and Hearing-Impaired Patrons*].

12. Melanie J. Norton, "Effective Bibliographic Instruction for Deaf and Hearing-Impaired College Students," *Library Trends* 41 (Summer 1992): 118-50.

13. Darlene E. Weingand, "The Invisible Client: Meeting the Needs of Persons With Learning Disabilities," *The Reference Librarian* 31 (1990): 77-88. Fay Zipkowitz, " 'No One Wants to See Them': Meeting the Reference Needs of the Deinstitutionalized," ibid., 53-67. Sally Gardner Reed, "Breaking Through: Effective Reference Mediation for Nontraditional Public Library Users," *The Reference Librarian* 37 (1992): 109-19.

14. Barbara T. Mates, *Library Technology for Visually and Physically Impaired Patrons,* (Westport: Meckler, 1991).

15. John J. Jax and Theresa Muraski, "Library Services for Students with Disabilities at the University of Wisconsin-Stout," *The Journal of Academic Librarianship* 19 (July 1993): 166-68.

16. Wallace C. Grant and Dorothy E. Jones, "The Three T's for a Talking Online Catalog: Technology, Teamwork, Teaching," *Information Technology and Libraries* (June 1993): 193-202. Readers will note that some equipment specifications in this article are already inappropriate for current software.

17. "Online Resources Useful for Librarians Seeking to Improve Services to Individuals with Disabilities," a list of electronic resources compiled by Chris Lewis is available from Chris Lewis, The American University Library, Media Services Department, 4400 Massachusetts Ave. NW, Washington, DC 20016 or CLEWIS@AUVM.AMERICAN.EDU.

18. For information on EASI, contact the EASI chair, Norman Coombs, Ph.D. at NRCGSH@RITVAX.ISC.RIT.EDU or the EASI office at EASI@EDUCOM.EDU and (310) 640-3193.

19. The Rehabilitation Act of 1973, Public Law 93-112, 26 September 1973, Section 504.

20. Technical specifications for the first workstation: Northgate 486 with 8 Mb of RAM and a 200 Mb hard drive, 3.5" and 5.25" floppy disk drives, large screen VGA monitor, Logitech Mouse, Vert Pro card, Vista card, Lynx card, network card, CCD camera, video/TV monitor, HP Laser Printer, Telesensory Everest Braille Embosser, and software including DOS 5.0, Wordperfect 5.1, Vert Pro, Lynx, Vista, Telnet, AMELIA. Technical specifications for the second workstation: Northgate 486 with 8 Mb of RAM and 157 Mb hard-drive, 3.5" and 5.25" floppy disk drives, super VGA monitor and card, Logitech Mouse, HP Scanner,

Vert Pro card, OsCar card, Network card, HP Laser Printer, Telesensory Everest Braille Embosser, and software including DOS 5.0, Wordperfect 5.1, Windows 3.1, OsCar, Vert Pro, Zoomtext, Telnet, and AMELIA.

21. Zipkowitz, " 'No One Wants to See Them'," 54-5.

22. Black, *Surveying Public Libraries,* O'Donnell, [cited n. 2 above].

23. Phyllis Dalton, "Exemplary Library Programs and Services for Those with Disabilities," 27-33 in Joanne L. Crispin, *The Americans with Disabilities Act.*

Ethnicity and Information Seeking

Mengxiong Liu

SUMMARY. Our society is becoming more and more culturally and ethnically diverse. It is important that libraries respond to this fact by reflecting diversity in both their collections and services. In order to do so, reference librarians must understand other cultures, be aware of the information needs and information seeking behavior of patrons with multicultural backgrounds. Through a literature review, some characteristics of multiethnic groups in the information seeking process are summarized. Barriers to effective communication in the libraries include language, conceptual awareness of library services, and philosophy of education. Among ethnic groups, informal social networks and gatekeepers play a crucial role in seeking information. Guidelines are suggested to achieve effective communication with patrons for whom English is a second language. Recommendations are also made for meeting the goals of diversity in reference service. Important topics discussed are: effective communication, special program development, needs assessments and outreach, and training and recruitment.

The demographics of the population in the United States are changing. According to the U.S. Bureau of the Census, more than 20 percent of the population is composed of ethnic minority groups, with African Americans, Hispanics, Asian Americans/Pacific Islanders, and American Indians as the significantly sizable groups. By the year 2000, these ethnic groups will make up approximately one-third of the population.[1]

Mengxiong Liu is Associate Librarian, Clark Library, San Jose State University, One Washington Square, San Jose, CA 95192.

[Haworth co-indexing entry note]: "Ethnicity and Information Seeking." Liu, Mengxiong. Co-published simultaneously in *The Reference Librarian* (The Haworth Press, Inc.) No. 49/50, 1995, pp. 123-134; and: *Library Users and Reference Services* (ed: Jo Bell Whitlatch) The Haworth Press, Inc., 1995, pp. 123-134. Multiple copies of this article/chapter may be purchased from The Haworth Document Delivery Center [1-800-3-HAWORTH; 9:00 a.m. - 5:00 p.m. (EST)].

A primary role of libraries is to meet the information needs of the communities which they serve. The increasing change of the composition of these communities is having a significant impact on library services. It is important that libraries respond to this fact by reflecting diversity in both their collections and services. Reference service is at the forefront of the library. Reference librarians are the first ones who encounter patrons when they come into the libraries. Face-to-face communication in the library takes place mainly at the reference desk. Therefore, a reference librarian must be an information specialist and a skilled interpersonal communicator. And the latter part is becoming more and more essential in a multicultural environment.

In order to serve the culturally and linguistically diverse communities, reference librarians must understand other cultures, and the information needs and information seeking patterns of the diverse groups. Information seeking patterns/behavior describes how people go about finding answers to solve a problem. The term also involves a wide range of perceptions, attitudes, activities, and outcomes associated with the pursuit and use of different forms of information. It is important to keep in mind that "information-seeking behavior must be viewed within the context of the end user's cultural experience."[2]

Culture influences people's behavior and their way of communication is influenced by the values they hold. The information needs and information seeking behavior of a library user from another culture could be very different from the traditional library users due to the different cultural experiences, language, level of literacy, socioeconomic status, education, level of acculturation and value system. There are quite a few studies investigating people's information seeking behavior, however, very few focusing on the ethnic groups. By reviewing the available literature, some characteristics of multiethnic groups in their information seeking process have been summarized.

COMMUNICATION

There are more than 100 different languages spoken in this country. On one hand, it presents diversity. On the other hand, it poses problems during the intercultural communication. Language could be a barrier for America's linguistically diverse population, especially those foreign-born individuals, when seeking information in the libraries and elsewhere. Insufficient English proficiency and lack of adequate English vocabulary make it difficult for them to understand library terminologies. A common complaint is that they could not fully understand what the librarian said during orientation tours. Shy about their poor communication skills in English and inexperienced with using reference assistance because of the lack of attention to reference services in their native countries, they rarely ask reference questions. This hinders them from clearly and fully understanding a library's policies and practices.[3] For similar reasons, they prefer to use their native languages when communicating among themselves. Reading activities as well as mass media use are primarily characterized by the native language. However, studies also found that the dependency on ethnic materials decreases based on the length of their stay in the country. The longer they stay in this country, the less they use ethnic media to satisfy their information needs. The length of stay was a significant predictor of the degree of communication gap between the first and the second generation.[4,5] Because of their relatively poor communication skill in English, they very often suffer from communication apprehension, the fear of talking. People from different ethnic groups all have certain degree of anxiety associated with oral interaction with another person when using English. However, if they want to survive in a very verbal society like America, where and how do they search for information to solve their problems? Studies reported that social networks play a critical role in their information seeking process.

Latinos maintain frequent communication with relatives and friends on an individual basis. There are also various types of "barrio-oriented" ethnic organizations as well as clusters of gatekeepers who facilitate access to resources for others to solve problems. There are channels of information available through various types of activities: mass media use, reading activity, use of the public library or other formal institutions, and participation in formal voluntary associations and other types of groups.[6]

Asian Americans rely more heavily on informal social networks than other whites, blacks, Chicanos, other Hispanics, and native

Americans. Word of mouth plays a critical role for Chinese to shape their personal problem-solving strategies. However, individuals who obtained information principally from informal networks tended to be female, older, and to have lower incomes, and fewer years of schooling.[7] A majority rely on Chinese-language newspapers printed in the U.S. as their major source of news information. Country of origin, English proficiency, and educational level were found to be the three most important determinants of information-seeking behavior of Chinese in the San Francisco Bay area.[8] In addition, job information acquisition of minority groups, especially Koreans, is linked to levels of social assimilation and the extent of their interpersonal network. It is also noted that, among Korean groups, females have more frequent conversation with American friends than males.[9]

Among the Afro Americans, the typical communication pattern is "call-and-response" which exemplifies traditional African world view. This standard communication pattern impedes Black-White communication since the White does not respond.[10] Among the urban aged black adults, many are struggling in their literacy efforts, however, women and those who are considered to have good reading ability tend to be more active learners.[11] There are also group differences in the use of languages to request information in conversational discourse among professional-class and working-class Blacks and Whites.[12]

CONCEPTUAL AWARENESS

In addition to lack of command of the English language and disadvantaged communication skills, the absence of the conceptual awareness of the self-service system are major obstacles to comprehension of American information systems. The prevalent philosophy of education and library service led to the consequences of the lack of libraries and of sources in libraries in many other cultures. Most Asian libraries are far different from the American standard. Many serve primarily as study halls. Most have closed stacks, with little self-service needed or encouraged, little service-attitude on the part of the library, and little emphasis on reference. The only practice of asking in the library is to request a book or journal from the closed stacks. Reference assistance is not a common practice. And there is no need to do comprehensive library research since independent research projects are not emphasized in education.

In many foreign countries, there are very few publicly supported libraries. Few privately owned libraries are accessible to the general public. Therefore, the idea of a public facility that not only houses thousands of volumes but also provides services is new to them.[13] To make things further complicated, people from other cultures are unfamiliar with the American classification system and subject headings. They have little or no idea about the reference tools, such as indexes and abstracts, online service, and interlibrary loan. The lack of information retrieval skills prevents them from taking advantage of automated bibliographic access system.[14] Occasionally when they try to use them, they are often frustrated and confused when online catalogs and databases retrieve too many results.[15] Inevitably, they feel unsure about their ability to use the library.

LEARNING PATTERN

For those immigrants and foreign students newly come to America, they are in a strange environment, where they feel insecure and doubtful about what behavior is expected of them. The means that they usually use to identify and react to these expectations are no longer with them: their language, the presence of their peer group, their ability to observe the culture and read the proper responses. Hence, they have to substitute three means of learning instead: observing specific behavior situations, the appropriate behavior for each situation, and active participation in the culture or society. However, some of them resent being in a dependent position. And the fear that they are being pressured to adopt the host culture's norms hampers their adoption of "explicit communication," which implies being told how to respond or behave.[16] In such cases, when using the library, they would feel more comfortable being directed rather than instructed.

Foley developed a list of Pacific attitudes and culture traits which might affect reference services. The following is her list:[17]

1. In general, the people belong to a non-book society.
2. The respect for printed materials is missing in the Pacific area. Books are not the first source of information. (China and Japan are exceptions.)
3. It is a non-technological society.
4. The Pacific mind is not the Western mind. Non-inquiring (don't ask), non-questioning (don't challenge), non-judging (accept both sides).
5. A lack of interest in, and little knowledge of the huge body of Western common knowledge, geography, history and so on. Even the alphabet can cause problems.
6. Special language difficulties.
7. Logic difficulties. People in many cultures are not taught to think in the same way as Westerners. This can cause problems with subject catalogs and encyclopedia organization.
8. Respect for elders and persons in authority. This may inhibit questions.
9. Fear of revealing ignorance. Inability to speak even when fear is absent.
10. Hopelessness in the face of a large task or a large body of material.

In addition, other observations include that Pacific students are not accustomed to jokes in an academic setting, some students give cues that they understand when they do not, nodding and smiling do not mean comprehension, some students look away from the speaker when they are listening intently, feedback is undesirable, respect for age and authority leads to shyness and reluctance to speak out.

GATEKEEPERS

Gatekeepers play an important part in the information seeking process of ethnic communities. Metoyer-Duran defines gatekeepers as the agents of acculturation when they disseminate information within their ethnic communities. Gatekeepers provide linkages between their communities and the appropriate information resources. An NIMH study which focused on culturally specific behaviors of gatekeepers examined the gatekeepers' use of language, kinship networks, and organizational attitudes. As a result, the study recommended that health service institutions should develop bonds with neighborhood members who functioned as information gatekeepers.[18] Some gatekeepers perceive their primary mission as preserving cultural integrity and "guarding" their ethnic enclaves from the cultural and value incursions of the external culture. Others function as opinion leaders and information resources because the community identifies them as influence individuals within their communities. In general, gatekeepers interact and network within their reference group and with clusters of other gatekeepers for purposes of sharing information and maintaining linkages outside their immediate sphere of influence.[19]

Through an extensive study, Metoyer-Duran presented a model of information-seeking behavior of gatekeepers in ethnolinguistic communities. She examined the information environment of ethnolinguistic gatekeepers from five culturally diverse groups: American Indian, Chinese, Japanese, Korean and Latino. Findings show that the U.S.-born ethnolinguistic gatekeepers demonstrate higher levels of data and concept usage than foreign-born gatekeepers; there is a positive relationship between a gatekeeper's position in the affective and cognitive domains and his or her length of U.S. residency; ethnolinguistic gatekeepers utilize more English and non-English information resources than other members of their ethnic communities; they also utilize more institutionally based information resources (i.e., libraries and social service agencies) than non-gatekeepers in their ethnic communities. In addition, she found that most of the gatekeepers are either bilingual or trilingual, they perceive the public library positively despite their limited use of the library as an information resource, and they have the interest in using information technologies.[20]

MEET THE GOALS FOR DIVERSITY

By reviewing the characteristics of information seeking patterns of ethnically diverse groups, it becomes obvious that, the survival of a library will be dependent on its acceptance of ethnic minorities both as providers and users of library services. Great efforts are needed to remove barriers to ethnic minorities and develop services sensitive to the needs of multiethnic users. What can reference librarians do to meet the goals for diversity?

Effective Communication

More effective reference work in a multicultural environment must be based on communication skills and cultural awareness, as well as library professionalism. The reference librarian must know enough about communication to differentiate the user whose problem is lack of clarity about his/her information needs from the user whose problem is conversation apprehension. Foley presented some practice examples with questions, answers and the comments.[21] Ormondroyd offered some rules to follow for effective communication with patrons who speak English as a second language. The rules include:

1. Keep sentence structure and vocabulary simple.
2. Make no assumptions.
3. Articulate clearly and use a slow pace.
4. Rephrase what you have said–do not repeat it.
5. When a student has difficulty communicating a complex idea, rephrase it in your own words to be sure that you have understood what was said and to provide an English-language model for the student's idea or question.
6. Hone your listening skills.
7. Be sensitive to the emotional state of your patrons.
8. Make yourself as knowledgeable as possible about other cultures.
9. Be aware of resources for foreign students on your campus.
10. Politeness, consideration, caring, and sensitivity will yield positive responses in all people.[22]

Special Programs and Instructions

Special programs of library instruction are needed to overcome problems derived from users' cultural differences, difficulties in oral communication, lack of an adequate vocabulary, and the inability to conceptualize and apply the English alphabet. Studies found that library tour is the most popular form of orientation for people who lack conceptual awareness of American library systems. Library tours provide them with more visualized pictures of how the collections are organized, the actual locations of the materials, and the directions they can follow. Tours should be offered in multi-languages if possible, and the tour leaders should articulate clearly and avoid library jargon. The handouts on the library materials accompanied with the glossaries of library terminologies can be written in the multi-languages. Multi-lingual tape tours are good practices in some academic libraries. Liu offered some specific recommendations to academic libraries to help students from developing countries.[23] By understanding their learning patterns, reference librarians are in a good position to tailor their services to multiethnic users, especially foreign students on academic campuses. Librarians may want to avoid "overexplaining and acting oracular," which poses less threat while allowing them to use observation and participation, thus, contributes more to their learning process. After such minimal help, the invitation to return for more help is necessary.[24] A good strategy could be informing them about the problems they might encounter in using the libraries, so that they could be mentally prepared and avoid some frustration.

Needs Assessment and Outreach

For libraries which serve increasingly diverse groups, community needs assessments are more important than library use studies. A traditional user study could miss significant members of the community, especially gatekeepers, because, although gatekeepers hold a high opinion of the library, they do not use it to any significant degree.[25] Metoyer-Duran recommended some specifics in doing community needs assessments. The fact that even gatekeepers do not fully understand the relationship between a library and an information agency makes it necessary for the library to promote its information services.

Outreach is a good approach to achieve this goal. Libraries may want to engage in outreach programs, such as participating in major ethnic events, conducting story hours in other languages, doing selected publicity pieces and signage in languages other than English, and establishing and maintaining contact with community groups and organizations. Berkeley Public Library's *Partnerships for Change* program is a successful example.[26]

Training and Recruitment

No single factor is more important than library staff that are trained to deliver a high level of quality service to the multicultural communities. Reference librarians need to be trained to become more sensitive to cultural differences, and to develop more effective communication skills by acquiring knowledge about multicultural information seeking behavior. These components should also be added to the library school's reference curriculum. And the entire library school curriculum needs to be continually updated to incorporate the elements of multicultural librarianship.

It is vital that we do not overlook the crucial need to reflect the society's diversity by including, accepting, and retaining representatives of all the society's ethnic groups in the professional work force of our library institutions. Diversity within a library's workforce should be viewed as a source of strength and richness.[27] A shift from affirmative action to more broadly based diversity programs is necessary.

Traditionally, very few librarians with ethnic background are hired. And even if they are hired, they are hired for technical services instead of public services. The ethnic composition of the reference librarians is at its minimal level. Now, it is time to change. Ethnic librarians at the reference desk may have an inside understanding about the behavior of and the nature of the questions asked by patrons with ethnic backgrounds. With the understanding and awareness in mind, they are capable of responding more effectively. They can also bring unique insight and perspective to the development of library programs, services, and collections designed to meet the needs of varied users. It is highly recommended that a diversity or outreach or multicultural services librarian position be developed in order to target library services to diverse ethnic communities.

However, building strong diversity programs requires a good understanding of multicultural issues, an overall strategy, and support from all levels of the institution. It is praiseworthy that library management has come to realize the importance, as Trujillo and

Weber stated "we should recruit from diverse racial and ethnic groups into the field of librarianship and build a significant pool of both practitioners and leaders needed for the immediate and long-term future."[28]

This paper focuses on the discussion of information seeking behavior from the perspective of the multicultural communities. The patterns and models discussed above represent significant departures from the traditional approach. Our knowledge about human information seeking behavior especially in a multicultural environment is far from enough. Reference librarians need to further explore human cognition in the context of multi-ethnicity. With the awareness of multiculturalism, the understanding of cross-culture information seeking behavior, and a sense of professionalism, librarians can meet the goals for diversity.

REFERENCES

1. U.S. Bureau of the Census, *Statistical Abstract of the United States: 1990.* Washington D.C.: Govt. Printing Office, 1990, pp. 14-15.

2. Metoyer-Duran, Cheryl. *Gatekeepers in Ethnolinguistic Communities.* Norwood, NJ: Ablex Publishing Corporation, 1993, p. 1.

3. Liu, Ziming. "Difficulties and Characteristics of Students from Developing Countries in Using American Libraries." *College and Research Libraries* 54 (January 1993): 25-31.

4. Kim, Y. Y. "A Communication Approach to the Acculturation Process: A Study of Korean Immigrants in Chicago." *International Journal of Intercultural Relations* 2 (2) (1978): 197-224.

5. Jun, S. "Communication Patterns Among Young Korean Immigrants." *International Journal of Intercultural Relations* 8 (4) (1984): 171-389.

6. Duran, Daniel F. *Latino Communication Patterns: An Investigation of Media Use and Organizational Activity Among Mexican, Cuban, and Puerto Rican Residents of Chicago.* (Ph.D. dissertation, University of Wisconsin-Madison, 1977).

7. Endo, R. "Use of Informal Social Networks for Service-Related Information." *Psychological Reports* 54 (1984): 354.

8. Pang, W. *Information-Seeking Behavior Among Chinese in the Bay Area.* (Unpublished master's thesis, San Jose State University, 1986).

9. Kim, K.C., and Hurh, W.M. "Social and Occupational Assimilation of Korean Immigrant Workers in the United States." *California Sociologist* 3 (2) (1980): 125-142.

10. Daniel, J.L. and Smitherman, G. "How I Got Over: Communication Dynamics in the Black Community." *Quarterly Journal of Speech* 62 (1976): 26-39.

11. Heisel, M.A. *Learning and Information Seeking Activities of Urban, Aged, Black Adults.* (Ph.D. dissertation, Rutgers University, 1983).

12. Hall, W.S., Bartlett, E. and Hughes, A.T. "Patterns of Information Requests." *New Directions for Child Development* 42 (Winter 1988): 43-58.

13. Mood, Terry Ann. "Foreign Students and the Academic Library." *RQ* 22 (Winter 1982): 175-180.

14. Allen, Mary Beth. "International Students in Academic Libraries: A User Survey." *College and Research Libraries* 54 (July 1993): 323-333.

15. Liu, "Difficulties and Characteristics of Students."

16. Mood, "Foreign Students and the Academic Library."

17. Foley, May. "Reference and Information Services in a Multi-cultural Environment." *Journal of Library & Information Science* 10 (October 1984): 143-162.

18. Snyder, Peter. "Neighborhood Gatekeepers in the Process of Urban Adaption: Cross-ethnic Commonalities." *Urban Anthropology* 5 (1976): 35-52.

19. Metoyer-Duran, Cheryl. "Information-Seeking Behavior of Gatekeepers in Ethnolinguistic Communities: Overview of a Taxonomy." *Library and Information Science Research* 13 (1991): 319-346.

20. Metoyer-Duran, *Gatekeepers in Ethnolinguistic Communities*; Metoyer-Duran, "Information-Seeking Behavior of Gatekeepers."

21. Foley "Reference and Information Services."

22. Ormondroyd, Joan. "The International Student and Course-Integrated Instruction: The Librarian's Perspective." *Research Strategies* 7 (Fall 1989): 148-158.

23. Liu, "Difficulties and Characteristics of Students."

24. Mood, "Foreign Students and the Academic Library."

25. Metoyer-Duran, *Gatekeepers in Ethnolinguistic Communities*.

26. Minudri, Regina. Presentation at CLA Annual Conference, Oakland, California, November 14, 1993.

27. Jones-Quartey, Theo S. and Byunn, Kit S. "Ethnic Minorities in Librarianship: A Selected Bibliography." *Special Libraries* 84 (Spring 1993): 104-111.

28. Trujillo, Roberto G. and Weber, David C. "Academic Library Responses to Cultural Diversity: A Position Paper for the 1990s." *Journal of Academic Librarianship* 17 (1991): 158.

Knowledge Gap, Information-Seeking and the Poor

Elfreda A. Chatman
Victoria EM Pendleton

SUMMARY. The purpose of this chapter is to address the issues of information seeking behavior within a context of an information poor life style. Several factors can be attributed to an information poor world. For example, it is one in which the mass media are not viewed as providers of useful information. Moreover, this is a world in which there is a parsimony of helpful interpersonal channels. Thus, both formal and personal sources are devoid of everyday practical information of the kind that is needed by poor people.

In addressing reasons to explain this phenomenon, knowledge gap theory is examined. The conclusion drawn from this analysis is that, although the mass media are perceived as sources of information for some (the "media rich"), they do not respond to the needs of the poor. Unfortunately, the role that interpersonal sources might play in this process, have not been adequately addressed by knowledge gap researchers.

INTRODUCTION

An item of discussion for researchers interested in information-seeking behaviors and poverty pertains to the issue of "knowledge

Elfreda A. Chatman is Associate Professor at the School of Information and Library Science, University of North Carolina, Chapel Hill, and Victoria EM Pendleton is a doctoral student at the School of Information and Library Science, University of North Carolina, Chapel Hill, 100 Manning Hall, CB # 3360, Chapel Hill, NC 27599-3360.

[Haworth co-indexing entry note]: "Knowledge Gap, Information-Seeking and the Poor." Chatman, Elfreda A., and Victoria EM Pendleton. Co-published simultaneously in *The Reference Librarian* (The Haworth Press, Inc.) No. 49/50, 1995, pp. 135-145; and: *Library Users and Reference Services* (ed: Jo Bell Whitlatch) The Haworth Press, Inc., 1995, pp. 135-145. Multiple copies of this article/chapter may be purchased from The Haworth Document Delivery Center [1-800-3-HAWORTH; 9:00 a.m. - 5:00 p.m. (EST)].

gap." The basis for this argument is that, sources of information are available to both poor and non-poor. However, there appears to be an enormous difference in the ways in which the information rich and the information poor search for, use, and share information.

In our opinion, this observation leads to a number of interesting questions. For example, what exactly is an impoverished lifestyle? And, more importantly, are there characteristics about this lifestyle that might be generalizable to other populations?

To begin to respond to these questions, it might be worthwhile to explore these issues within a needs/wants categorization. Wilson, Derr, and others have engaged in a long-standing debate regarding factors that constitute "needs" and "wants."[1] Although it is not our intent to engage in further discourse regarding these notions, a word about the difference between them does appear to be in order.

A consensus that seems reasonable is that "a need" is somehow linked to a state of dependency. In other words, if the information is absent, our current state-of-affairs is in *jeopardy*. It is more than advantageous to have it; not to possess the information is to make our circumstances worse.

On the other hand, "want" conveys some degree of enhancement. That is, we would not be worse off if we didn't have the information, but it would be an added benefit if we possessed it. It seems to us, therefore, that what constitutes an impoverished lifestyle is the inability of poor people to resolve their need for critical information.

So, in response to our first question: what constitutes an impoverished lifestyle? It seems that a primary contributor is a dysfunctional life-world. We want to make clear that our use of this term, dysfunctional, occurs because members of this social milieu are themselves aware that items of information within their worlds do not lend themselves to solving problematic situations. A plausible explanation is three-fold. For one, because they perceive that sources of information are unusable in a timely manner. Secondly, because, when sources are both available and useful, they are insufficient to respond to their needs. Finally, the channels of information, both mass and interpersonal, are viewed with suspicion and skepticism.

MEDIA AS SOURCES OF EVERYDAY INFORMATION

Repeated findings from the communication research literature link media exposure to information awareness and use. Regarding the use of the media by poor people, studies revealed that television is the medium of choice. Related to this finding, is that television is an important source that could be used by the poor in their everyday lives. Sorts of things documented include crime, health and safety concerns, and programs that reflect true-life situations, primarily of a disruptive nature.[2]

However, there is some debate about the utility of television (and, for that matter, the media, generally) to enrich the knowledge stock of poor people.[3] In fact, the research suggests that, in particular, television, is mainly viewed as a source of escape and diversion.[4]

The second medium typically associated with poor people is newspapers. An observation noted is that newspapers have more utility than television.[5] Items of interest include the following: crime and violence, news dealing with location-interests, and events that were of minority interests.[6] For example, Bogart's work with blue-collar workers reported that the disadvantaged's use of the mass media was restricted, depended upon concrete details, and required a heightened degree of timeliness.[7] Later, Chatman would extend Bogart's description to include a first-order knowledge world.[8] Essentially, this world requires information to respond to localized concerns. These concerns demand immediate attention, and acceptance depends upon the ability to be tested against lived experiences of potential receivers.

To sum up our discussion thus far, mass media are not used by poor people to assist them in coping with problems. Whatever roles are being played in their information environment are those that generally reflect their places in non-poor environments. Namely, mass media are sources of recreation, to give them a general sense of local and national affairs, and (with sensational news events) as topics of pastime conversations. Thus, if mass media are not sources of relevant information, do poor people make greater use of the interpersonal communication process?

INTERPERSONAL SOURCES
AND INFORMATION-SEEKING

By now, it should come as no surprise that the interpersonal picture researchers have of poor people is one of familiarity. In a sense, research contends a more restricted world view might enhance their knowledge of, and reliance on, information contacts from people very much like themselves. For example, Garfinkle defines this as shaping a world in which most issues are resolved through a taken-for-granted attitude.[9] Wilson, on the other hand, argues that it is one in which "understanding is . . . on . . . local and personal matters."[10] However, no hard evidence exists to support the notion that the poor rely on each other for information of an important or critical nature.

If this is the case, what sorts of information exchanges occur on a social network comprised of family and neighbors? And, is this information sufficient to address problems and concerns? Research which addresses the information exchanges among poor people discovered these exchanges contributed little to one's information stock.[11] The finding that channels of information, capable of instrumental resolution to problems are rare in low-income environments is supported by Dervin and Greenberg who acknowledge that:

> . . . interpersonal mistrust is high. The idealized image of a tight-knit lower-class community may have applied to a community of several decades ago.[12]

In describing the interpersonal channels as providers of information, researchers acknowledge that they are not perceived as very helpful or desirable. For example, findings from research conducted by Cohen and Hodges, and Black revealed that the social exchanges among poor people are ones astonishing devoid of support or mutual caring.[13]

Despite a few exceptions, the overwhelming evidence is that poor people have a minimal association with neighbors. Moreover, when family members are asked for advice, it is with the understanding that their difficulties remain within the family unit. Significantly, the impression provided by this information world is that it is one in which people live alienated from each other, where there are few, if any, interpersonal contacts, and one in which neighbors and friends are seen through hostile and protective eyes. As a consequence, Ireland and Besner's convincing argument is that the disadvantaged are the most socially isolated from each other.[14] We can reasonably assume then, that if this is indeed the case, the interpersonal channels that might serve as providers of needed information are also mutually exclusive.

In weighing the implications for purposes of our examination, we conclude that there is precariously little margin for information exchanges. Our observation is supported by research conducted by Chatman in which the information world of low-skilled workers was studied.[15] One of the things she learned was that the poor live in an environment in which they are alienated from each other and have few, if any, social supports. Thus, poor people can be characterized as living in an impoverished information world. It is one in which mass media exposure does not yield new information to assist them and one in which interpersonal channels are closed. The findings from that research were considered so significant that the study led to a formulation of alienation theory in order to explain the destitution of this information world.

Before we proceed to a discussion of the broader issue of knowledge gap and its implications to the information-seeking patterns of poor people, we want to readdress our initial question, namely, factors that constitute an impoverished information environment. Our examination thus far contributes the following. The mass media do not hold a magical well-spring of new knowledge. Poor people view these sources primarily to be entertained or to pass time. When a medium, e.g., a newspaper, was specifically scanned for particular items, research shows that those items were extremely localized and responded to immediate lived experiences. However, because interpersonal channels were parsimonious, verification of facts (such as crime), which contained mutual interest and curiosity, was also closed. With this solemn picture of an information world in mind, we turn to an examination of supporting evidence that researchers have used to describe the "information poor."

THE KNOWLEDGE GAP AS AN EXPLANATION

Since the late 1940's, researchers tried to identify and describe reasons why portions of the population acquire public information at differing rates. Knowledge gap, communication effects gap, and information gap are synonymous terms used by different researchers to describe the phenomenon.[16] Inequitable access, psychological or educational barriers, and social systems explanations were advanced as to why gaps occurred in the acquisition of new information.

A seminal work addressing this issue was introduced in 1970 by Tichenor, Donohue and Olien.[17] What the authors found was that people with greater economic means also had better informational sources than people of lesser means. Despite a few exceptions, also noted as contributing factors supporting the stratification argument are communication skills; prior exposure to a topic of interest or concern; social contacts; and attitudes of the individual regarding the relevance of the information in light of his needs.

In contrast to a description of differences between the haves and the have-nots, other researchers, attempted to identify conditions which narrowed gaps.[18] For instance, Donohue, Tichenor, and Olien found that a crisis in an homogeneous community reduced gaps in knowledge about the local issue. Interpersonal communication increases when conflict is intense, and any knowledge gap declines as public interest wanes.[19]

Another cause for the narrowing of knowledge gaps, is the evidence of ceiling effects. Ettema and Kline argue that there are two critical imposed ceilings: the "naturally occurring," i.e., the sources contain a limited amount of information; and an "audience imposed" ceiling effect, one created by the members themselves. In other words, the ceiling is subjectively self-imposed.[20] We suspect the phenomenon happens because persons, particularly poor people, will retreat from acceptance of sources that seem irrelevant to their situations.

THE SITUATIONAL MODEL

The introduction of situational factors into this discussion is the result of several researchers who noted a curious situation. Namely, that *the context* in which information acquisition and use were occurring, was being ignored. For example, in their literature review, Ettema and Kline summarized the two major causes of knowledge gap. As we indicated in the preceding paragraphs, these were ceiling effects and audience related factors. A significant contribution these authors made was a useful description to explain idiosyncratic traits; for example, communication skills, predisposition for a particular medium, and motivation to acquire information. In particular, Ettema and Kline concluded that a knowledge gap will always widen when only socioeconomic traits are considered. Whereas, an examination of situation specific differences is a better predictor of knowledge gaps. Why? Because this approach considers the interest or motivation level of a person, and because it addresses whether or not the information is functional in the member's life world.[21]

Other researchers also support the notion of linking motivation and functional information as predictors of knowledge gaps.[22] For example, Genova and Greenberg differentiates interest by its functional utility. In this view, "self-interest" pertains to daily coping needs. "Social interest" is information that is perceived to have utility for one's social networks. The authors acknowledge that these interests may be shaped by social norms and by the mass media. "Thus, changes in the individual's spheres of activity and/or social milieu should result in changing perceptions of informational utility, and perhaps the formation of new interest areas."[23]

A reasonably accurate view provided thus far, suggests several findings pertinent to our discussion. In the first place, it indicates that the mass media do indeed play less significant roles in the lives of poor people. Why? Because their interest is generally viewed as being irrelevant in responding to everyday concerns. In this case, we note that it is probably due to an inability or lack of interest in addressing the contextual use of information. The absence of context or situational use of information as a concern is hardly limited to the poor. But because they have so few information contacts, this omission is significant.

To recapitulate the major points addressed in this section. The findings reveal that some members of any social milieu (including an impoverished one) might be motivated enough to find means by which to narrow knowledge gaps. In this light, Dervin's typology to predict information use is a helpful extension to the situational model. In her model, she proposes specific conditions in which individuals might seek information: decision situations; worry situations; barrier situations; and in problematic situations.[24] Dervin's model is particularly appreciated because it indicates the urgency in which people approach information sources. Moreover, she does not hesitate to suggest barriers to the information-seeking process.

Dervin's contribution to our discussion boils down to this. In focusing on a particular segment of the information environment, we have concentrated on the factors that make for an impoverished life-world. In our assessment of that world, we note minimal attention by researchers to reasons why some people live in a knowledge gap milieu. We conclude that, among factors already addressed, is a mistrust by poor people of sources that originate outside their information environment. We suspect this is due to their inattention to the context in which the information is being directed. Dervin, on the other hand, places the context or situation that brought about the information-seeking behavior as paramount to the total process. Although her work is not specifically directed at studies for the poor, we believe that she makes a significant contribution to studies of information and poverty.

CONCLUSION

In conclusion, most of the knowledge gap research has applied several conceptual models to explain how people acquire and use information. However, there is no consensus as to what are the defining characteristics of the knowledge gap. A factor for this is minimal attention to the situational use of information, particularly within communities comprised of poor individuals. We contend that issues dealing specifically with the poor and discussions of knowledge gap or gain, has yet to be fully explored.

What then, do our findings suggest to members of our profession? We suggest a preliminary picture which might provide usefulness for practice and research. Having studied poor populations, and being engaged in critical analysis of pertinent literature, we conclude the following.

If disadvantaged members of a social environment experience gaps, perhaps it is gaps in second-level knowledge, or knowledge *about* which they do not know; nor does anyone else know. In trying to examine what information poverty is, an approach providing some credibility is to conceptualize information poverty in terms of first and second-level knowledge. We concur that first-level knowledge is knowledge *of* things. That is, things are known to us and to those whom we share lived experiences. These things are readily accessible and sources have immediate verifiability. We simply check it out for ourselves or ask others until the collective assessment of the situation satisfies us.

However, as noted above, information poverty pertains to second-level knowledge. This is knowledge that originates outside our lived experiences. Because it addresses things we have not previously experienced, its relevance to our specific circumstances is questionable. Verification of its truthfulness is also problematic. So, even if the poor are exposed to a wide variety of information, they might not accept these sources as ways in which to better their situations.

One way in which we might begin to bridge the gap between ourselves and the poor would be to introduce both ourselves and the items we provide as trustworthy, reliable, and useful to their situation. It is not sufficient to just respond to inquiries. We suggest a more active role in which we engage in some basic research that would identify all members of our information community. This might necessitate a linkage with the community's social service providers. Whatever choices we make, in today's world with its heightened emphasis on information acquisition and use, we need to find ways which better serve those members of our society who are the information poor.

REFERENCES

1. Patrick Wilson, *Second-hand Knowledge: An Inquiry into Cognitive Authority* (Westport, CT: Greenwood Press, 1983); and Richard Derr, "A Conceptual Analysis of Information Need," *Information Processing and Management* (1983):273-278.

2. Ralph E. Carter and Peter Clark, "Suburbanites, City Residents and Local News," *Journalism Quarterly* 40 (1963): 548-559; George Comstock, Stephen

Chaffee, Nathan Katzman, Maxwell McCombs, and Donald Roberts, *Television and Human Behavior* (New York: Columbia University Press, 1978); and Thomas H. Allen, "Mass Media Use Patterns in a Negro Ghetto," *Journalism Quarterly* 45 (1968): 525-527.

3. S.T. Eastman, "Uses of Television Viewing and Consumer Life Styles: A Multivariate Analysis," *Journal of Broadcasting* 23 (1979): 491-500; and Gerald F. Klein, "Media Time Budgeting as a Function of Demographics and Life Styles," *Journalism Quarterly* 48 (1971): 211-221.

4. Elfreda A. Chatman, "Life in a Small World: Applicability of Gratification Theory to Information-Seeking Behavior," *Journal of the American Society for Information Science* 42 (1991): 438-449; Leonard I. Pearlin, "Social and Personal Stress and Escape Television Viewing," *Public Opinion Quarterly* 23 (1959): 255-259; and Brenda Dervin and Bradley Greenberg, "The Communication Environment of the Urban Poor," In *Current Perspectives in Mass Communication Research,* vol.I, edited by Floyd G. Klein and Peter J. Tichenor (Beverly Hills, CA: Sage Publications, 1972): 195-234.

5. Harold L. Wilensky, "Mass Society and Mass Culture: Interdependence or Independence?," *American Sociological Review* 29 (1964): 173-197; and M.M. Gordon and C.H. Anderson, "The Blue-Collar Worker at Leisure," In *Blue-Collar World: Studies of the American Worker,* edited by A.B. Shastah and W. Gomberg. (Englewood Cliffs, NJ: Prentice-Hall, 1964): 407-416.

6. C.A. Stroman and L.B. Becker, "Racial Differences in Gratifications," *Journalism Quarterly* (1978): 767-769; and Elfreda A. Chatman, "Information, Mass Media Use and the Working Poor," *Library and Information Science Research* 7(1985): 97-113.

7. Leo Bogart, "The Mass Media and the Blue-Collar Worker," In *Blue-Collar World,* pp.416-428.

8. Chatman, "Life in a Small World."

9. Harold Garfinkle, "Studies of the Routine Grounds of Everyday Activities," *Social Problems,* II (1964): 225-250.

10. Wilson, *Second-Hand Knowledge,* p.152.

11. Nathan Glazer, "The Alienation of Modern Man," *Commentary* 3 (April 1947): 378-385; and David Riesman, Nathan Glazer, and Revel Denney, *The Lonely Crowd* (New Haven, CT: Yale University Press, 1961).

12. Dervin and Greenberg, "The Communication Environment of the Urban Poor," p.212.

13. Albert K. Cohen and Harold M. Hodges, Jr., "Characteristics of the Lower-Collar Class," *Social Problems* 10 (1963): 303-334; and Carle E. Block, "Communicating with the Urban Poor: An Exploratory Inquiry," *Journalism Quarterly* 45 (Spring 1970): 3-11.

14. Lola M. Ireland and Arthur Besner, "Low Income Outlook on Life," *Welfare in Review* 3 (September 1965): 13-19.

15. Elfreda A. Chatman, "Alienation Theory: Application of a Conceptual Framework to a Study of Information Among Janitors," *RQ* 29 (1990): 355-368.

16. See literature reviews by: James S. Ettema and F. Gerald Kline, "Deficits, Differences, and Ceilings: Contingent Conditions for Understanding the Knowledge Gap," *Communications Research* 4,2 (April 1977): 179-202; and Cecilie Gaziano, "The Knowledge Gap: An Analytical Review of Media Effects," *Communication Research* 10,4 (October 1983): 447-486.

17. P.J. Tichenor, G.A. Donohue, and C.N. Olien, "Mass Media Flow and Differential Growth in Knowledge," *Public Opinion Quarterly* 34 (Summer 1970): 159-170.

18. Gaziano, "The Knowledge Gap."

19. G.A. Donohue, P.J. Tichenor, and C.N. Olien, "Mass Media and the Knowledge Gap: A Hypothesis Reconsidered," *Communication Research* 2,1 (January 1975): 3-23.

20. Ettema and Kline, "Deficits, Differences, and Ceilings," pp.197-199.

21. Ettema and Kline, "Deficits, Differences, and Ceilings;" and Brenda Dervin, "Communication Gaps and Inequities: Moving Toward a Reconceptualization," In *Progress in Communication Sciences*, vol.II, edited by Brenda Dervin and Melvin J. Voigt. (Norwood, NJ: Ablex Publishing, 1980): 73-112.

22. B.K.L. Genova and Bradley S. Greenberg, "Interests in News and the Knowledge Gap," *Public Opinion Quarterly* 43,1 (Spring 1979): 79-91; James S. Ettema, James W. Brown, and Russell V. Luepker, "Knowledge Gap Effects in a Health Information Campaign," *Public Opinion Quarterly* 47,4 (Winter 1983): 516-527; and Reinhold Horstmann, "Knowledge Gaps Revisited: Secondary Analyses from Germany," *European Journal of Communication* 6 (1991): 77-93.

23. Genova and Greenberg, "Interests in News," p.82.

24. Dervin, "Communication Gaps and Inequities," pp.103-104.

A Matter of Focus:
Reference Services for Older Adults

Connie Van Fleet

SUMMARY. Older adults comprise a diverse clientele who require opportunities for lifelong learning and leisure. Reference librarians can adapt existing services to serve the majority of patrons over the age of fifty. Patience, sensitivity, and flexibility are essential to effective interviewing. Information about issues of concern to older adults, including family relationships, health, death and dying, housing, legal and financial affairs, and leisure activities, can be gathered from selected, readily available sources. Reader's advisory services, programming, and outreach activities should be focused to more effectively target older adult users. Adhering to common service philosophy based on lifelong learning and a commitment to provide equal service to all individuals will facilitate tailoring services to meet the needs of the older adult patron.

INTRODUCTION

Elizabeth Brown, a high school graduate, is the manager of a credit union with over 500 members and 4 million dollars in assets. She purchased a new home three years ago, owns a VCR and answering machine, and spends a great deal of her free time with a significant other or celebrating (almost anything) with her family.

Connie Van Fleet is Associate Professor at the School of Library and Information Science, Louisiana State University, 267 Coates Hall, Baton Rouge, LA 70803.

[Haworth co-indexing entry note]: "A Matter of Focus: Reference Services for Older Adults." Van Fleet, Connie. Co-published simultaneously in *The Reference Librarian* (The Haworth Press, Inc.) No. 49/50, 1995, pp. 147-164; and: *Library Users and Reference Services* (ed: Jo Bell Whitlatch) The Haworth Press, Inc., 1995, pp. 147-164. Multiple copies of this article/chapter may be purchased from The Haworth Document Delivery Center [1-800-3-HAWORTH; 9:00 a.m. - 5:00 p.m. (EST)].

She subscribes to several popular magazines, including *Modern Maturity* and *Prevention*. She drives to the public library branch near her home, and reads mysteries and adventure stories when not working crossword puzzles.

Martha Green checks out groceries at the neighborhood market to supplement her income and rents the house in which she used to live with her husband (now deceased). She walks to work, but is somewhat overweight. She is troubled by arthritis when the weather is cold, but she "don't let it slow her down none." Her family lives at some distance, but they write and phone frequently.

David Black recently retired from the University after a long career as an educator and researcher. He owns his home and has retirement income as well as social security. He attends the symphony and other musical events, as well as the theater. He has an active social life and travels a great deal. He continues to receive journals in his discipline and subscribes to several popular magazines, including *Architectural Digest* and *Gourmet*.

Adelle White retired from a position as a teacher's assistant 18 years ago and lives in the house where she and her husband raised five children. With the help of a visiting nurse/aide and children who live nearby, she is able to live independently in spite of lower back problems, diabetes, and macular degeneration, a condition that results in low vision. She attends church each Sunday (driven by a church or family member) and reads letters and magazines with the aid of a lighted magnifier. She watches soap operas on a large television and receives books on tape by mail through the National Library Service for the Blind and Physically Handicapped. While she used to prefer romances (particularly nursing romances), her taste has become more eclectic since she has had to depend on the NLS collection, and she currently reads mysteries, westerns, adventures, and general fiction as well.

Though their educational levels, working experiences, health profiles and socio-economic statuses are very different, Elizabeth, Martha, David, and Adelle are all considered members of the same group: older adults. This group continues to be the fastest growing segment of American society, and one that has increased in political influence at an even greater pace.

In 1990, there were 53 million Americans over the age of 55,

31.6 million of whom were over age 65.[1] One in every eight Americans is over the age of 65, making the older adult population of the U.S. greater than the entire population of Canada.[2] The American Association of Retired Persons (AARP), which admits to membership anyone over the age of 50, has over 30 million members, and has become a political force of enormous power. This is hardly surprising, given that people over 65 control two in five consumer dollars and almost one in three federal budget dollars is spent for their benefit. Couple this with the fact that 20% of voters are seniors and that Americans age 55-74 have had the highest voting rates in last five national elections, and it is not difficult to understand the attention politicians give to the concerns of older adults.[3]

The sheer numbers provide a compelling argument for library services for the group of older adults, but there are dangers inherent in identifying individuals as group members. The tendency to think in terms of stereotypes or averages is overwhelming. Yet effective library service is based on awareness of the needs of the individual. So while we may think of the "average" older adult as having 12 years education, being married and living with a spouse in a home which they own, having an income in the low $20,000s, a savings account, life insurance, and no debt and who retired by choice at age 62, that precise profile fits only a minority of group members.[4] Sociologists recognize groups within the group: ethnic minorities, rural populations, prisoners, women, and the "vulnerable elderly" or "old old."[5]

Such diversity in the older adult population merely reflects the diversity within library communities. The current emphasis on community analysis, appropriate planning, and targeted marketing draws attention to specific groups; the unswerving commitment to serve all patrons provides a foundation for effective library service. Services to older adults, as services to all special populations and specific groups, draw from a common service philosophy based on lifelong learning. Applying basic strategies and techniques of library service to older adults is simply a matter of focus.

LEARNING PATTERNS OF OLDER ADULTS

The greatest barrier to full participation for older adults is often ageism. Myths about the horrors and sadness of growing old permeate American thinking, yet studies indicate that such ideas are unfounded. Older adults learn better, live more independently, are more active, and are healthier and safer than is generally realized.[6]

Lifelong learning is a widely recognized phenomenon, and support for lifelong learning theory draws from a variety of disciplines, including education, sociology, psychology, and management and business administration.[7] Librarians with a commitment to providing services to older adults will find they have they have much in common with other service professionals. Waters and Goodman, in their book, *Empowering Older Adults: Practical Strategies for Counselors,* target "the 95 percent of older persons who live in the community and wish to remain independent as long as possible" and work from the conviction that "older adults can learn, change, and take control of their lives."[8]

It is clear that learning is a process that may continue from birth to the grave, provided that the learning process is established, positive attitudes are developed, and opportunities are provided to encourage continued growth. While learning patterns of older adults may be different from those of younger people, there is significant evidence to support the claim that adults continue to learn effectively throughout the lifespan. Older adults tend to have greater wisdom—that is, assimilate learning into a context based on broader experience. Verbal skills seem to increase with age, while mathematical skills appear to decline. Older adults generally work more slowly and do poorly in timed tests, but often commit fewer errors because they avoid a trial and error approach.[9]

Research on learning patterns suggests that adults demonstrate learning preferences that are markedly different from the typical pedagogical approach. Adults prefer to control the pace of learning activities, to learn independently, to use discussion to reinforce and stimulate ideas, and generally to take a more active and controlling part in the learning activities in which they are engaged.[10] The greatest factor affecting continued learning is not age, but a personal predisposition developed over the course of a lifetime.[11]

Turock, however, notes that despite the significant body of research to the contrary, "it remains a fact that librarians subscribe to the myth of an intellectual decline in aging."[12] Her series of studies tracing the development of public library services to older adults leads her to conclude that the provision of services has not kept pace with the growth of older populations,[13] a finding reinforced by several other researchers.[14] It should be noted, however, that these studies tend to focus on specialized services to older adults, and may not reflect the level of service provided by librarians who have chosen a more integrated approach to service provision.

ALA GUIDELINES FOR SERVICE

ALA documents demonstrate that some segments of the library community, most notably the RASD Library Service to an Aging Population Committee and ASCLA's Library Service to the Impaired Elderly Forum, have been aware of the need for services to older adults. Two documents in particular will provide guidance for those implementing or expanding services to older adult populations.

"The Library's Responsibility to the Aging," developed by RASD's Library Service to an Aging Population Committee, was first adopted in 1964 and revised in 1970, 1971, and 1981. This very brief document offers ten broad areas in which librarians may offer service, beginning with "contributing toward a positive attitude toward aging and the aged."[15]

The 1987 "Guidelines for Library Service to Older Adults" prepared by the Library Services to an Aging Population Committee of RASD supersedes the 1975 "Guidelines for Library Services to an Aging Population."[16] These guidelines provide specific activities for accomplishing service goals, and will prove invaluable in planning services to older adults. This document in many ways parallels the earlier "Responsibility" document, but provides much greater detail.

Library services for older adults have essentially the same goals as services for all of our patrons–to provide the means for enriched leisure, the information for effective living, and the opportunity for continued growth and learning throughout the entire lifespan. The specific articulation of these services will vary according to the community's needs and demands. The difficulty is in ensuring that the special needs of older adults are met while remembering that "an older adult has a range of interests and abilities similar to any adult, and that . . . it is imperative that our programs be entirely free of any condescending nuances associated with aging."[17]

INTERVIEWING AND INTERPERSONAL SKILLS

Public services librarians already possess the skills necessary for successful interaction with older adults. They are accustomed to dealing with diverse clienteles with varying levels of education, different information needs, and unique personalities. The essential component is attitude. Reference librarians must be alert to special needs, while avoiding a paternalistic attitude on one hand or an abrupt and impatient approach on the other. Self-awareness is the first step, and librarians should begin by examining their own attitudes to ensure that they have not unconsciously accepted stereotypes about older adults, whether those stereotypes are positive or negative.

Providing special guidelines for interaction with older adults must be viewed with some trepidation. Most older adults will require no special treatment, and providing techniques for those who do tends to reinforce stereotypes and lead to inappropriate generalizations. Nevertheless, a few suggestions may enhance awareness. Special techniques required for interviewing older adults are relatively simple.

The reference librarian may require patience. An interview with an older adult may take more time for a number of reasons. Studies indicate that as people age they may become more internally directed, more egoistic, and less concerned about the opinions of others, so they may feel less inclined to come to the point and hurry along just for the convenience of others. Learning theory also suggests that older adults are more likely to take time to fully understand situations and tasks before beginning, while younger people may prefer immediate action and a trial and error approach. Many older adults also develop a more relaxed attitude toward time; they slow down and genuinely enjoy and savor life in a way they couldn't when their lives were governed by timeclocks, careers, and family responsibilities. They may also view their trips to the library as opportunities for socialization, and they may actually enjoy visiting with the staff. Recognition of these factors will not help the busy librarian eliminate the situation, but it may help with acceptance and understanding of the patron's needs. Nolan's article, "Closing the Reference Interview: Implications for Policy and Practice," provides an excellent overview of factors influencing the length and success of reference interviews.[18] Public services librarians will find the section on establishing reference goals and objectives particularly useful, and will want to consider the needs of older adults in reviewing their own expectations for reference transactions.

The reference librarian must be sensitive to unspoken needs. Most older adults will require no special treatment. Some, however, will be reluctant to ask for help they need for fear of seeming troublesome or demanding. The librarian will need to be doubly conscientious in confirming that the patron's needs have been met by asking closing questions such as "Is this what you needed?" or "May I do anything else for you?" and articulating a willingness to help–"Please don't hesitate to ask if you need anything else."

The references librarian will need to be flexible in applying service strategies. As a result of the Americans with Disabilities Act (ADA), many public services librarians are becoming more skilled in meeting the special needs of patrons. Gradual loss of vision and/or hearing are a part of the aging process, though most older patrons don't consider themselves "disabled." They might be "slowing down a little bit," a trifle "hard of hearing," or need "bigger print or longer arms." Some older adults will need service accommodations, as will some younger people with disabilities.

Public services librarians will find it second nature to utilize basic techniques for enhancing the reference interaction. It is rather natural to repeat a comment if a patron leans forward, places a hand behind the ear, looks puzzled, or asks what was said. Looking directly at the patron, speaking in a measured and clear, but not exaggerated, voice and keeping hands, gum, and hair away from the mouth will also enhance interaction. Keeping a pad and pencil handy for writing notes will help clarify information for all patrons, not just those who have difficulty in hearing.

A patron with a visual impairment may need additional service, particularly in libraries that have not met ADA standards for signage. Range signs, the card catalog or OPAC may all be unreadable. A patron who can read regular print with a magnifier may need help in locating the correct volume on the shelf. Some patrons who can read large print books may have difficulty in reading spines, and those who listen to tapes may need help in reading titles. Again, the accommodation is second nature to most public service librarians; the librarian "points with the feet" by getting out from behind the reference desk and walking with the patron to the stacks. In addition, librarians will find that it is a simple matter to provide enlarged photocopies and a variety of magnifiers for use with reference materials, but that such accommodations result in more effective reference service for many patrons.

Those librarians who will be working with the institutionalized older adult or the older adult with severe disabilities may wish to consult Anne Ring's *Read Easy,* Waters and Goodman's *Empowering Older Adults,* or library literature dealing with ADA compliance for more specific and appropriate strategies.[19]

INFORMATION AND REFERRAL SERVICES

The section above gives some suggestions for interviewing and general guidelines for interacting with older adults. There are a number of important elements in providing adequate information services to older adults. Coupled with the necessity for a personal attitude that demonstrates respect for older adults and results in treating all patrons with dignity is the need for knowledge of significant information needs and resources for fulfilling them. Scanning the literature of various fields such as social work, sociology, counseling, gerontology, and medicine is helpful, and there is a great deal to be learned from this activity, but it is time consuming and requires a great deal of synthesis. More effective is using a good basic source, such as Turock's *Serving the Older Adult,* or Casey's *Library Service for the Aging* to become familiar with areas of information need common to older adults.[20] Especially helpful in identifying library resources are Brazil's *Building Library Collections on Aging,* Rubin and McGovern's *Working with Older Adults* and Hudson's *Libraries for a Lifetime.*[21] *Working with Older Adults: a Handbook for Libraries* (California State Library) and *Libraries for a Lifetime* (Oklahoma Department of Libraries) provide essential background and procedures for librarians wishing to implement older adult services.

Modern Maturity, Mature Outlook and other magazines that are published for the older adult audience and newspaper columns written for seniors help to keep reference librarians aware of issues and may provide current information for vertical files. Establishing links with other community service agencies will aid in planning programs, gathering information for vertical files, establishing networks for referral, and developing entries in community information databases. Brochures and catalogs from the National Council on Aging, Inc. and other associations are focused and timely. Traditional collection development tools are useful for keeping collections current, and some of these will provide special features on resources for older adults.[22] Attending ALA conference programs offered by RASD's Services to an Aging Population Committee or ASCLA's Library Services to the Impaired Elderly Forum is an interesting and painless way to keep current.

Areas of interest to older adults fall broadly within interest areas of the general adult population, but different specific topics are of primary concern. Listed below are areas in which reference librarians are most frequently called upon to supply information.

Changing family relationships are often a cause for concern. Older adults may need information about second marriages, especially if they are recently widowed or if their children feel compelled to become involved in their selection of a spouse. Because of the increased lifespan, many older adults are finding themselves responsible for their own aged parents and may need to know about alternatives for care and mechanisms for social, emotional, and economic adjustments. Of critical importance to many older adults is maintaining autonomy in the face of concerned and well-meaning children. Because many people have accepted the myth that roles become reversed and adult children are required to parent the parent, older adults may need to find ways to accept nurturing without compromising autonomy and integrity. Another area of family relations that has recently found more widespread interest is that of parenting grandchildren. As a result of a number of sociological trends, including drug addiction, single parenting, and teenage pregnancy, a growing number of older adults are finding themselves acting as parents to grandchildren, a responsibility that most did not expect to assume and feel ill-equipped to fulfill.

Health, fitness, and sex absorb the interest of many older adults, reflecting the popular trend common to all age groups. It is predictable that older people have concerns about some specific health problems that become more acute with age: heart disease, Alzheimer's, high blood pressure and stroke, and more recently, prostate and breast cancer. The alert librarian will recognize that conventional information sources and treatments may be geared to younger people. For instance, a recent newspaper article revealed that older women often neglect to conduct regular breast self-examinations because they lack the mobility and vision to do so.[23] An alternative method has been developed, but it is recent enough that the information may not be included in books that provide traditional approaches to women's health. Fortunately, publishers and medical experts appear to be aware of the need for materials targeted for the older adult audience, and titles such as *Ourselves, Growing Older: Women Aging with Knowledge and Power* are more common.[24]

Information on drugs and drug interactions are of vital importance to older adults who want to be informed consumers. Statistics reveal that the typical older adult averages 15 prescriptions annually and is taking six different prescription medicines simultaneously.[25]

Additionally, while some seniors recognize a natural change in their patterns of sexual activity, there is a growing recognition that older adults are attractive, social, and still interested in sexual relationships. Surveys indicate that "there are as many variations in attitudes and [sexual] practices as within any other group."[26]

It may seem natural that *grieving, death and dying* are important concerns for older adults. Studies report, however, that only 24% of older adults worry about death, as compared to 55% of 18 to 24 year olds.[27] Many older adults take a rather pragmatic view about their own deaths, and want information for estate planning and making funeral arrangements so as to relieve the burden on surviving spouses and children. Seniors may need support and guidance in dealing with loss of a spouse, a child, friends or a pet.

Living arrangements are of primary concern. Librarians can help older adults make intelligent choices by providing information about a wide variety of options, including retirement apartments, nursing homes, and services that enable older adults to maintain independent households. In addition, the Americans with Disabilities Act has heightened awareness, and many of the young old (50-65 years old) are seeking information for remodeling and adapting their homes in anticipation of some of the mobility problems that might arise in old age. Personal safety and security measures are important to older adults, though the image of senior as victim is not a particularly accurate or empowering one. Violent crime against older adults is frightening, but scams and ripoffs are more common. Providing information that allows seniors to protect themselves by alerting them to potential danger areas affords them control and independence.

As with most Americans, *legal and financial affairs* are of continuous interest. Older adults may be preparing for retirement, or concerned about the financial effect of working after retirement. Information regarding wills and trusts is important to most adults, but many avoid any decision-making about such devices until the need seems more eminent. Indeed, many older adults are, at some point, attempting to transfer assets to children prior to death because there may be substantial tax benefits. Because financial well-being for many seniors is so closely linked with federal programs and local social services, political and legal information is another area in which older adults evidence a lively interest.

Finally, older adults now have time to pursue *leisure activities*. Travel information is of particular and perennial interest. Librarians will want to check their regular sources to ensure that information about senior discounts is included. Hobby information, particularly about sewing and gardening, is popular. Some sources will provide techniques for participating in favorite activities while accommodating problems such as arthritis, rheumatism, or reduced mobility or vision.

READER'S ADVISORY SERVICES

The provision of fiction guidance has emerged (again) as a growing part of the reference librarian's opportunity for service. Many older adults continue to use the library for recreational reading, reflecting their own established patterns as well as the general pattern of public library use. As Casey notes, "leisure time is, and probably will continue to be, a challenge for the aged and an opportunity for the library."[28] Reader's advisory interviews provide the opportunity for intellectual stimulation and socialization for both the librarian and the patron, as well as for establishing a foundation of trust for future transactions.

Again, librarians will be aware of diverse interests within the older adult population. Some prefer mystery or romance while others like westerns or anything on the *New York Times* Best Seller Lists. Some will be offended by anything more than a chaste kiss; others will want to know if you have anything "juicy." Some want graphic true crime novels, others want a genteel murder mystery with no blood. And some patrons will want to read sensitive novels about growing older or will enjoy seeing an older adult as the protagonist in genre fiction.

There are a number of excellent tools available to reader's advisors. The best general introductory source on the reader's advisory process is Saricks and Brown's *Reader's Advisory Service in the Public Library,* which provides planning and interviewing strategies.[29] *Genreflecting* and *What Do I Read Next?* are important bibliographic resources.[30] In addition, genre-specific sources such as Mackler's *Murder by Category* will be of value in serving patrons whose preference is for a certain type of literature.[31] Librarians who want the convenience of sources that concentrate on literature featuring older adults will find Rubin's *Of a Certain Age* and Donavin's *Aging with Style and Savvy* invaluable. Monroe and Rubin's *The Challenge of Aging* is a classic, and older fiction and nonfiction materials may be found here.[32] These sources are helpful in recommending books and materials for patrons and serve the valuable secondary function of enhancing the librarian's understanding of the issues and concerns of the older adult population.

Booklists, bookmarks, and publicity provided by reader's advisors should be printed clearly, in an uncluttered font and with high contrast between letters and background. Large print versions should be readily available.

PROGRAMMING

Programming for older adults inevitably receives high marks from participants. Programs range from those targeted for a general audience but attended by older adults to intergenerational programming planned with interaction among age groups as a primary focus to programs planned exclusively for older adults. Within each of these categories, there exists a wide variety of topics and goals.[33] While lecture programs provide information for daily living, formal elderhostel programs offer educational opportunities, book discussions stimulate intellectual activity and socialization, and reminiscence programming encourages older adults to validate their experiences and communicate them to a younger generation.

Informational programs on current issues are popular among older adults. These topics are in areas of importance throughout the lifespan, but are reflective of the developmental tasks, life changes, and consumer needs of the group. For instance, programs on financial planning may focus on estate planning or retirement planning; programs on exercise may emphasize swimming and low-impact workouts; programs on taxes may include such topics as the effect of a second marriage on social security income and benefits. Skimming *Modern Maturity,* the magazine of the American Association of Retired Persons, will keep the librarian abreast of topics of interest to seniors.

Older adults often attend the National Endowment for the Humanities (NEH) Let's Talk About It programs. These discussion programs, led by humanities scholars, are planned for general audiences, but Durrance and Rubin report on attendance by older adult participants and accommodations made for them.[34]

Silver Editions, the National Council on Aging, Inc. (NCOA) program series, follows the Let's Talk About It format and are planned around topics designed to appeal to older adult audiences. Evaluation of the NCOA program provides practical information for program planners: (1) Participants are generally already library users; (2) Smaller groups (no more than 15 participants) seem to be most effective. Attrition over the span of the series seems inevitable; (3) Factors such as scheduling (daytime preferred), facility (smaller, cozier room with comfortable chairs), and refreshments (coffee and desserts) are very important; (4) Brief, but focussed training for presenters enhances success, even if the presenters are experienced educators drawn from universities and colleges.[35] Interestingly, while program topics are chosen to reflect past experiences and history, comments from participants indicate that older adults are well-informed about current events and open to innovation. For example, discussions of the internment of Japanese in America during World War II evoked analogies to the then-current treatment of Arabs in America during Desert Storm. Suggestions for ways to improve the programs included requests for tours and training on online public access catalogs and electronic databases.[36]

Reminiscence programming, in which adults reflect on past experiences, are sometimes offered with the aid of Bifolkal kits, which offer scripts, audiovisual aids, and instructions and materials for activities.[37] As with the humanities discussion programs listed above, these centrally developed programs are great time savers for local librarians. Reminiscence programming provides opportunities for socialization and validation, and they are sometimes regarded as bibliotherapy for participants. Some librarians, however, have combined reminiscence programming with oral history projects, thus enhancing local history collections and providing tangible evidence of an appreciation of the value of older adults.

Services such as the popular VITA/IRS tax help program involve older adults on both sides of the desk, as both information providers and recipients. Such programs offer recognition of the contribution senior volunteers can make. Many librarians have recognized that older adults can provide valuable service to the library, and seniors are often willing volunteers.[38] While volunteer programs offer benefits by promoting positive attitudes towards aging and older adults, librarians must remember that it is the library that receives primary benefit from such activities. The notion that libraries are doing older adults a favor by providing opportunities for meaningful activity is condescending and demeaning. Care should be taken to follow ALA's *Guidelines for Library Service to Older Adults* regarding use of volunteers.[39]

OUTREACH

Outreach, referral, and delivery services are essential elements of service for older adults who are institutionalized or homebound. These services, per se, are not within the purview of this article. It is well to remember, however, that many adults, both young and old, are often hospitalized or temporarily in need of such services. Selecting and reserving materials, adapting service policies that allow family members or other designees to check out materials, and offering flexible eligibility criteria for delivery and books by mail services will ensure continuous service for those with temporary problems.

Librarians will also want to think of outreach in the broader terms of "stimulation," "public relations," and "marketing." Involving older adults in planning for peers promotes effective service. Announcements (in large print) of library services and activities can be placed in appropriate newsletters or posted in retirement communities, nursing homes, local offices of aging councils, churches, or senior centers. As noted earlier, liaisons with other community agencies and local associations will be valuable in informing older adults and caregivers of opportunities provided by the library and in predicting the need for library services. Library newsletters and mailings can be made available in large print formats and sent on request, or mailing lists with a "large print" designation can be developed.

CONCLUSION

This article is offered as a primer of practical advice for reference and other public services librarians. Librarians have basic reference, collection development, and planning skills. Their expertise and commitment in dealing with diverse clienteles is supported by the common thread of lifelong learning theory. As they recognize the diversity among patrons, librarians demonstrate their understanding of varied needs by offering a variety of services from which individuals may choose.

Older adults are one group among many, and the individuals who comprise that group may belong to other groups as well. Librarians will continue to demonstrate their concerns and to offer service–one patron at a time. Serving older adults is not a matter of developing new and unfamiliar services. It is often not a matter of serving new patrons–just patrons who, for the convenience of demographers, have entered a new classification. It is the application of a bit of specialized expertise to a broad foundation of experience, knowledge, and service. It is a matter of doing the same things we've always done, but with greater sensitivity, more awareness, stronger commitment and enthusiasm. It is, after all, a matter of focus.

REFERENCES

1. Elizabeth Vierck, *Fact Book on Aging* (Santa Barbara, CA: ABC-CLIO, 1990): 3.

2. Vierck, xix, xii.

3. Vierck, 71.

4. Vierck, xix-xxi.

5. Anita S. Harbert and Leon H. Ginsberg, *Human Services for Older Adults: Concepts and Skills*, 2nd revised (Columbia, SC: University of South Carolina Press, 1990): 3, 54-80.

6. National Council on Aging, Inc. *Aging in the Eighties: America in Transition: a Survey Conducted for the National Council on Aging, Inc. by Louis Harris and Associates, Inc.* (Washington, D.C.: National Council on the Aging, 1981) in Connie Van Fleet, "Public Library Service to Older Adults: Survey Findings and Implications," *Public Libraries* 28 (March/April 1989): 110-111.

7. Connie Van Fleet, "Lifelong Learning Theory and the Provision of Adult Services" in *Adult Services: an Enduring Focus for Public Libraries*, ed. Kathleen M. Heim and Danny P. Wallace (Chicago: ALA, 1990), pp. 166-265.

8. Elinor B. Waters and Jane Goodman, *Empowering Older Adults: Practical Strategies for Counselors* (San Francisco: Jossey-Bass Publishers, 1990): p. xi.

9. A. J. Cropley, *Lifelong Education: a Psychological Analysis* (New York: Pergamon, 1977), pp. 57-58; Willis W. Harman, "Recent Psychological and Psychic Research: Implications for Science and Society," in *The Future of Education: Policy Issues and Challenge*, ed. Kathryn Cirincione-Coles (Beverly Hills: Sage, 1981), p. 218.

10. Patrick Penland, "Adult Self-Planned Learning," *Public Libraries* 17 (Summer 1978): 6-8; Allen Tough, *The Adult's Learning Projects: a Fresh Approach to Theory and Practice in Adult Learning*, 2nd ed. (Austin, TX: Learning Concepts, 1979); Malcolm S. Knowles, *The Modern Practice of Adult Education*, revised and updated (Chicago: Association Press, 1980).

11. J. Roby Kidd, *How Adults Learn* (New York: Association Press, 1959), p. 90; K.A. McClelland, "Self-conception and Life Satisfaction: Integrating Aged Subculture and Activity Theory," *Journal of Gerontology* 37 (1982): 723.

12. Betty J. Turock, *Information and Aging* (Jefferson, NC: McFarland, 1988), p. 1.

13. Betty J. Turock, "Public Library Service for Older Adults: Update 1984," *Library Quarterly* 57 (April 1987): 143.

14. See Celia Hales-Mabry, "Serving the Older Adult," *The Reference Librarian* 31 (1990): 69-76 or reports of the Adult Services in the Eighties Project, including Betty J. Turock, "Serving Older Adults" in Kathleen M. Heim and Danny P. Wallace, eds. or Connie Van Fleet, "Public Library Service." Other studies include Elliott E. Kanner, "Library Service to Older Adults: Progress in Research Application," *Public Libraries* 23 (Fall 1984): 93 and Eleanor Phinney, "A Study of Current Practices in Public Library Services to an Aging Population: Report on a PostCard Survey," *ALA Bulletin* 51 (September 1957): 607-609.

15. "The Library's Responsibility to the Aging," Prepared by the Library Service to an Aging Population Committee, Reference and Adult Services Division, American Library Association. *RQ* 21 (Fall 1981): 27.

16. "Guidelines for Library Service to Older Adults" Prepared by the Library Services to an Aging Population Committee, Reference and Adult Services Division, American Library Association, *RQ* 26 (Summer 1987): 444-447.

17. Elaine Landau, "The Challenge of Film Programming for Older Adults," *The Bookmark* 42 (Winter 1984): 102.

18. Christopher W. Nolan, "Closing the Reference Interview: Implications for Policy and Practice," *RQ* 31 (Summer 1992): 513-523.

19. Waters and Goodman; Anne M. Ring, *Read Easy: Large Print Libraries for Older Adults* (Seattle: CAREsource Program Development, Inc.: 1991).

20. Betty J. Turock, *Serving the Older Adult: a Guide to Library Programs and Information Sources* (New York: Bowker, 1982); Genevieve M. Casey, *Library Services for the Aging* (Hamden, CT: Library Professional Publications, 1984).

21. Mary Jo Brazil, *Building Library Collections on Aging: a Selection Guide and Core List* (Santa Barbara, CA: ABC-CLIO, 1990); Rhea J. Rubin and Gail McGovern, *Working with Older Adults: a Handbook for Libraries,* 2nd. (Sacramento, CA: California State Library, 1988); Elizabeth A. Hudson, *Libraries for a Lifetime* (Oklahoma City: The Oklahoma Department of Libraries, 1989).

22. See, for example, Karen McNally Bensing, "Rejuvenating Your Books on Aging," *Library Journal* 118 (October 1, 1993): 55-58.

23. "Researcher Promotes Ways for Elderly to Do Cancer Checks," *The Advocate* (Baton Rouge, LA), 10 February 1993, p. 11(A).

24. Paula Brown Doress and Diana Laskin Siegal, *Ourselves, Growing Older: Women Aging with Knowledge and Power* (New York: Touchstone, 1987).

25. Vierck, 103-104.

26. Denise Perry Donavin, *Aging with Style and Savvy* (Chicago: ALA, 1990), p. 27, reporting on *Love, Sex, and Aging: a Consumers Union Report*, Edward M. Brecher and the Editors of Consumer Reports Books (PLACE, Little, Brown, 1984).

27. Vierck, 143.

28. Casey, *Library Services for the Aging*, p. 7.

29. Joyce G. Saricks and Nancy Brown, *Reader's Advisory Service in the Public Library* (Chicago: ALA, 1989).

30. Betty Rosenberg and Diana Tixier Herald, *Genreflecting: a Guide to Reading Interests in Genre Fiction* (Englewood, CO: Libraries Unlimited, 1991); *What Do I Read Next?* (Detroit: Gale Research Inc., 1991).

31. Tasha Mackler, *Murder . . . by Category: a Subject Guide to Mystery Fiction* (Metuchen, N.J.: Scarecrow Press, 1991).

32. Margaret E. Monroe and Rhea Joyce Rubin, *The Challenge of Aging: a Bibliography* (Littleton, CO: Libraries Unlimited, 1983).

33. Danny P. Wallace, "The Character of Adult Services in the Eighties: Overview and Analysis of the ASE Questionnaire Data," pp. 27-165 in Kathleen M. Heim and Danny P. Wallace, eds.; Connie Van Fleet, "Public Library Service," pp.110-112.

34. Joan C. Durrance and Rhea J. Rubin, "Let's Talk About It: Lessons in Adult Humanities Programming," *Public Libraries* 28 (March/April 1989): 90-91.

35. For the complete evaluation of the project, see Connie Van Fleet, *Silver Editions II: Advancing the Concept of Library-Centered Humanities Programs for Older Adults. an Evaluation Prepared for the National Council on the Aging.* (Baton Rouge, LA: School of Library and Information Science, Louisiana State University, November 11, 1991). ERIC ED 342 416. A brief overview of the Silver Editions project is provided in Sylvia Riggs Liroff and Connie Van Fleet, "Silver Editions II: Humanities Programming for Older Adults," *RQ* 31 (Summer 1992): 473-476.

36. Connie Van Fleet, *Silver Editions II: Advancing*, pp. 128-146.

37. BiFolkal kits are produced by BiFolkal Productions, Inc. in Madison, Wisconsin.

38. Vierck (p.71) reports that 47% of those between the ages of 55 and 64 participate in some volunteer activity, while 40% of those between 65 and 74 and 29% of those 75 years and older are volunteers.

39. "Guidelines," p.445.

Kids Count:
Using Output Measures
to Monitor Children's Use
of Reference Services

Virginia A. Walter

SUMMARY. The author discusses *Planning and Role Setting for Public Libraries* and *Output Measures for Public Libraries* as tools for evaluating reference services and demonstrates how the newer *Output Measures for Public Library Service for Children* can contribute to our understanding of informational services for young people.

Since the late 1980s, public libraries have increasingly tried to adopt a marketing approach to their service delivery, surveying community needs and then responding with targeted programs and services to meet those needs, finding the market niche for which they are uniquely suited. This effort has been a response to growing fiscal constraints and has been bolstered by the publication in 1987 of two important documents, *Planning and Role Setting for Public Libraries* (PRSPL) and *Output Measures for Public Libraries,* second edition (OMPL). In this article, I will show how these docu-

Virginia A. Walter is Assistant Professor in the Department of Library and Information Science, Graduate School of Education and Information Studies, University of California, Los Angeles.

[Haworth co-indexing entry note]: "Kids Count: Using Output Measures to Monitor Children's Use of Reference Services." Walter, Virginia A. Co-published simultaneously in *The Reference Librarian* (The Haworth Press, Inc.) No. 49/50, 1995, pp. 165-178; and: *Library Users and Reference Services* (ed: Jo Bell Whitlatch) The Haworth Press, Inc., 1995, pp. 165-178. Multiple copies of this article/chapter may be purchased from The Haworth Document Delivery Center [1-800-3-HAWORTH; 9:00 a.m. - 5:00 p.m. (EST)].

ments have contributed to our understanding of reference services in public libraries. I will also show the potential of a subsequent document, *Output Measures for Children's Services in Public Libraries,* for contributing to the development of better information services for children.

THE PUBLIC LIBRARY PLANNING AND ROLE SETTING PROCESS

As part of the ongoing Public Library Development Program, the Public Library Association and the American Library Association presented a revised planning process in 1987. *Planning and Role Setting for Public Libraries: A Manual of Options and Procedures* was based on the assumption that library services should reflect the needs of specific communities and should be based on planning and decision making done at the local level.[1] The manual presents a process for reviewing the existing levels of service and defining the mission of the library based on community needs.

One of the key elements in developing the resulting library plan is the selection of a limited number of roles which the library intends to fill in its community. The authors of the manual explain that the roles are " . . . profiles of library service emphases."[2] Eight roles are presented as a menu from which public library decision-makers may select:

1. Community Activities Center: The library is a central focus point for community activities, meetings, and services.
2. Community Information Center: The library is a clearinghouse for current information on community organizations, issues, and services.
3. Formal Education Support Center: The library assists students of all ages in meeting educational objectives established during their formal courses of study.
4. Independent Learning Center: The library supports individuals of all ages pursuing a sustained program of learning independent of any educational provider.
5. Popular Materials Library: The library features current, high-demand, high-interest materials in a variety of formats for persons of all ages.

6. Preschoolers' Door to Learning: The library encourages young children to develop an interest in reading and learning through services for children, and for parents and children together.
7. Reference Library: The library actively provides timely, accurate, and useful information for community residents.
8. Research Center: The library assists scholars and researchers to conduct in-depth studies, investigate specific areas of knowledge, and create new knowledge.[3]

The authors point out that no library can fulfill all eight roles with excellence. Therefore, they encourage library decision-makers to prioritize possible roles and place them into one of three categories: primary, secondary, or maintenance. Libraries, depending on size and resources, should select one or two roles for the primary category and one or two for the secondary category. They recommend that approximately 80% of the library's efforts and resources be channeled into the primary and secondary roles. Roles relegated to the maintenance level are not necessarily dropped; they simply receive much less emphasis and support.[4]

Output Measures for Libraries was the companion volume to *Planning and Role Setting for Public Libraries*.[5] It provided specific techniques for measuring a library's progress towards achieving quantifiable objectives in the fulfillment of its selected primary and secondary roles. For example, if a library had selected Popular Materials Center as its primary role, PRSPL suggested that it consider Turnover Rate, Browsers' Fill Rate, Subject and Author Fill Rate, Title Fill Rate, Circulation per Capita, and Registration as a Percentage of the Population as possible output measures that might usefully help to determine how successfully the library is fulfilling that role.[6] OMPL provides detailed instructions for collecting the data and analyzing and interpreting the results for each of those output measures.

LIMITATIONS OF THE PLANNING AND ROLE SETTING PROCESS

It is difficult to know exactly how many public libraries have adopted the planning and role setting process, but there are at least some indicators. Of the 562 libraries reporting data for the *Public Library Data Service Statistical Report '91*, for example, only

228–less than half–included information on role selection.[7] A qualitative study of the adoption of the planning process in smaller libraries showed that the directors of the six case study libraries were all aware of the PLA planning process and that 2/3 of them had implemented some form of role setting.[8]

Regardless of how many public libraries have formally adopted the planning and role setting process, the eight roles have become part of the common knowledge of most public library directors. Recently, some library leaders, including Charles McClure, one of the architects of the original role menu, have suggested that the roles should be revisited and revised to reflect new realities, particularly the implications of the latest information technology which suggest the possibility of an "Electronic Networked Library" role.[9] Nonetheless, the original eight roles create a convenient frame of reference for understanding and talking about what public libraries do, and the output measures provide some standardized ways to monitor the results.

There are some limitations to the output measures, which comprise the evaluation tools for the planning process. They are strictly quantitative and only measure how much of something in comparison to how much of something else. They only measure tangible outputs and do now attempt to assess the quality or the significance of those outputs. They are not "outcome measures" which David Osborne and Ted Gaebler define as measures of quality and the effectiveness of production.[10]

The measures for reference services, for example, do not attempt to assess the accuracy of the information given or its value to the user, two dimensions of reference service which have sometimes been determined through unobtrusive testing or patron surveys.[11] The output measures are, nevertheless, useful tools for monitoring progress towards quantifiable goals and hold out the promise of standardizing data collection definitions and techniques in public libraries throughout the United States.

OUTPUT MEASURES FOR PUBLIC LIBRARY SERVICE TO CHILDREN

Almost as soon as PRSPL and OMPL were published, there were concerns expressed about the relative invisibility of service to children in these general documents. Some advocates for public library service to children were concerned that literal-minded library directors would spot the one role which targeted children, Preschoolers Door to Learning, and assume that this was the only role which could be applied to children. Managers of children's and youth services were concerned that the general output measures did not allow a library to pinpoint and monitor specialized services for children. A joint committee of ALSC and PLA, chaired by Kathleen Reif and Clara Bohrer, began immediately to develop a set of specific output measures for public library service to children. In 1990, the ALSC/PLA Output Measures for Children's Services Committee submitted a grant request to the U.S. Department of Education for a project to develop evaluative measures for library services for children age 14 years and under and their care givers. The request was funded, and Virginia Walter was hired as the principal investigator responsible for developing and field testing these measures, as well as writing the new manual, *Output Measures for Public Library Service to Children* (OMPLSC).[12] Before publication, these new measures were pretested in three Southern California libraries and field tested in four sites across the country. In addition to the members of the ALSC/PLA Output Measures for Children committee, another thirty readers reviewed the final manuscript.

Before presenting detailed instructions for implementing the output measures, OMPLSC revisits the eight public library roles and shows how each of them could be used to focus on a particular aspect of public library service to children. For example, the library with a primary role as Popular Materials Center would provide high demand, high-interest materials for children as well as adults. The library would highlight materials reflecting the current popular culture as children perceive it, including mass market items, as well as the more traditional "quality" materials found in most children's collections.

The children's output measures differ from the more general output measures in a number of ways. They focus on children age 14 and under as a segment of the total service population of any public library. They take into account the seasonal nature of public library service to children, with the different use patterns typically found during the school year and during the summer. They also take into account the fact that adults are often the intermediaries between children and the library. Teachers, child care providers, parents, and scout leaders are all adults who frequently find materials at the library and check them out for children to use elsewhere. Library staff may never see the children who are the end users of the materials. Whenever appropriate, OMPLSC directs data collectors to count care givers, or adults acting on behalf of children, as well as the children themselves.

ACCOUNTING FOR PUBLIC LIBRARY REFERENCE SERVICES

As noted earlier, PRSPL designated Reference Library as one of the eight public library roles. The role description specifies that the library

> . . . actively provides timely, accurate, and useful information for community residents in their pursuit of job-related and personal interests. . . . Information provided may range from answering practical questions (how to remove garden pests, what to feed a guinea pig, how to apply for a job, what is the name of a poem that starts with . . .), to specialized business-related research (finding patent information), to answering questions about government (locating regulations for a grant program), to providing consumer information.[13]

The role description for Reference Library neither mentions children nor gives any examples of a typical children's reference question, unless one is to presume that only a child wants to know what to feed a guinea pig. It does, however, indicate that the collection emphasizes informational materials which are available for all ages and reading levels.

So many public libraries adopt Reference Library as a primary or secondary role that some people have suggested that it has become a de facto universal public library role. A study by Nancy Van House and Thomas Childers showed that public librarians ranked Reference Library as the most important role that their library plays. Van House and Childers find that Reference Library clusters with three other roles–Popular Materials Center, Formal Education Support Center, and Independent Learning Center–to form a composite definition of the traditional public library role. This contrasts with an emerging alternative role definition which is made up of the four remaining roles–Community Activities Center, Community Information Center, Research Center, and Preschoolers Door to Learning. [14]

The suggested output measures for Reference Library are Reference Transactions per Capita, Reference Completion Rate, and In-Library materials Use per Capita. OMPL defines a reference transactions as

> . . . an information contact which involves the knowledge, use, recommendations, interpretation, or instruction in the use of one or more information sources by a member of the library staff. It includes information and referral services. Information sources include printed and nonprinted materials, machine-readable data bases, catalogs and other holdings, records, other libraries and institutions, and people inside and outside the library. The request may come in person, by phone, or mail, from an adult or child.[15]

Specifically excluded are directional questions, questions about rules and policies, and telephone requests for known items, which are counted instead in Materials Availability Measures. [16]

Reference Questions per Capita is the total number of reference questions asked in a year divided by the total population of the library's service area. The data is collected by reference staff through a tally of reference questions during a one-week sample period. The directions do not specify that tallies should be taken at the children's services public desk, but one presumes that this is the intent, that questions asked by children in any part of the library will be included in the overall count. In the "Further Possibilities" section, the final suggestion is to measure reference transactions separately for children's and young adult services.[17]

The Reference Completion Rate is " . . . the proportion of reference transactions successfully completed on the same day that the question is asked, in the judgment of the librarian."[18] It is computed from the same data collected for the Reference Transactions per Capita measure. Again, a further possibility is to measure separate Reference Completion Rates for children's and young adult services.[19]

In-Library Materials Use per Capita measures the number of materials used in the library per person in the community served.[20] It is categorized as one of the Materials Use measures, along with Circulation per Capita and Turnover Rate. It may be linked with a high Reference Transactions per Capita rate in a library that is focusing on the Reference Library Role, indicating a large usage of in-house reference materials. The data is collected for this measure by asking users not to reshelve materials for one sample week and then counting all materials used and left unshelved. The directions do not specify that unshelved children's materials be counted as well as adult materials, but presumably that is the intent. OMPL does not suggest any "further possibility" for applying this measure to children's services.

OUTPUT MEASURES FOR CHILDREN'S REFERENCE SERVICES

In discussing how the Reference Library role could be applied to children, OMPLSC points out first that the library should be certain that children have access to all information resources, including referrals and online data bases. The author cautions that all library staff, not just the children's specialists, should be trained to answer children's questions and to use the specialized reference tools available in the children's collection. The children's collection should emphasize information materials in all formats and at all reading levels. The staff must learn to adapt their reference interview techniques to the special communication styles of children. They help children formulate research strategies and retrieve information.[21]

The output measures suggested to help monitor a library's performance in filling this role are parallel to the general output measures, segmented to focus on children: Children's Information Transactions per Child, Children's Information Transaction Completion Rate, and In-Library Use of Children's Materials per Child. The ALSC/PLA Output Measures for Children Committee and the author of OMPLSC decided to use the more generic term Information Transaction instead of Reference Transaction. There was some concern that the label "Reference Transaction" might lead some librarians to assume that readers' advisory questions, traditionally a large part of public service to children, are not included. A children's information transaction is defined as " . . . contact between a library user who is 14 and under or an adult acting on behalf of a child and a library staff member who provides help with or knowledge, interpretation, or instruction in the use of an information source."[22] Examples given are similar to those in the general output measures with two additions: "general or specific requests for something to read" and "requests by adults on behalf of children." [23]

Data collection for Children's Information Transactions per Child and Children's Information Transaction Completion Rate is similar to the methods outlined in OMPL, with two crucial differences. First, for the children's measure, data is collected during *two* sample weeks during the year, a typical week in summer and a typical week during the school year, in order to account for the difference in children's library usage during those two seasons. In computing the measure, the count for the typical week during the school year is weighted by a factor of three because the school year is three times longer than the summer. Second, the children's measure counts only those questions asked by children and by adults asking questions on behalf of children. The librarians taking the tally must make an assumption about the age of the library user and the intended user of the information if the question asker is an adult. The manual gives advice about how to handle both of these issues, and, in fact, libraries who have implemented this measure have not found either to be particularly difficult. The manual does point out that for every young-looking fifteen-year-old who is counted in error, there is probably a mature thirteen-year-old who is missed. The assumption is that this evens out in the long run. Context provide many clues about the ultimate use of the information, and a good reference interview will elicit this information as well.[24]

As with the measures of information services for children, In-library Use of Children's Materials per Child requires some adjustments to target just the use of children's materials. The method for data collection is exactly like that of the general output measure, except that only children's materials are counted and the count is taken in two sample weeks, one during the school year and one in summer. Further possibilities include calculating the In-Library Use of Children's Materials per Child for particular parts of the collection or types of materials or calculating the measure for particular times of day, such as the notorious after school rush.[25]

In spite of the fact that the output measures relating to children's reference services are relatively easy to implement, they have not been widely adopted by public libraries. This information is not among the data elements required by the federal government. The Federal Center for Educational Statistics is now collecting statistics on children's circulation and children's programming, but not on children's reference transactions. This may limit the incentive to collect the data.

The Public Library Data Service collected some statistics on children's output measures in 1991, before OMPLSC was published, but they too did not request data on children's reference use. (The 1994 survey will include this information.) A recent survey of public library service for children conducted by Keith Curry Lance and Barbara Immroth showed that only 62% of the respondents reported data on children's information transactions and only 33% had statistics on in-library use of children's materials.[26] Rosemarie Riechel found in her survey of reference services to children and young adults that many librarians serving young people in schools and public libraries felt that they were doing a good job but just didn't have time to document their efforts.[27]

There is much to be gained from a more widespread implementation of children's output measures relating to reference services. The information that results from implementing these three measures of library service to children is extremely useful to a children's librarian. For example, a high Children's Information Transactions per Child probably indicates that patrons rely heavily on the staff for assistance. This may mean that the staff is friendly and approachable and successful in attracting young users. On the other hand, it could also indicate that the library is unreasonably difficult to use or that patrons lack basic library skills or that patrons have been kept unnecessarily dependent on professional staff for help. While a library that is focusing its efforts on the reference function would presumably aim for relatively high Children's Information

Transactions per Child rates, other libraries, such as those whose primary role is Popular Materials Center or Community Activities Center might not be interested in this. Professional judgment is thus necessary in interpreting the results.

The output measures are all particularly well-suited for monitoring progress towards quantifiable objectives. A library might aim, for example, to increase its Children's Information Transactions per Child from 3.6 to 5.0 during the next year. Then the children's services staff could pay attention to promoting reference and readers' advisory services that the library provides to children and their care givers. They could increase the visibility of the children's public service desk or make a single service desk more child-friendly. They could encourage staff to offer assistance rather than waiting for shy or reluctant library patrons to ask for help. They could monitor the quality of information transactions between children and staff to be sure that children are made welcome. The comparison of annual Children's Information Transaction per Child measures will confirm or deny that these efforts have been successful.

Library administrators should also be interested in the information to be gained from these measures of children's use of information services. It may be that staffing is poorly allocated between the adult and children's reference desks, reflecting old assumptions about usage. One library director in Southern California was astonished to learn that children's reference transactions accounted for more than 66% of all reference transactions in the branches of her system. Only the Central Library was used more by adults for information services. When the County Administrator asked for budget reduction packages, the director revised her original plan to reduce children's staff and suggested cuts in the adult reference staff instead. A high Children's Information Transactions per Child coupled with a low Children's Information Transaction Completion Rate may indicate a need for more cross-training of the adult staff in the special techniques and resources needed to answer children's questions effectively.

A close monitoring of children's use of a public library's information services may even indicate the need for more sweeping policy changes. In California, school libraries have been neglected for years and now rank 50th in the nation in funding.[28] Public libraries have finally begun to take a proactive approach to the information needs of school children and are providing Homework Centers with resources especially designed to support the curriculum. As Formal Education Support Centers, they are paying more attention to children's roles as information seekers and information users.[29] The output measures described here could help monitor how well California public libraries are making this shift in emphasis and perspective.

This is a different perspective than that which sees young library users primarily as story hour attendees or Summer Reading Program participants. Research which I completed recently on the information needs of ten-year-olds in Southern California indicated that children are lacking some of the most basic information which they need to thrive, and in some cases, to survive. The world they live in is increasingly complex, and the traditional providers of some of this basic information—parents and schools—are no longer capable of doing so, for a variety of reasons. Public libraries are not filling the gap, perhaps because they have not yet perceived children as active consumers of information.[30]

CONCLUSION

Since the publication of *Output Measures for Public Library Service for Children* in 1992, librarians have had access to standardized, easy-to-implement techniques for measuring the quantitative results of their reference services for children. There are a number of convincing reasons why children's librarians and library administrators should look more closely at the evaluation of age-level reference service. The data can help librarians and library administrators achieve objective goals, improve service, and allocate resources more effectively.

There is also some evidence that focusing on informational service to children might produce good results in the political arena. A recent Gallup poll showed that 90% of the general public rates the role of Formal Education Support Center "very important" for a public library. Eighty three percent rated the Independent Learning Center "very important." Preschoolers' Door to Learning won a "very important" rating from 82%. The role with the next highest percentage of people rating it "very important" was Research Center, with 67% responding favorably. The pollsters had limited the Reference Center role to Reference Library to Community Businesses, and this more limited reference role received a "very important" rating from only 54% of the respondents.[31] The very high ratings for Formal Education Support and Independent Learning suggest a high public support for the information functions of the library that are related to education. While this hopefully means lifelong learning, it almost certainly means support for information services for school age children, particularly when coupled with the high support for Preschoolers' Door to Learning. Even if they don't use libraries themselves, adults support public library services for children.

REFERENCES

1. Charles R. McClure et al., *Planning and Role Setting for Public Libraries: A Manual of Options and Procedures* (Chicago: American Library Association, 1987), p. xix.

2. *Ibid.*, p. 28.

3. *Ibid.*

4. *Ibid.*, p. 42.

5. Nancy A. Van House et al., *Output Measures for Public Libraries: A Manual of Standardized Procedures,* second edition (Chicago: American Library Association, 1987).

6. McClure, *op.cit.,* p. 36.

7. *Public Library Data Service Statistical Report '91* (Chicago: Public Library Association/American Library Association, 1991).

8. Verna L. Pungitore et al., *The Public Library Planning Process: Case Studies of its Implementation in Smaller Libraries* (Bloomington, Ind.: Indiana University, School of Library and Information Science, 1991): 68.

9. Charles R. McClure, "Updating *Planning and Role Setting for Public Libraries: A Manual of Options and Procedures,*" *Public Libraries,* Vol. 32, No. 4 (July/August, 1993): 198-199.

10. David Osborne and Ted Gaebler, *Reinventing Government: How the Entrepreneurial Spirit is Transforming the Public Sector.* (Reading, Mass.: Addison-Wesley, 1992).

11. Patricia Hults, "Reference Evaluation: An Overview," *The Reference Librarian,* No. 38 (1992): 141-150.

12. Virginia A. Walter, *Output Measures for Public Library Service to Children: A Manual of Standardized Procedures* (Chicago: American Library Association, 1992).

13. McClure, *Planning and Role Setting for Public Libraries*, p. 38.

14. Nancy A. Van House and Thomas A. Childers, *The Public Library Effectiveness Study: The Complete Report* (Chicago: American Library Association, 1993), p. 54.

15. Van House, *Output Measures for Public Libraries*, pp. 65-66.

16. *Ibid.*, p. 68.

17. *Ibid.*, p. 69.

18. *Ibid.*

19. *Ibid.*, p. 71.

20. *Ibid.*, pp. 44-47.

21. Walter, *op.cit.*, p. 12.

22. *Ibid.*, p. 50.

23. *Ibid.*

24. *Ibid.*, pp. 51-54.

25. *Ibid.*, pp. 37-39.

26. Keith Curry Lance and Barbara Immroth. *Children's Services in Public Libraries Survey 1993: Preliminary Results* (Denver, CO: Library Research Service, State Library and Adult Education Office, Colorado Department of Education, 1994).

27. Rosemarie Riechel. *Reference Services for Children and Young Adults* (Hamden, Conn.: Library Professional Publications, 1991): 113.

28. Howard D. White, "School Library Collections and Services: Ranking the States," *School Library Media Quarterly,* Vol. 19, No. 1 (Fall, 1990): 13-26.

29. See, for example, *Developing Public Library Service for Youth* by Jerry Tello and Laura Weber (Los Angeles: Los Angeles Public Library, 1993).

30. Virginia A. Walter, "The Information Needs of Children," *Advances in Librarianship* (in press).

31. Judy Quinn and Michael Rogers, "Public Would Double Library Support, Says National Survey," *Library Journal,* Vol. 17, No. 13 (August, 1992): 16.

Women Library Users and Library Users of Traditional Women's Subjects

Geraldine B. King

SUMMARY. In the studies of general library use, women use libraries more than men. When use studies of particular subjects are done, women nearly always are more likely to use libraries for information on that subject than men. Yet there are few studies on women's information needs or use studies of traditional women's subjects. When women's subjects are written about in the library literature, the articles are nearly always on collection development, not on information needs. Information on women's subjects is primarily requested in public libraries and is not considered worthy of scholarly concern. Five specific categories of women's subjects: traditional women's subjects like needlework, practical information for the home, information related to a change in life like returning to school or to work, information on women's health issues, and information about parenting are reviewed. Current trends in commercial electronic information systems and telecommunications technology make the issue of information needs research and analysis urgent.

Women's information needs and library use are not the specific and predictable sort that are associated with groups whose information needs have been studied. As a group, women's needs and

Geraldine B. King is Assistant Professor, Information Management and MALS Program, College of St. Catherine, 2004 Randolph Avenue, St. Paul, MN 55105.

[Haworth co-indexing entry note]: "Women Library Users and Library Users of Traditional Women's Subjects." King, Geraldine B. Co-published simultaneously in *The Reference Librarian* (The Haworth Press, Inc.) No. 49/50, 1995, pp. 179-193; and: *Library Users and Reference Services* (ed: Jo Bell Whitlatch) The Haworth Press, Inc., 1995, pp. 179-193. Multiple copies of this article/chapter may be purchased from The Haworth Document Delivery Center [1-800-3-HAWORTH; 9:00 a.m. - 5:00 p.m. (EST)].

179

interests are broad and varied. In many library use situations, most usually in academic and corporate libraries, there is little useful purpose in looking at women as a category of library user. But women are the majority of public library users. Subjects which are traditionally associated with women: cooking, needlework, home-making activities of all sorts, returning to school or work after a break as a mother/homemaker, female health issues, and child care–are the kind of practical lifestyle information that makes up much of public library reference.

There are two critical issues which women library users as a group and use of women's subjects in libraries have in common. While the users and topics make up the majority of information requests in public libraries, they are seldom covered in the professional literature of librarianship. They are not considered to be important enough or scholarly enough to be the subject of user needs research. The problem is aggravated because public librarians are not routinely expected to do research and publish as are many academic librarians. The second critical issue is that women's information needs and the resources to meet those needs are little covered in the education of librarians. The lack of published literature on these users and their information needs makes their inclusion in the education and training curriculum difficult. There is not a body of theory that can be presented nor written materials to support teaching.

There are also significant current issues which make women library users and library users of women's subjects a timely topic for the attention of professional information workers. Discussions of the demise of the public library in light of the "Information Highway" and potential electronic information access in all homes appear in the popular press as well as in library journals. Yet little attention is given to exactly what information the average citizen needs nor how best to deliver that information and make it useful. The issue of fee or free access to information, already difficult to resolve, is complicated by the new technology. Transaction and use fees versus public subsidies; access for the culturally, physically, and economically disadvantaged; and copyright and legal owner-ship issues are all currently much discussed, but with no resolution immediately in sight.

THE PUBLIC LIBRARY AND PRACTICAL INFORMATION

Through the first half of the twentieth century, public libraries were thought of primarily as educational and cultural institutions. Many public libraries in this country were established to help educate and prepare new immigrants for employment. Reference service was geared to assisting people with intellectual and cultural pursuits. After World War II, public libraries began to take on an informational function. Recognition of the public library as a place where the average citizen could find information useful to his everyday needs began to appear in the professional literature with the "Information & Referral" movement in the nineteen sixties. This movement in librarianship can be traced to the Citizens Advice Bureaux often developed or housed in public libraries in Great Britain during and after World War II. Subsequently there has been some literature on the public library as a place where people go for other practical information they need to use in their daily lives such as consumer product and service information of various kinds, recipes, nutrition information and house cleaning techniques and products, do-it-yourself auto and appliance repair, parenting and child behavior information, medical, drug, and legal information for the layperson, various kinds of information for the woman who wishes to resume education or employment after a period of full-time child rearing, etc.

This paper will attempt to survey the relevant publications on information needs of women and use of women's subjects and sample responses to the perceived needs. Because the potential number of topics which could be discussed in this paper is so large, the following criteria were established to limit the material to a manageable amount:

I. neglect of the topics in the professional literature and in research,
II. the need for discussions of the issues for educational and training materials,
III. frequency of requests at public library reference desks.

PUBLIC LIBRARY USE STUDIES

In the studies of general public library use in this century, women have always used libraries more than men. When use studies of particular subjects are done, women nearly always are more likely to use libraries for information on whatever subject than men.

The most recent of the general use studies, the 1978 Gallup Survey, the 1987 "Life Style Profile of the Public Library User" and the 1990 Equifax-Harris survey also found that women use libraries more than men although the spread between the two seems to be narrowing. The 1990 survey reported that 68% of the women used the library as compared to 63% of men.

Marchant (1991) analyzed "motivation" for adult public library use. His motivation categories were home and family life, vocational growth, religion, and politics. Among the many demographic characteristics which he included in his study was sex so that he was able to compare male and female motivation factors. Findings from this study will be mentioned as they are relevant to the various topics.

Words written in the popular library press in 1982 by Parikh and Broidy are just as true today: "The population of the U.S. is over 50% female, the library profession over 80%, yet analysis of and attention to women's issues and needs both as library users and library workers lags far behind our majority representation," and "Library doors have traditionally been open to help immigrants, cultural minorities, and the economically disadvantaged gain a toehold in American society. Women in this society are an economically disadvantaged cultural minority. Today, as in the past, it is the responsibility of the public library to open its doors and extend its resources to these immigrants in a man's world."[1]

WOMEN'S INFORMATION NEEDS AND USE

One of the few studies of women's information needs is Bates "Library and Information Services for Women, Homemakers, and Parents" published in 1974. At that time, she wrote, "The library literature appears to be devoid of information on the needs of these three groups as groups."[2] Bates looked at information needs found in Extension Service surveys, women's movement organizations, and general studies of the public's information needs. Bates categorized the information needs of these groups as survival related–crisis, survival related–general, and self enrichment and growth. The first category is the library role as an "information & referral" center for social services and various experts such as physicians, psychologists, lawyers. The second and third categories are subjects for which information can be acquired from usual public library materials.

The next significant addition to the analysis of practical information needs is Dervin's 1976 chapter: "The Everyday Information Needs of the Average Citizen: a Taxonomy for Analysis." While not limited to women, her taxonomy covers many of the same subjects which Bates associated particularly with women's information needs. Dervin's complete list of subjects is neighborhood; consumer; housing; housekeeping and household maintenance; employment; education and schooling; health; transportation; recreation and culture; financial matters or assistance; public assistance and social security; discrimination and race relations; child care and family relationships; family planning and birth control; legal; crime and safety; immigration, migration, and mobility; veterans and military; and public affairs, political, and miscellaneous.[3] Dervin concludes by saying "The clearest generalization which emerges from this discussion is that huge gaps exist in the knowledge base relating to average citizens and their information needs." [4]

A few studies of specific groups of women or of specific women's information needs have been published. One of the earlier ones is Turock's (1975) description of the establishment of a Women's Information & Referral Service in the Montclair, N.J., Public library in the 1970's. Initially, "agencies and organizations working with women were consulted to see what their primary areas of concern and assistance were."[5] This led to an initial data-bank on legal rights and aid, career and other counseling, family planning, self-awareness, educational opportunities, day care and nursery facilities, women's organizations, and sexism in the media.[6] However, once the service was in operation, "Most of our queries have to do with job information . . . the large majority of our patrons want to know how they can get into or return to the job market, where they can get help for writing a resume or upgrading job skills, where they can get day care for their young children."[7]

Chatman has done two studies of information needs of specific groups which are relevant to the information needs of women: one on the "working poor" (1985) and one on "older women" (1991). Both of her studies found interesting perceptions about libraries. The women urban poor in CETA training in the earlier article did not see the library as a source of useful information specific to employment,[8] and the older women seemed to see the library as a place to get recreational reading, but not as an information source.[9] One of the older women had a clear picture of what she thought the library should provide:

> I think a library can help older people by providing them with good books and things to assist them to learn. They could put out pamphlets about general tips on aging. Plus, put books on crafts in large print. They should have a newsletter for older people telling them about meetings of interest to them. If they request something special, the library should be willing to get it. I wanted a book to read so I called my daughter to pick it up for me at the library. It would be nice though if they would send it in the mail. If they weren't willing to pay for it, I would have. There are a lot of people here who have had heart attacks or are crippled. They can't get to a library. People assume that everybody can drive, and they can't. Plus older people are afraid of a lot of traffic.[10]

Whitt (1993) studied the information needs of lesbians. The subjects of this study went to the library "for lesbian fiction, for poetry, both popular and research-oriented psychological and sociological materials and for information on ethics and sexual behavior."[11] "The library figures very prominently in the initial effort to locate information,"[12] but less frequent library users expected the material to be outdated or not positive. One respondent remarked that librarians should "at least have the ability to conceal surprise about alternative lifestyles."[13]

LIBRARY USERS OF TRADITIONAL WOMEN'S SUBJECTS

There are few use studies of stereotypically women's subjects. When such subjects are written about in library literature, the articles are nearly always on collection development, not on use or users. Traditional women's subjects, such as cooking, needlework, sewing, and gardening are rarely treated in library literature except for papers on cataloging of fiber art or preservation of textiles or in book reviews or articles on collection development. *Library Journal* has done a series on collection development of popular public library subjects including crocheting and knitting and garden design. Chatman picked up an information need in her study of older women when one of the subjects mentioned the need for craft books in large type (see above). In addition to the technical information needs evident in the literature of these fields, there is much evidence of the need for sources of creative inspiration. For example, a much discussed topic in many of the current publications on needlework is the use of pictorial sources for design. Monitoring relevant subject lists on the Internet provides additional examples of information needs: sources for unusual materials, lists of continuing education, workshops, and conferences, information on institutions, organizations, museums, etc. For the information professional, this remains an unexplored area of information need and one which would prove fruitful to study.

LIBRARY USERS IN NEED OF PRACTICAL INFORMATION FOR THEIR HOME

This category is the broadest and most basic one for this paper. It includes homemakers of either sex; do-it-yourself repair persons including repair of appliances, automobiles, utilities (home improvements, generally); people seeking consumer product ratings, etc.

In Marchant's (1991) categorization of adult use of public libraries, men and women were equally involved with his category, "home and family affairs," but "women were twice as likely as men to use the library for this purpose."[14]

In a study of library use for practical information, Harris and Mitchell (1988) related attitudes about bibliographic instruction to male and female sex-typed topics. They found that "The standard that seems to be operating in this study is that when patrons know little about a topic (as is apparently assumed when a patron makes a cross-sex query), the librarian is obliged to teach; yet when a patron makes a sex-consistent request, library instruction should not be given."[15] Female topics were day care, planning a wedding, choosing a diet, selecting a knitting pattern, and flower arranging; male topics: fixing a washing machine, obtaining a patent, trout fishing, joining the armed forces, and getting a home electrical permit.[16]

Searches through the professional literature of librarianship for practical topics frequently yield no more than one article per topic. While auto repair is a stereotypically male topic, not only are more women now repairing their own cars, but anecdotal literature tells us that women have been sent to the public library to get information on auto repair to be used by the male members of their family. The one article on auto repair, Pankl (1992), considers some aspects of information need as well as collection development. Sources of needs information outside of library literature are included. "Provision of repair manuals in public libraries is not a subject to which the professional literature of librarianship has given significant attention. An online literature search revealed no postings. A manual search of *Library Literature* back to 1980 was almost equally fruitless. An Infotrac search revealed, however, that articles do appear in popular periodicals from time to time."[17] Those articles in the popular do-it-yourself literature do provide information on users (e.g., surveys of which models are most worked on by owners), and state motor vehicle licensing departments can provide the number of each model licensed in the state.[18] In preparing his discussion of the auto repair reference service at Tulsa Public Library, Pankl also surveyed nine public libraries, finding that questions on auto repair averaged 25% of total reference transactions.[19] Commercial vendors of auto repair information apparently have noticed this market; the Ford Motor Company Technical Publication Department was an A.L.A. Midwinter exhibitor in 1994 with special show prices for technical manuals.

Examples of other articles related to practical information for the home have less information needs content. In a collection development oriented article, Langstaff (1991), "Meet Mr. and Mrs. Fixit," quotes marketing statistics on the increase in home improvement activities by do-it-yourselfers prefatory to a discussion of the increase in publishing in this area.[20] The one article in library literature on appliance repair manuals deals with the acquisition of those materials.[21]

LIBRARY USERS WHO NEED INFORMATION FOR REENTRY TO EDUCATION OR WORK

While this is clearly not a topic confined to women, nearly every study of women's information needs finds this as a major, if not the highest, priority information need. Those studies include Javelin (1976) on information needs of local community organizations (women's vocational organizations), Chatman (1985) on urban poor women, Glass (1990) on minority women, and Marchant (1991) on general adult library use. Furthermore, this appears to be an area where the library is often the most frequently used information source. The many special sections on job or career information in public libraries have increased public awareness of the library as a job information source. However, the Chatman study had less promising results. Only 36% of her subjects "considered the library as a likely source of this specific type of information. A few respondents felt that the library may have some employment-type information such as Civil Service listings and general information about a career field but no information about how one goes about pursuing a job in a specific field." A general concern was "libraries are not up-to-date" (Chatman, 1985, p. 104).

LIBRARY USERS OF INFORMATION ON WOMEN'S HEALTH ISSUES

This topic is also one on which the articles in the library literature uniformly deal with collection development. However, information needs on this subject have been much written about in the feminist literature; currently both the popular literature and health-care literature are very concerned with women's health research and information needs. An example of a recent library article is Bibel (1993) "Consumer Health Information: a Selected List of Reference Sources for the Lay User." The Medical Library Association has published many similar collection development lists. With the present emphasis on health care reform, there is likely to be much more information published, both on information needs and on resources to meet those needs.

LIBRARY USERS WANTING INFORMATION ABOUT PARENTING

Parenting also is an issue which has been covered extensively in recent years in the non-library press–both popular media and sociological/psychological journals. The publishing industry has responded to this concern and many materials are available in public libraries. This topic is also one which is included in the *Library Journal* collection development series mentioned above. The ERIC Clearinghouse on Assessment and Evaluation announced in March 1994 the addition of fifty full-text essays on parenting to their resources.

A different parental function is the frequently described practice of parents doing their children's homework in the library. While this is a common discussion topic whenever public library reference librarians are together, there has been no apparent attempt to analyze the associated information needs, and very little has been written on the topic.[22]

CURRENT TRENDS

Much of the practical kinds of information resources discussed in this paper are available for various transaction and use fees from commercial and nonprofit organizations other than libraries. Those other vendors of practical information for the average citizen market their services far more extensively than do public libraries. Many people, and particularly those less able to pay, know of the fee-based services and not of the free tax-supported services. This has been a less significant issue in the past because there were not so many or so well-known fee-based alternatives. Computerization and the various network services, CompuServe, America Online, Prodigy, etc., are now making a big difference. Many more people know of and use the fee services. Far fewer know of and use the public library services. Low-income parents speak proudly of their children accessing encyclopedias to do their homework via CompuServe or Prodigy when there are comparable encyclopedias available for free computer dial-up from their local public library. Among solutions to this marketing problem touted in the library press are cooperation and collaboration with other public agencies which provide information to the general citizen like Extension services and social agencies. Maciuszko (1990) describes two kinds of organizations which go a step further, the community online systems like the Free-Nets and community online information systems organized by public libraries.[23] The report on the Equifax-Harris survey, *Using the Public Library in the Computer Age* (1991) also describes library-originated community computerized information systems.[24] Without the expense of initiating a local network, some public libraries are now providing access to online information systems via the Internet. In the 1980's, public libraries provided many adults with their first lessons in computer literacy when card catalogs were converted to OPACs; they are now continuing this educational mission with providing first access to information networks for many patrons.

NEEDED RESEARCH

Library information service has always tended to rush to provide the answer before finding out the question. Electronic information sources have not changed this sequence. Studying and analyzing the everyday information needs of women–for recreational, educational, vocational, health and family–as well as the needs of all people, regardless of sex or age or other demographic characteristics, for practical and lifestyle information has been little done. Public library administrators and jurisdictions should require research and publication on information needs of women and users of women's subjects for librarians' promotion and provide the opportunities for this research. Public libraries and librarians need to publicize their mission of responsibility for research and publication on information needs of the average citizen rather than their popular mission as purveyors of video movies and romantic novels. Forty hours a week of frantic reference work is no longer the best way to serve the public's information needs. Perhaps the impetus provided by commercial services and home electronic access will excite librarians about pursuing such research.

In 1976 Dervin concluded with "The clearest generalization that emerges from this discussion is that huge gaps exist in the knowledge base relating to average citizens and their information needs."[25] Still true!

REFERENCES

1. Parikh, Neel and Ellen Broidy. "Women's Issues: The Library Response" *Wilson Library Bulletin* 57 (Dec. 1982), p. 295, 297.

2. Bates, Marcia J. "Library and Information Services for Women, Homemakers, and Parents" in *Library and Information Service Needs of the Nation* (Washington, U.S. Govt. Printing Office, 1974), p. 129.

3. Dervin, Brenda. "The Everyday Information Needs of the Average Citizen: A Taxonomy for Analysis" in *Information for the Community,* ed. by Manfred Kochen and Joseph C. Donohue. (Chicago, A.L.A., 1976), p. 24-5.

4. *Ibid.,* p. 35.

5. Turock, Betty. "Women's Information & Referral Service Asks Community for Answers" *Wilson Library Bulletin* 49 (Apr. 1975), p. 568.

6. *Ibid.,* p. 570.

7. *Ibid.,* p. 571.

8. Chatman, Elfreda A. "Information, Mass Media Use and the Working Poor" *Library and Information Science Research* 7 (1985), p. 110.

9. Chatman, Elfreda A "Channels to a Larger Social World: Older Women Staying in Contact with the Great Society" *Library and Information Science Research* 13 (1991), p. 296.

10. *Ibid.,* p. 295.

11. Whitt, E. J. "The Information Needs of Lesbians" *Library and Information Science Research* 15 (Summer 1993), p. 281.

12. *Ibid.,* p. 278.

13. *Ibid.,* p. 283.

14. Marchant, Maurice P. "What Motivates Adult Use of Public Libraries?" *Library and Information Science Research* 13 (July-Sept. 1991), p. 233.

15. Harris, Roma M. and Gillian Michell. "Home Insulating and Home Births: Do Patrons' Sex-typed Questions Influence Judgments about the Competence of Reference Librarians?" *RQ* 28 (Winter 1988), p. 184.

16. *Ibid.,* p. 181.

17. Pankl, Robert R. "Automobile Service Information in the Public Library" *RQ* 32 (Winter 1992), p. 230.

18. *Ibid.*, p. 230-31.
19. *Ibid.*, p. 233.
20. Langstaff, Peggy. "Meet Mr. and Mrs. Fixit" *Publishers Weekly* 238 (Oct. 4, 1991), p. 15.
21. Bredeson, Peggy. "Appliance Repair Manuals Sources" *Unabashed Librarian* 50 (1984), p.6.
22. Loorie, Nancy S. "Whose Homework is it Anyway? Helping Parents at the Reference Desk" *New Jersey Libraries* 26 (1993) 15-17.
23. Maciuszko, Kathleen L. "A Quiet Revolution: Community Online Systems" *Online* 14 (Nov. 1990), p. 31.
24. Westin, Alan, and Anne Finger. *Using the Public Library in the Computer Age: Present Patterns, Future Possibilities.* (Chicago, A.L.A., 1991) p. 44-47.
25. Dervin, *op. cit.*, p. 35.

SELECTED BIBLIOGRAPHY

Alloway, Catherine S., Edward Cool, and Sherry Feintuch. "Health Index Plus: a CD-ROM Product for Consumer Health Information" *Medical Reference Services Quarterly* 11 (Spring 1992) 39-45.

Bates, Marcia J. "Library and Information Services for Women, Homemakers, and Parents" in *Library and Information Service Needs of the Nation: Proceedings of a Conference on the Needs of Occupational, Ethnic, and Other Groups in the United States* ed. by C. A. Cuadra and M. J. Bates (Washington, U.S. Govt. Printing Office, 1974).

Bibel, Barbara. "Consumer Health Information a Selected List of Reference Sources for the Lay User" *Booklist* 89 (Jan. 1, 1993) 828-29.

Blake, M. "Homeworkers and their Information Needs" *Library and Information Research News* 16 (Spring 1993) 14-16.

Bredeson, Peggy. "Appliance Repair Manuals Sources" *Unabashed Librarian* 50 (1984) 6.

Cassell, Kay Ann and Kathleen Weibel. "Public Library Response to Women and Their Changing Roles" *RQ* 20 (Fall 1980) 70-75.

_____ . "Librarians, Politics, and the ERA" *Wilson Library Bulletin* 57 (Dec. 1982) 292-94.

Chatman, Elfreda A. "Channels to a Larger Social World: Older Women Staying in Contact with the Great Society" *Library and Information Science Research* 13 (1991) 281-300.

_____ . "Information, Mass Media Use and the Working Poor" Library and Information Science Research 7 (1985) 97-113.

Demo, Bill. "Fixing Up Your Home Repair Collection" *Library Journal* 116 (Sept. 1, 1991) 161-65.

Dervin, Brenda. "The Everyday Information Needs of the Average Citizen: A Taxonomy for Analysis" in *Information for the Community,* ed. by Manfred Kochen and Joseph C. Donohue. Chicago, A.L.A., 1976.

Doman, Dave. "Community Connections: Local Information Databases" *Colorado Libraries* 18 (March 1992) 35-6.

Ensor, Pat. "Prodigy: Bellwether or Pariah?" *Online* 15 (July 1991) 61-63.

Fairer-Wessels, Felicite A. "Basic Community Information Needs of Urban Black Women" *Mousaion* 5 (1987) 54-65.

Geffert, Bryn. "Community Networks in Libraries: A Case Study of the Freenet P.A.T.H." *Public Libraries* 32 (Mar./Apr. 1993) 91-9.

Glass, Betty J. "Information Needs of Minority Women and Serials Resources: A Selected Bibliography" *The Reference Librarian* 27/28 (1990) 289-303.

Harris, Jill. "The Demand for Health and Sickness Information in a Large Public Library" *New Zealand Libraries* 47 (March 1992) 3-10.

Harris, Roma M. and Gillian Michell. "Home Insulating and Home Births: Do Patrons' Sex-typed Questions Influence Judgments about the Competence of Reference Librarians?" *RQ* 28 (Winter 1988) 179-84.

"Home Repair/Renovation Best Sellers" *Library Journal* 117 (Apr. 1, 1992) 109.

Jackson, Mary E. "Sew Good" *Wilson Library Bulletin* 68 (Nov. 1993) 120.

_____ "Videos for the Sewing Collection" *Library Journal* 116 (June 1, 1991) 100.

Javelin, Muriel C. "Analyzing Information Needs of Local Community Organizations: A Case Study" *Library Trends* 24 (Jan. 1976) 527-35.

Langstaff, Peggy. "Meet Mr. and Mrs. Fixit" *Publishers Weekly* 238 (Oct. 4, 1991) 15-22.

Leonard, Peter C. "Remodeling a Home Renovation Collection" *Library Journal* 117 (Feb. 1, 1992) 53-6.

Lind, Judith. "Threading Your Way Through the Sewing Books" *Library Journal* 116 (Feb. 1, 1991) 57-60.

Loorie, Nancy S. "Whose Homework is it Anyway? Helping Parents at the Reference Desk" *New Jersey Libraries* 26 (1993) 15-17.

Maciuszko, Kathleen L. "A Quiet Revolution: Community Online Systems" *Online* 14 (Nov. 1990) 24-32.

Marchant, Maurice P. "What Motivates Adult Use of Public Libraries?" *Library and Information Science Research* 13 (July-Sept. 1991) 201-235.

Marshall, Joanne. "A Development and Evaluation Model for a Consumer Health Information Service" *Canadian Journal of Information Science* 17 (Dec. 1992) 1-17.

Murray, Joan V. "Public Libraries" *Catholic Library World* 48 (Apr. 1977) 400-01.

Pankl, Robert R. "Automobile Service Information in the Public Library" *RQ* 32 (Winter 1992) 230-37.

Parikh, Neel and Ellen Broidy. "Women's Issues: The Library Response" *Wilson Library Bulletin* 57 (Dec. 1982) 295-99.

Pasterczyk, Catherine E. "Handspinning Periodicals" *Serials Review* 12 (Spring 1986) 27-33.

Pritchard, Sarah M. "Linking Research, Policy, and Activism: Library Services in Women's Studies" *The Reference Librarian* 20 (1987) 89-103.

Quint, Barbara. "Real Research for Real People" *Wilson Library Bulletin* 65 (March 191) 97-100.

Turock, Betty. "Women's Information & Referral Service Asks Community for Answers" *Wilson Library Bulletin* 49 (Apr. 1975) 568-72.

Van de Streek, David. "Tuning Up Your Auto Repair Collection" *Library Journal* 116 (June 1, 1991) 91-2.

Westin, Alan, and Anne Finger. *Using the Public Library in the Computer Age: Present Patterns, Future Possibilities.* Chicago, A.L.A., 1991.

Whitt, E. J. "The Information Needs of Lesbians" *Library and Information Science Research* 15 (Summer 1993) 275-88.

Zlendich, Janice. "Knit One, Read, Too" *Library Journal* 117 (Oct. 1, 1992) 55-9.

Fee-Based Services:
An Option for Meeting
the Information Needs
of the Business Community

Helen B. Josephine

SUMMARY. Information needs of the business community vary considerably depending on a number of factors including size and type of business, competitive environment, state and local support, and managerial expertise, among others. This paper will explore some of these information needs and discuss the ways libraries meet these diverse needs including the offering of fee-based information services.

INTRODUCTION

Businesses large and small operate in competitive environments. Work smarter not harder is the new business motto. Many of the day to day information needs of business can be filled by the informal information networks of colleagues, government agencies and friends. Eventually every business reaches a point where they need

---

Helen B. Josephine is Associate Director, Office of Technology Transfer and Economic Development, University of Hawaii and Program Director of the Library External Services Program, Hamilton Library, University of Hawaii, Honolulu, HI 96822.

[Haworth co-indexing entry note]: "Fee-Based Services: An Option for Meeting the Information Needs of the Business Community." Josephine, Helen B. Co-published simultaneously in *The Reference Librarian* (The Haworth Press, Inc.) No. 49/50, 1995, pp. 195-203; and: *Library Users and Reference Services* (ed: Jo Bell Whitlatch) The Haworth Press, Inc., 1995, pp. 195-203. Multiple copies of this article/chapter may be purchased from The Haworth Document Delivery Center [1-800-3-HA-WORTH; 9:00 a.m. - 5:00 p.m. (EST)].

195

"library" information. "Library" information for businesses has expanded from the standard directories and business periodicals to include full text CD-ROM, real time electronic SEC filings, and government information on the Internet. "The ability to access and process information on competitive intelligence, new product information, research and development, market trends, and environmental and regulatory impacts is critical to a company's future," observed Robert Muir in his recent article on marketing library or information service to businesses.[1]

All libraries must continually market their business information resources if they want to provide service to the business community. While the corporate information center or law firm library may be physically a part of the company, the services offered must still be marketed to potential users. If the public, college, or university library wants to serve the information needs of the business community, then a commitment to marketing the resources is just as important as the commitment to purchase, catalogue and shelve the resources.

In order to serve the information needs of businesses the library must become an active partner. The role of the librarian or information professional is changing, As Barbara Quint observes in a recent editorial in *Searcher*, "Information professionals must know the value of the information they supply, how it supports the institution's activities, what new or external clients might pay for it, and the cost of supplying the information."[2]

Briefly discussed here are the various responses to the information needs of large and small corporations, professional firms, and small business. While some companies have the advantage of in-house libraries or information centers, all businesses to some extent depend on the collections of their local public, college or university libraries.

THE CORPORATE INFORMATION CENTER

The information needs of large corporations are usually handled by the Corporate Information Center. Staffed by a professional librarian, these centers order, catalogue, circulate, interpret, and research the books, journals, and technical reports needed by the various divisions of the company, marketing, research and development, legal, etc. Intimately knowledgeable about the details of the company, its products, markets, competitors, the librarian becomes an information partner of every staff member in the company. The challenge is to keep current with the information tools needed to stay on the fore front and at the same time market the library as an important function in the company.

Left to their own devices, business managers and researchers would rely almost exclusively on their informal information networks–friends and colleagues in other departments of the company. One role of the librarian is to educate company employees in the value of using the resources of the corporate information center. Some centers use weekly newsletters of hot topics or new acquisitions to keep potential library users informed and interested in using the library. Other centers may circulate the table of contents of key journals and reports received by the library. Electronic table-of-contents routing is now easier with company networks linked to the Internet and such services as Uncover's Reveal, a table-of-contents electronic mail service available on the Internet. Once again, however, it is the librarian who alerts the company to the availability of these new services.

In his article on marketing information services to business, Muir list three key elements the information center needs to be able to sell to be successful:

- the ability to alert customers to the presence of the information service;
- the information products and services needed by the company;
- the value of the service to the company.[3]

The challenge facing businesses today is to make informed decisions faster. The role of the corporate information center librarian is to assist this by becoming an active information gathering partner. In many instances this includes scanning relevant literature, keeping managers up-to-date on competitive markets, preparing "briefing packets" on hot topics, and synthesizing data from a variety of sources. As Jack Borbely, the director of a corporate information center for a firm in New York observed in his paper, "This new role has required that corporate libraries increasingly act as the 'information interpreters' for the clients they support."[4] The library fulfills its mission as the provider of information allowing the company mangers to devote their time to acting on the information.

An additional challenge for the corporate information center is harnessing the power of the Internet and the sources available on the "information superhighway." The responsibility for evaluating the usefulness, accuracy and appropriateness of the hundreds of Internet sources falls to the corporate information center librarian. Managers and research personnel from a variety of business divisions want access to the government, university, and private information resources available via the Internet and various gateway services. Knowledge of the existence of these resources is not sufficient. The corporate information center librarian also trains end users in the research and retrieval protocols used by the variety of sources on the Internet as well as evaluates the pertinence of the sources to the information needs of the business.

PROFESSIONAL CORPORATIONS: LAW FIRMS, ACCOUNTING FIRMS, ARCHITECTURAL FIRMS

To stay competitive, professional corporations must maintain a viable client base, provide quality services, and keep current with all legal and regulatory changes affecting the firm and its area of specialization. The role of the information center is critical to the successful completion of these tasks.

Because of the specialized and narrow focus of the professional corporation, the librarian's role is more clearly seen as an information partner of the firm. The specialized legal, financial, or architectural information required by the firm often demands an additional master's degree or hands on experience with specific research tools and electronic databases.

In addition the librarian collects, organizes, retrieves and interprets the specialized collection of books, journals, and reference materials required by the firm. The use of electronic information sources including the Internet has increased the role of the librarian to include evaluation of electronic resources and end-user searching training.

The librarian must also be aware of external sources of information which can be used on an as needed basis. These sources include trade and industry associations, experts and consultants, translators, university library collections, and other specialized information "brokering" agencies.

SMALL BUSINESSES AND THE SOLE PROPRIETOR

The small business and the sole proprietor does not enjoy the advantage of having an in-house library or information center. As Raymond Paolino of the New York State Department of Economic Development observed in his article on economic development, "the small business must depend upon outside resources to supply its particular information needs."[5] While information gathering may have taken place when the original business plan was formulated, small businesses often work in an information vacuum. Owners are too busy to do the research themselves and don't know where to go to get help.

Agencies, such as the Small Business Administration, local chamber of commerce or local small business development centers often have library collections and pamphlets on various business topics. Public libraries have special business collections created for the needs of the small business owner and entrepreneur. The challenge again is marketing these services to the business client. In his research on information services and the business community, Doug Ernest concludes, "libraries everywhere may not be receiving heavy external use of their business resources simply because business people do not visualize libraries as sources of information in their decision-making processes."[6]

Some of the marketing techniques used by public libraries to overcome the perception that libraries do not have resources for the business community have included participation at local "business-to-business" exhibitions, public service announcements on the radio, information columns in the local business newspaper or on the business page of the local newspaper. Others have participated in joint sponsorship of programs with the Small Business Administration or local chamber of commerce on specific topics such as trademarks, patents, government contracting, census information, etc.

The key is being committed as a library organization to meeting the information needs of the local business community by doing more than subscribing to business journals and directories. A committed effort requires staff dedicated to listening to the needs of the business community, working toward fulfilling those needs, and an active marketing plan to reach out to the business community. Libraries wanting to serve the needs of the business community must also be willing to invest in the electronic resources currently available as well as those just on the horizon and promote them to potential users through demonstrations or seminars.

FEE-FOR SERVICE OPTION

All the information needs of a large corporation or professional firm cannot be answered by the in-house information center. The local public, college, or university library is often used as a back-up resource for seldom used reference sources, electronic databases, journals and books. For the small business owner the local public, college or university library may be the only source of business information.

However, the local public, college, or university library may feel overwhelmed by the increased demands of the business community for information and rapid access to journal articles. One solution to this problem is to establish a fee-based information service to handle requests from the business community and other external or non-primary users.

Fee-based services are found in a variety of institutional settings including public, academic and special libraries. The fourth edition of *The FISCAL Directory of Fee-Based Research and Document Supply Services* lists 445 services in public, academic, and special libraries world-wide. The Directory also includes 61 commercial document delivery suppliers not affiliated with a library.[7]

In some instances library policy may dictate that some services remain free while others may have a fee attached. Careful review of the local business community, potential donor partnerships, staff expertise, current funding for core services and the overall mission of the library must take place before initiating a fee service.

After determining that a fee service might be useful to the business community and beneficial to the library, then a working proposal for the service should be developed. The areas to consider include:

- full or partial cost recovery,
- target date for cost recovery (three, four or five years),
- startup funding for new equipment or share current equipment,
- new staff required or share current staff,
- current levels of service offered at no charge versus enhanced or expanded service offered on a fee basis.

For further discussion and approval by the library administration or other governing body, a business plan for the service should be drafted. The plan should include projected first year revenues and expenditures, equipment needed, and proposed staff. A separate marketing plan with expenditures for advertisement, brochure design and exhibit costs should also be prepared.

Surveys of local business will provide the information needed for determining the types of services the fee-based service could offer. Typically these include:

- document delivery of articles, books, government documents, technical reports, patents from the home institutions collections;
- expedited interlibrary loan from the network of other fee-based services in public and academic libraries;
- computer database searching of commercial databases, CD-ROM indexes and Internet resources;
- custom research including computerized retrieval, manual research, and fact checking with experts or trade associations;
- consulting on information resource purchases or data organization;
- training and seminars on information topics and electronic sources.

Only after information on the needs of the business community is gathered and analyzed can planning for fee-based service take place.

Partnerships with other state or local agencies involved with small business development or state-wide economic development may provide additional start-up funding for a fee-based service for the business community. Certainly joint programming with these agencies will expose the library's fee-based service to a wider audience of potential clients.

Any new service offering designed for the business community will need to take into account the business requirements for speed, reliability and accuracy. In addition marketing efforts must overcome any negative stereotypes of the library as difficult to get to, difficult to use and not worth the effort. An "image" audit of the library and its services, while potential painful, will yield valuable information about how the business community views the library and its resources. For example selected businesses could be asked to rate the library in regard to: types of resources, availability of resources, staff helpfulness, and staff expertise.

An open ended question asking for comments on one area for improvement should also be added. Even if one area over which the library has no control consistently comes out on top, such as parking, just asking the question and acknowledging the response increases communication between the library and the business community. A frank and open discussion of the needs of the business community is the goal; especially if the library is intending to market a fee service to the business community.

CONCLUSION

Information needs of the business community will continue to grow. Libraries have the option of struggling to meet those demands with limited staffing and resources or establishing partnerships with the business community. These partnerships can include funding for specific business research tools, especially electronic access and computer equipment. At the same time businesses can be asked to pay their fare share for expedited and custom service by establishing a fee for service to meet the specific information needs of the business community. In his article on academic libraries and fee-based information services, Doug Ernest concludes, "fee-based services offer an alternative whereby academic libraries can serve the needs of the local business community without having an impact on the needs of their primary clientele."[8]

As members of the larger community, libraries have an obligation to support the economic health of the community by contributing information resources to help large companies remain competitive and small businesses get started. The new electronic sources currently available and those promised on the information "superhighway" make the role of the librarian as an evaluator, interpreter and supplier of information even more crucial. The resources available in libraries are not instinctively known to those who need them. A strong marketing plan which highlights all of the library's services, fee and free, is an important element in serving the information needs of the business community.

REFERENCES

1. Robert Muir, "Marketing Your Library or Information Service to Business," *Online* (14:4 July 1983) p. 41.

2. Barbara Quint, "Write if You Get Work," *Searcher: The Magazine for Database Professionals* (2:1 January/February 1994) p. 4.

3. Muir, p. 42.

4. Jack Borbely, "The Emerging Role of the Corporate Library; Restructuring Information Service to Fit the Times," *The Bookmark* (47:1 Fall 1988), p. 57.

5. Raymond G. Paolino, "New York's Resurging Economy and State Economic Development Information," *The Bookmark* (47:1 Fall 1988), p. 4.

6. Douglas J. Ernest, "Academic Libraries, Fee-Based Information Services, and the Business Community," *RQ* (32:3 Spring 1993) p. 396.

7. Steve Coffman and Pat Wiedensohler, *The FISCAL Directory of Fee-Based Research and Document Supply Services* (Chicago: ALA, 1993).

8. Ernest, p. 400.

The Changing Instructional Paradigm and Emerging Technologies: New Opportunities for Reference Librarians and Educators

Lorene Sisson
Donna Pontau

SUMMARY. As the next millennium approaches, libraries must change and evolve in the very near future in order to survive. Reference services can no longer stay behind a desk or within a building's walls. Instead, reference librarians must examine their clientele, determine their unique information needs, and develop and market appropriate collections and services. The changing instructional paradigm in America's classrooms provides an opportunity for reference librarians to modify and expand their efforts to encourage information use and literacy for education faculty, student teachers, classroom teachers and administrators. This paper briefly discusses present day information seeking and library use by educators and then suggests new overtures to this library patron community.

A suburban newspaper article prominently highlights a training session for teachers about the Internet. These middle school teach-

Lorene Sisson and Donna Pontau are Reference Librarians with Curriculum and Education academic assignments, San Jose State University Library, One Washington Square, San Jose, CA 95192-0028.

[Haworth co-indexing entry note]: "The Changing Instructional Paradigm and Emerging Technologies: New Opportunities for Reference Librarians and Educators." Sisson, Lorene, and Donna Pontau. Co-published simultaneously in *The Reference Librarian* (The Haworth Press, Inc.) No. 49/50, 1995, pp. 205-216; and: *Library Users and Reference Services* (ed: Jo Bell Whitlatch) The Haworth Press, Inc., 1995, pp. 205-216. Multiple copies of this article/chapter may be purchased from The Haworth Document Delivery Center [1-800-3-HAWORTH; 9:00 a.m. - 5:00 p.m. (EST)].

205

ers, according to the news report, are excited and enthralled with this new resource. One teacher states "Instead of having to go to the library and in the conventional way look up resources on shelves of books, you do research with this program and it's at your fingertips."[1] Is this teacher in-service workshop sponsored or taught by any local school, public or academic librarians? No–a representative from the local telephone company!

Libraries, in order to survive, must change and evolve before the next millennium arrives. Reference services can no longer stay behind a desk or within a building's walls. It is no longer sufficient for libraries to unlock their doors at their posted opening hour, have a professional at the Reference Desk and wait for patrons to appear. The ever expanding "information superhighway" provides alternatives and options for many patrons. Instead, libraries, like other organizations, must more closely examine who their various clients are, determine their information needs, behaviors and desires, then develop and market appropriate collections and services, and finally assess the effectiveness of their services.

As the opening paragraph indicates, libraries must re-examine their services for the education community: education faculty, student teachers, classroom teachers and school administrators. Neglecting to do so diminishes or eliminates the Library's role in the information society and hurts educators at a time when they need more information and skill due to the changes occurring in the profession and the classroom.

American educators are shifting their paradigm. Instruction is gravitating toward a learner centered environment where individual student learning style, knowledge, and background are incorporated into a meaningful learning experience. The individuals comprising the class will require differing methods, strategies, and examples to achieve academic success. Consequently, classroom instructors will need to become "teacher-researchers." While school administrators are more prone to seek information, they too must become more skilled and adept. As the classroom environment changes, so too must individual schools, and school districts. Education faculty and student teachers must be exposed and encouraged to explore and incorporate new information sources and technologies. In short, all members of the education community will need more information literacy than in the past.

This paper will examine the issues and opportunities academic libraries face in the provision of reference and information services for education faculty, student teachers, classroom teachers and administrators. A brief discussion highlighting present knowledge about information and library use by educators will be followed by examples and suggestions for new overtures to this patron community.

BACKGROUND

Researchers through the years have documented the lack of use of a variety of information sources–including libraries–by educators. Several factors contribute to this lack of use: the sources themselves, teacher training, teacher autonomy, and the old, disintegrating paradigm. Teachers, like others, make judgments about the net benefits of time, convenience and applicability of a source for their needs. Not surprisingly, ease of access and use directly affects source utilization. Consequently, classroom teachers in K-12 "prefer close-at-hand, traditional sources of information such as textbooks, curriculum guides, and other school based materials."[2] The literature also indicates that "many teachers, especially those who did little research in college, do not have a good foundation in even the traditional information skills."[3] Another writer states that teachers often receive "inadequate" preparation for finding information; they often are unfamiliar with the system of a library, the wide range of resources published, and the strategies for locating desired information.[4] The result of this lack of library and information literacy directly impacts selected information sources. Library or more research oriented sources are underutilized in favor of more internal, traditional sources.

A 1991 user survey of the ERIC database illustrates this point. Over a thousand college and university professors, librarians, school administrators, classroom teachers, policymakers, education researchers, graduate students, parents, counselors and journalists answered a 21 item questionnaire. The survey project's goal was to "access the education information needs of respondents, as well as the extent of their use of ERIC, their evaluation of ERIC services and products, and their suggestions for system improvement and expansion."[5] Fourteen percent of the respondents were classroom teachers compared to librarians–25%, professors–27% and school administrators–17%. Most respondents sought journal article citations for research purposes. Classroom teacher respondents, who were most likely to be ERIC non-users, stated little interest in research, but preferred items on "practical ideas of teaching."[6]

Teachers, whether at the K-12 or college level, generally exercise great autonomy in their work. While frameworks, course descriptions, and curricular statements exist, instructors command their classrooms as they see fit. This "expectation" is created during the professional preparation for the field. Educators are not generally taught to "look outward" for assistance–or even to work in teams. Consequently, the expectation of autonomy and self-reliance erects a barrier toward cooperative ventures with colleagues as well as professionals other than teachers. A school librarian writes, "One reason is that teachers don't know or don't see the need for librarian-teacher partnering. Few teacher credential programs include team-teaching models, particularly including librarians as the collaborators. High school teachers, in particular, tend to be credentialed in a specific subject area, and they consider themselves experts in their field. How could a librarian know more about their subject than they–how could a librarian tell them how to teach their courses?"[7]

The sole reliance on traditional and practical sources may have worked in the old teaching paradigm, but the dependence on them may well be detrimental to effective teaching in a learner centered classroom. "The role of the teacher is changing from that of a "dispenser of knowledge" to that of a "facilitator of learning."[8] Why? The increasing diversity of America's population and a greater understanding and recognition of different learning styles may be two very important factors.

Newspapers, magazines and television whether via news, programming or advertising are a constant reminder that America is a multiracial, multiethnic, and multicultural country. America's schools reflect its population. In the Fall of 1986, 70.4% of the country's students enrolled in public elementary and secondary schools were white, 16.1% Black, 9.9% Hispanic, 2.8% Asian or

Pacific Islander, and 0.9% American Indian/Alaskan Native. The percentages a mere five years later in Fall 1991 were: 67.4%, 16.4%, 11.8%, 3.4% and 1.0%. The population changes in particular states such as California and New York are even more impressive.[9] The resulting heterogeneity in student language, cultures, background, values, and opportunities requires alternatives to past methods. When Limited-English-proficient students comprise 34.2% of all California public school students, educators must adapt.[10]

Recent recognition of different learning styles and aptitudes has also contributed to the need for teachers as teacher-researchers. The research of Gagne exposed five different kinds of learning outcomes—verbal knowledge, intellectual skills, cognitive strategies, attitudes and motor skills. These categories are similar to the three major strands of Bloom's taxomony: cognitive, affective, and psychotomotor domains. The research by Gagne, Bloom and others has "substantial use in the planning and design of instruction."[11] Therefore, a more adaptive learning environment is necessary. As two researchers write, "The majority of students will need more aptitude support than conventional teaching provides, and different kinds of specialized support will likely be needed for different kinds of students."[12]

Educators will need access to information which assists them in fulfilling the individual instructional needs of their diverse students.

Teachers need to see that information skills are the tools needed to be the "facilitators" of learning which the new paradigm requires. Further, teachers "need to know that information skills are part of everyone's curriculum, not just a subject taught in elementary school or in language arts class."[13]

OPPORTUNITIES

The paradigm shift and changing technologies offer new opportunities for developing or expanding services to all educators by academic librarians. It is no longer sufficient to encounter only education faculty or student teachers at the Reference Desk or through Bibliographic Instruction presentations. Further, technology frees librarians from facilitating information needs solely at the

Reference Desk. Electronic resources and accompanying technology can permit librarians to model the teacher-researcher ideal. All members of the education community–faculty, student teachers, classroom teachers and administrators–must be actively recruited to become not only information users, but also information producers, disseminators and evaluators.

Tried and true practices, however, will not achieve the desired goals. Since educators generally "do not come to us," librarians must reach out to them. Examples of this perspective are already evident. The 1991 ERIC survey results mentioned earlier suggested " . . . not only a need for better marketing of existing products and services but a potential shift in system resources in order to disseminate practitioner oriented information to a new target audience."[14] Hence, the AskERIC Service for K-12 Educators was developed by the ERIC Clearinghouse on Information and Technology at Syracuse University.

The AskERIC Service debuted in 1993 after pilot testing. The service already is more heavily used than anticipated. A January 1994 flyer for the service states it is "an Internet-based question-answering service for teachers, library media specialists, administrators, and others involved in K-12 education. The hallmark of AskERIC is a human intermediary who interacts with the information seeker and personally selects and delivers information resources within 48 working hours. AskERIC staff use an array of relevant resources, both from the ERIC system and from the vast resources of the INTERNET, to respond to information requests." Interested persons simply send an e-mail message with their question to *askeric@ericir.syr.edu.* The system facilitates users in their information quest by providing an average of ten items related to their topic. AskERIC is a means of introducing and encouraging forays into the ERIC database for traditional non-users; it also promotes remote access to information.

Another example of a well-researched, expansive project to connect teachers to information is the Eisenhower National Clearinghouse for Mathematics and Science Education (ENC). E-mail correspondence with Nancy O'Hanlon, Associate Director for Library and Information Systems for the ENC has supplied the authors with facts about both the mission and products for this new resource.

This Center's stated mission is "to provide better access to resources for all who are interested in creating a better learning environment. The Clearinghouse will accomplish this by creating and maintaining a comprehensive, multimedia collection of materials and programs which will be distributed in a timely manner through a national system using both traditional formats and advanced computing and telecommunications technologies."

The ENC is developing a number of products to accomplish its mission. One product is the catalog of mathematics and science curriculum materials from Federal agencies and other sources which will be available via INTERNET and a toll free number sometime in 1994 and CD-ROM in 1995. This catalog will include information not usually found in library catalogs: abstract, evaluations, grade level(s), target audience, geographic focus, standards, availability and ordering information, cost category, sample pages or photos, material type, physical and pedagogical formats, and funding information. It is hoped that making this vital information available to the teacher-practitioner will entice him or her back to the ENC resource as a repeat user. Becoming a repeat user changes the practitioner into a teacher-researcher. The ENC is yet another illustration of efforts to reach educators regardless of their location or position in the education community.

Efforts in the cataloging arena also demonstrate a desire to make relevant materials of interest to educators easier to locate in library online catalogs and other databases. MARC format has long been the standard for database records, yet its usefulness for curriculum materials is lacking due to the vagueness about which fields should contain which item details and the absence of some pertinent fields altogether! The Curriculum Enhanced MARC (CEMARC) proposed standards would, for the first time, permit effective searching for curriculum materials via characteristics pertinent to educators in online catalogs and databases.

In a 1992 paper, *National Curriculum Enhanced USMARC Standard or What Information Should a MARC Record Contain?*, Roger W. Minier, Educational Technologist at Bowling Green State University, states that due to variations and inconsistencies in how the MARC Standard is applied, a new MARC Standard that helps meet curriculum objectives is needed. This enhanced record will include fields and information not currently in standard cataloging records: learner characteristics, state curriculum objectives linked with media resources, grade level indicator for interest, and grade level indicator for content. In addition, some fields which are currently in use have been targeted for modifications: curriculum specific terms not included in Library of Congress Subject Headings, minimum of five subject headings, etc. At the 1993 annual conference of the American Library Association, the CEMARC proposal was approved by the Machine Readable Bibliographic Information (MARBI) Committee and sent to the Library of Congress as a recommendation for adoption. Again, standardizing the MARC format will allow more precise and pertinent searching for characteristics which are essential for effective use of education materials on large electronic databases such as library online catalogs and OCLC for both educators and librarians.

Cooperative and collaborative efforts are emerging as effective means of facilitating information use and exchange. San Jose State University is an example. The Library's Curriculum librarian also serves as the Director of the College of Education's Learning Resources Display Center. This center acquires and organizes the instructional materials being considered for adoption and those materials already adopted for use in California public schools. The interaction between the education faculty and the librarian is a mutually enlightening experience. The faculty learn more about the Library's resources from a person with firsthand knowledge and expertise in their field of study. The librarian develops a more intimate understanding of the needs of the faculty and students in the program. Librarians are no longer perceived to be merely "book readers" chained to an immobile Reference Desk. Instead, faculty begin to view reference librarians as professionals and peers. This occurrence also encourages faculty to consult with the reference librarian for advice and recommendations about information needs and library resources–a desirable situation given the new instructional paradigm.

Often school librarians promote the teacher/librarian collaboration as an effective method of bringing research and technology to the classroom. Adding academic reference librarians to the loop enhances the collaboration. While school librarians often see their primary mission as bringing advanced technology and teaching research to their school colleagues, school library collections or electronic services may not always provide the scope or extent of desired materials for either the school librarians or, hopefully, more and more classroom teachers. Academic library collections, services and staff could be tapped–especially in these days of shrinking resources for all types of libraries and the trend toward remote access.

One example from the literature illustrates a nice collaborative effort with respect to secondary school student use of academic libraries. University, school, and public libraries in the Waterloo, Ontario, Canada region collaborated on a program which lessened the disruption for the academic libraries, improved student use of library resources in all types of libraries, developed a manual and skills chart checklist, enhanced the consultative role of the teacher-librarian at the secondary school, and created a greater awareness and skills in secondary school teachers about library and information resources available in the region.[15] Collaboration efforts benefited all libraries.

Academic reference librarians with designated liaison roles with the secondary school librarians was a component of the successful venture among the Waterloo libraries. Liaison relationships can be quite beneficial to the information needs of educators in other ways too. For example, reference librarians at some universities are assigned liaison roles for particular academic departments or colleges. Often the liaison is a member of the college or school curriculum committees. This participation benefits both parties. It aids librarians through advance notice of new courses and changes in the curriculum; it aids the teaching faculty by the early connection between their changes in curriculum and available resources. For example, the SJSU College of Education recently developed a distance education program for secondary science and mathematics teachers. No provisions in the program plan were made for access to library and research materials except a course reader. Upon discussion with the library liaison, the Curriculum Committee and the program proposers were amazed to discover how much access and instruction the Library could provide in this area–despite the fact that the students would probably never come to the campus!

Reference librarians throughout academia are integrating e-mail and INTERNET resources into their repertoire of tools. Such technology and resources can easily be incorporated into liaison responsibilities. E-mail lists can be created for College of Education faculty, students in targeted courses, various school administrators and district personnel. Messages about new resources and services can be disseminated. Similarly, school and district information and questions could be relayed back to the academic liaisons, thus improving reference librarian knowledge about community resources. This *exchange* between librarians and educators encourages facilitation and cooperation between all players in the local education community–even academic librarians.

Broader facilitation could occur through other electronic avenues. Particularly good gopher sites, directories and files could be linked to local library gophers as well as details describing them such as the ERIC Clearinghouse on Assessment and Evaluation at the Catholic University of America. Contributions could be consistently submitted to present related electronic discussion groups or bulletin boards, or locally-mounted listservs could be created for discussion, instruction, and assistance of educators. With heightened interest in using and developing multimedia instructional materials, keeping educators abreast of image, sound and animation files available on the INTERNET for retrieval using MOSAIC or other software is important as well. Through the use of these emerging technologies, academic reference librarians could contribute not only to the information literacy of their local educators, but to educators anywhere in the world! Such assistance and "exposure" to the education community may very well lessen the likelihood that money making corporations will be viewed as the "only" experts or "information professionals" in the decades ahead; collaboration and outreach may well insure that academic reference librarians are "librarian-teachers" during future inservice workshops.

Such liaison activities may seem like pipe dreams to already overworked and stressed reference librarians. Much of the information disseminated to a new, broader clientele would need to be unearthed anyway in order to provide good traditional reference desk service. Emerging technologies allow broader distributions with minimal investment of time, supplies and money. The bottom line is that reference librarians, as information professionals, must play a role in ensuring the information literacy of the education community. Traditional methods and definitions of library clientele are no longer sufficient.

CONCLUSION

Learner centered instruction represents a major attitude change on the part of educators. The change will not happen overnight, and not all educators will immediately embrace it. Those who do will need more than their files of handouts, adopted textbooks, office collections and media sources–they will need information in order to tailor their instruction and professional endeavors to the individual needs of their students.

Experience has shown that educators often will not actively seek information in libraries no matter how strong the services or extensive the collections. Increasing efforts in remote access of information resources and human facilitation or coaching are strategies to explore in the years ahead. "The concept of off-hours, off-site availability of information will become the norm and more providers of information will seek methods of offering their indexes, abstracts and texts whenever, wherever and however users will require. The successful providers will be those who heed the need of the customer by offering the best service at the best cost in the best way."[16] Access is important, but quality, personalized human service is essential, too. Just ask American business.

Reference librarians in academic libraries cannot stay static or traditional in their services or outreach to educators. To do so is to run the risk of becoming a dinosaur in the next millennium! Instead, librarians must harness technology and its capabilities in order to move via "warp speed" to provide the information and literacy skills needed today by the next generation of American educators.

REFERENCES

1. "Students are introduced to Internet," *Tri-Valley Herald,* 20 February 1994, sec. A.

2. Patricia Vertinsky, "Information Source Utilization and Teachers' Attributes in Physical Education: A Preliminary Test of a Rational Paradigm," *Research Quarterly for Exercise and Sport,* 60 (September 1989): 268-279.

3. Mary Alice Anderson, "Information Skills for the 90s," *Book Report* 10 (November/December 1991): 30.

4. Priscilla C. Geahigan and George Geahigan, "Library Research: Answering the Information Needs of Art Teachers," *Art Education,* 35 (May 1982): 34-39.

5. Educational Resources Information Center, *REPORT: ERIC User Survey.* (Rockville, Maryland: ACCESS ERIC, 1991.) ERIC Microfiche Document ED349032.

6. Ibid., p. 5.

7. Lesley S. J. Farmer, *Creative Partnerships: Librarians and Teachers Working Together.* (Worthington, Ohio: Linworth Publishing, 1993).

8. Kris Mesicek, "Quality in the Teaching Professional and our Schools," *NCATE Quality Teaching,* 2 (Winter 1993): 8-9.

9. U.S. Department of Education. National Center for Education Statistics. *Digest of Education Statistics 1993* (Washington, DC: GPO, October 1993).

10. Jim Greco, "LEP Student Enrollment Up 6.3 Percent in 1993," *BEOutreach,* 5 (Spring 1994): 18-19.

11. R. M. Gagne, "Learning Outcomes, I" in *Encyclopedia of Psychology, Vol. 2, 2nd ed,* ed. Raymond J. Corsini (New York: John Wiley and Sons, 1994), 323-326.

12. Lyn Corno and Richard E. Snow, "Adapting Teaching to Individual Differences Among Learners," in *Handbook of Research on Teaching 3rd ed.,* ed. Merlin C. Wittrock (New York: Macmillan Publishing Co., 1986), 605-627.

13. Anderson, p. 30.

14. Educational Resources Information Center, p. vi.

15. Margaret Hendley, "Community Cooperation in Reference Service via a Librarians' Liaison Committee," *The Reference Librarian,* no. 33 (1991):191-205.

16. Ernest A. DiMattia, Jr., "Total quality management and servicing users through remote access technology," *The Electronic Library,* 11 (June 1993): 187-191.

Reference Accuracy

Loriene Roy

SUMMARY. This article explores aspects of accuracy as applied in a reference setting. Accuracy is defined in terms of correctness and precision as measured against some benchmark. Some factors that might influence accuracy are identified: education, attitude, reference setting, reference collection, the nature of the request, and the patron. Finally, some assumptions are presented that challenge the use of accuracy as a gauge of reference success. Accuracy will largely be discussed in the context of question answering rather than other facets of reference service, such as library use instruction or the creation of bibliographies.

INTRODUCTION

Reference service has been offered in American libraries since the nineteenth century yet it was not until the late 1960s that refer-

Loriene Roy is Associate Professor, Graduate School of Library and Information Science, The University of Texas at Austin, Austin, TX 78712-1276.

[Haworth co-indexing entry note]: "Reference Accuracy." Roy, Loriene. Co-published simultaneously in *The Reference Librarian* (The Haworth Press, Inc.) No. 49/50, 1995, pp. 217-227; and: *Library Users and Reference Services* (ed: Jo Bell Whitlatch) The Haworth Press, Inc., 1995, pp. 217-227. Multiple copies of this article/chapter may be purchased from The Haworth Document Delivery Center [1-800-3-HAWORTH; 9:00 a.m. - 5:00 p.m. (EST)].

ence librarians began to examine objectively their ability to answer patrons' queries[1,2] Up to this time, reference evaluation, the determination of the quality or goodness of reference service, was largely answered by indicators of traffic (the greater the number of questions posed, the better the service), self or patron assessment (the more confident the librarians felt in handling transactions or the greater the degree of satisfaction the patrons felt after a reference query, the better the service), or responses to scheduled testing situations (the greater the number of questions answered correctly on paper and pencil tests, the better the service). It was the results of unobtrusive testing that first indicated that there was a gap between librarians' impressions of reference provision and the verity of the responses they provided to even factual questions posed by patrons.[3] When unaware that their responses to simulated patron queries were being analyzed, reference librarians provided correct and complete answers to just over half of the questions.[4] Since the 1960s, replication studies have only confirmed these results.[5]

DEFINING AND MEASURING ACCURACY

The term accuracy suggests two concepts. The first is correctness: "freedom from mistake."[6] The second is precision as measured against truth or a recognized standard.[7] These definitions imply that accuracy can be measured.

ACCESSING CORRECTNESS

Childers reminds us that reference service is broader than the context of question answering and includes such activities as current awareness services and the creation of bibliographies.[8] When answers are requested, common practice and common sense indicate that it is difficult and, in some cases, impossible to provide an answer to all questions. For those questions that can be answered, there exist informal and formal approaches in defining accuracy. Informal approaches include unsolicited positive and negative verbal and nonverbal feedback from patrons or intuitive clues.[9] Formal approaches follow a planned schedule of events, the ultimate purpose of which is to assess accuracy and, hopefully, identify some factors that contribute to or reduce accuracy. In undertaking a formal approach to examining correctness, librarians may pursue qualitative and/or quantitative avenues.

While accuracy may be viewed as a continuum, quantitative approaches have been applied to measure the discrete quantity of truth within an answer. Measurements may be made on a variety of scales, such as a dichotomous (right or wrong) or a graded (50 percent accurate) scale.

Quantitative assessments of correctness may be based on a narrow definition of what constitutes a reference question; it is for this reason many reference evaluation studies are centered on answering questions with known factual answers. Once questions and their answers are known, the questions are posed to librarians and the answers they supply compared to the acceptable answer. Shades of correctness may be used. To qualify as correct, an answer might need to be not only completely match the known answer, but the librarian might be required to provide the patron with a reference to the source used to provide the answer.[10] The ratio of the number of questions answered correctly divided by the number of total questions asked is sometimes referred to as the correct-answer fill rate. Hernon supplies additional advice in measuring correct-answer fill rate and interpreting the results.[11]

Qualitative measurements of accuracy entail attaching a personal judgement to the reference result. Typically, user studies are used to gather qualitative data.[12,13] Hernon suggests another qualitative measure, that librarians study whether or not a relationship exists between some indicator of patron satisfaction and how important the patron perceives the anticipated answer to be.[14] Applegate reviews the research on user satisfaction in the literature of computer systems, library and information science, marketing, and clinical psychology.[15] She employs three scenarios to explain user satisfaction. The Material Satisfaction Mode is primarily used in evaluating reference sources, including online databases. Here, satisfaction is based on the ability of the source to retrieve items that are judged to be useful or valuable. A second scenario is labeled the Emotional Satisfaction Model–Simple Path. Patron satisfaction is measured when he or she responds directly or indirectly to one or a number of questions indicating happiness or unhappiness with the product of the reference encounter. In the third scenario, the Emotional Satisfaction Model–Multiple Path, a patron's assessment of a reference transaction is based on three sets of conditions: (1) those related to the patron's expectations of the librarian's response; (2) those related to the reference setting or policies associated with the provision of the reference service; and, (3) those associated with the actual end product or answer.

ASSESSING PRECISION

The Standards and Guidelines Committee of the Reference and Adult Services Division of the American Library Association prepared guidelines for librarians providing reference, outlining the responsibility of the library in terms of accuracy: "The Library should provide users with complete, accurate answers to their information queries regardless of the complexity of those queries."[16]

Librarians have not agreed on a level of reference accuracy that would denote an acceptable, base level of service.[17] Rather than striving for, and perhaps failing to achieve, a uniform high standard of precision for the wide range of questions that may be posed in a reference setting, librarians might do better to set varying levels of precision based on a taxonomy of types of reference questions.[18] For example, a given library may set as its goals the need to correctly answer 99 percent of all directional questions and 80 percent of all short answer-factual questions, with the provision that all reference encounters close with an appropriate and/or feedback loop.

FACTORS AFFECTING ACCURACY

While Aluri indicates that there is no known explanation for error in reference, a number of authors have investigated factors that may or may not impact accuracy.[19] Results from some of these studies are summarized as follows.[20]

Professional preparation and education may have a bearing on accuracy. Librarians in Whitlatch's study felt that when users succeeded in finding the information they needed, the librarians contributed to this successful outcome through their own subject related knowledge while the librarians' belief in the importance of suggesting alternative approaches to solving the problem, such as turning to resources outside the library, was a negative influence.[21] In gathering data on sixty-five variables that might affect scores on a reference test, Benham indicated that high scores were predicted by several factors, including their ability to name a number of sources that would correctly provide answers as well as the librarians' achievement on the quantitative portion of the Graduate Record Examination.[22]

Could additional training, such as introductory on-the-job training for new librarians or continuing education for all staff, improve performance? Kemp and Dillon promote collaborative efforts in the work environment.[23] The most cited result of a statewide unobtrusive test of reference service in Maryland public libraries was Gers and Seward's reminder to librarians to close a reference encounter with, "Does this answer your question?"[24] They found that this approach to inviting patrons to provide feedback increased the number of correct answers from 52 percent to 76 percent. Whitlatch found that both librarians and users indicated that success in locating information was tied to their ability to provide each other with appropriate feedback.[25]

Are there personal attributes that contribute or even predict whether or not a reference librarian might be able to provide accurate answers? There is mixed evidence regarding whether or not attitude affects reference results. Olszak indicated that one type of error librarians might make is to wrongfully assume a particular attitude, such as overconfidence or a dislike of the public, and associate it with their role as a reference librarian.[26] Elzy et al. found that perceived helpfulness and approachability, as rated by surrogate patrons, only slightly influenced accuracy.[27] Benham said attitude, defined as whether or not recent graduates of ALA-accredited master's programs found their reference work satisfying, was a moderate predictor of accuracy.[28]

Is there something in the nature of specific questions that

influences accuracy? Elzy et al. reported that accuracy was not tied to the difficulty level of the question asked.[29] Canadian public librarians indicated that they had difficulty using legal and medical sources and feared that they provided incorrect answers.[30]

How could the reference setting and/or local policies contribute to increased accuracy? Olszak differentiates between mistakes and failures.[31] Mistakes stem from individual error while failures result when the question or questioner is at odds with system frameworks such as library policies and occupational definitions of service. Instead of listing one or two tactics for improving success, some authors recommend changing the institutional milieu. Thus, the onus for failure falls not on the individual reference librarian but on the setting under which he or she operates. Durrance recommends alterations in the physical environment under which the reference encounter takes place.[32] Weech advocates a reference personnel performance evaluation program that draws from techniques online searchers have used to evaluate their results, especially the peer review process.[33] Nolan itemizes seven questions that librarians should answer in developing goals and objectives for local reference service.[34] Elzy et al., as well as Gers and Seward, found that the length of time spent on answering questions did not affect accuracy.[35]

Might the collection be developed in such a manner as to increase reference accuracy? Powell's findings point to a possible minimum and maximum collection size to provide reference service: librarians needed to have access to at least 800 volumes in reference before they could answer correctly at least half of the test questions Powell supplied, but reference accuracy actually declined after reference collections reached 3,500 or more volumes.[36] Benham, on the other hand, concluded that size of the collection was not as important a predictor of reference accuracy as were other variables.[37]

How might users influence reference accuracy? Patrons participating in Whitlatch's study in five academic libraries indicated that they contributed to accurate results when they made efficient use of their time with the reference librarian.[38] Their own familiarity with the subject was not an important factor influencing success in locating needed information.[39]

SHOULD ACCURACY BE USED AS A MEASURE OF USER SUCCESS?

Attending to accuracy focuses on the end result of a reference interaction, ignoring the events that led the patron to pose the question, how the librarian interpreted the query, the mental processes undertaken to arrive at a possible answer, and the complexities of communicating the results. Smith indicates that evaluation of reference service is necessarily complex because it is dependent upon individuals communicating with each other.[40] Whether or not accuracy is an appropriate measure of reference service is based on a number of assumptions. Each assumption presents a statement that, if taken as truth, serves to help define the reference function of a library. If not accepted as truth, these assumptions may serve as a rationale for altering, limiting, or discontinuing reference activity.

First is the assumption that librarians should continue to attempt to provide answers to reference questions. Nolan provides examples of reference service that are successful yet do not result in the provision of an answer.[41] Lester asks whether reference librarians provide clues, instead of answers, to patrons who then conduct their own searches for information.[42]

A second assumption is that accuracy can be determined and error detected. Olszak points out the difficulty in testing this assumption by providing two reasons why workers are reluctant to discuss occupational mistakes. It is often difficult to arrive at a consensus regarding error and, if workers openly discuss these mistakes, there is fear that their professional image may suffer. Additionally, colleagues are empathetic with peers who commit mistakes and are not apt to criticize others for errors they themselves might have made.[43] Weech suggests that researchers of reference service may be reluctant to investigate the individual librarian's role in reference out of concern for preserving privacy and observing the ethics of human subject research.[44]

Third, that someone else than the patron can understand the patron's need and assess the validity of the answer.[45] Lancaster differentiates between needs and demands: patrons may vocalize demands that may or may not be representations of their true needs.[46] Dervin proposes that little is known about how individuals need, create, and use information.[47]

Fourth, that librarians are, or should be, held accountable for improving accuracy rate.[48] While this appears to be a loaded question, Olszak points out that reference accuracy and completeness is but one goal of reference service that is sometimes in conflict with the need to satisfy other demands such as those of bibliographic instruction and efficient use of reference staff time.[49] Aluri recommends involving management with continuous reference accountability to chart and illustrate reference transactions through using quality control devices such as check sheets, control charts, Pareto charts, and cause and effect diagrams.[50]

Last, there is the assumption that patrons are concerned with accuracy. Are they interested, capable, and/or willing to evaluate the librarians' response? If yes, what will they do if the answer is found to be incomplete or incorrect? Even if correct, patrons may reject them if they do not conform to what Kelly terms the individual's personal constructs, an internal map or template against which new data are tested.[51] There is some evidence of false positives: some patrons are emotionally satisfied with the answer the librarian provides, even though the answer is faulty or incomplete.[52] In some cases, when such patrons are aware that the librarian's service is inadequate, they still report satisfaction and might justify the results.[53] Accuracy may not be the sole determinate of patron satisfaction. Usefulness of an answer may be a more appropriate assessment tool than accuracy in that usefulness incorporates both measures of quantity (degree of truth) and quality (patron perception of value).[54] Durrance defined success as the willingness of the patron to return to the staff member who provided assistance in the past.[55]

Hutchins, an early pioneer in education for reference librarians, indicated that librarians were motivated by two interests: "the desire to help other people" and "the desire to achieve success in the hunt."[56] Assessment of accuracy will provide one answer to whether or not a hunt by a librarian on behalf of a patron is indeed successful. Aluri eschews the use of the word error, preferring the phrase, "opportunity for improvement."[57]

Accuracy is a step in the diagnosis of where improvements might be needed. Accuracy helps arrive at answers to two questions in relation to the ability to provide correct reference services: What is possible? What is acceptable?

REFERENCES

1. Bunge, Charles A. "The Personal Touch: A Brief Overview of the Development of Reference Services in American Libraries." in *Reference Service: A Perspective,* edited by Sul H. Lee. Ann Arbor, Mich.: Pierian Press, 1983, p. 2.

2. Allen, Bryce. "Evaluation of Reference Services." in *Reference and Information Services: An Introduction,* edited by Richard E. Bopp and Linda C. Smith. Englewood, Colo.: Libraries Unlimited, 1991, p. 172.

3. Crowley, Terence and Childers, Thomas. *Information Service in Public Libraries: Two Studies.* Metuchen, NJ: Scarecrow Press, 1971.

4. A number of authors have criticized the methodology and results of unobtrusive reference evaluation. Childers, Thomas, "The Quality of Reference: Still Moot After 20 Years," *Journal of Academic Librarianship* 13 (May 1987): pp. 73-74. Douglas, Ian, "Reducing Failures in Reference Service," *RQ* 28 (Fall 1988): pp. 94-101. Durrance, Joan C., "Reference Success: Does the 55 Percent Rule Tell the Whole Story," *Library Journal* 114 (April 15, 1989): pp. 31-36.

5. For citations to other research studies employing unobtrusive testing see the bibliography in Douglas, pp. 94-101.

6. *Webster's New Collegiate Dictionary,* (1973), s.v. "accuracy."

7. Ibid.

8. Childers, p. 74.

9. Olszak noted that excessive time spent on a patron's question or repeat questions from a given patron were signals librarians reported using as indicators that they may have made a mistake. Olszak, Lydia, "Mistakes and Failures at the Reference Desk," *RQ* 31 (Fall 1991): pp. 42-43.

10. See, for example, the scoring used in the following studies. Elzy, Cheryl et al., "Evaluating Reference Service in a Large Academic Library," *College and Research Libraries* 52 (September 1991): p. 456. Gers, Ralph and Seward, Lillie J., "Improving Reference Performance: Results of a Statewide Study," *Library Journal* 110 (November 1, 1985): p. 32. Rodger, Eleanor Jo and Goodwin, Jane, "To See Ourselves as Others See Us: A Cooperative, Do-It-Yourself Reference Accuracy Study," *The Reference Librarian* 18 (Summer 1987): p. 141. Wallace, Danny P. "An Index of Quality of Illinois Public Library Service." in *Illinois Library Statistical Report Number 10,* Springfield, Ill: Illinois State Library, 1983, p. 38.

11. Hernon, Peter, "Utility Measures, Not Performance Measures, for Library Reference Service?" *RQ* 26 (Summer 1987): pp. 455-456.

12. Allen, p. 180.

13. See the following review article. Hewins, Elizabeth T. "Information Need and Use Studies." in *Annual Review of Information Science and Technology* 25 (1990): pp. 145-172.

14. Hernon, p. 457.

15. Applegate, Rachel, "Models of User Satisfaction: Understanding False Positives," *RQ* 32 (Summer 1993): pp. 525-539.

16. "Information Services for Information Consumers: Guidelines for Providers," *RQ* 30 (Winter 1990): p. 263.

17. Allen, p. 174. See his discussion of reference evaluation standards.

18. See the following article for a discussion of classifying reference questions. Childers, Thomas; Lopata, Cynthia; and Stafford, Brian, "Measuring the Difficulty of Reference Questions," *RQ* 31 (Winter 1991): pp. 237-243.

19. Aluri, Rao, "Improving Reference Service: The Case for Using a Continuous Quality Improvement Method," *RQ* 33 (Winter 1993): p. 225.

20. Other summaries of factors affecting accuracy are found in the following. Baker, Sharon L. and Lancaster, F. Wilfrid. *The Measurement and Evaluation of Library Services*. 2nd edition. Arlington, VA: Information Resources Press, 1991, pp. 247-260. Crews, Kenneth D., "The Accuracy of Reference Service: Variables for Research and Implementation," *Library and Information Science Research* 10 (1988): pp. 331-355. Lancaster, F. Wilfrid. *If You Want to Evaluate Your Library . . .*, Champaign, IL: University of Illinois, Graduate School of Library and Information Science, 1988, pp. 115-124. Lester, Ray, "Clues or Answers? Which Response to Library Users' Questions?" *The Reference Librarian* 10 (Spring/Summer 1984): pp. 85-92. Powell, Ronald, D., "Reference Effectiveness: A Review of the Literature," *Library and Information Science Research* 6 (1984): pp. 3-19. Weech, Terry L., "Who's Giving All Those Wrong Answers?, Direct Service and Reference Personnel Evaluation," *The Reference Librarian* 11 (Fall/Winter 1984): pp. 112-115.

21. Whitlatch, Jo Bell, "Reference Service Effectiveness," *RQ* 30 (Winter 1990): pp. 211, 213, 218.

22. Benham, Frances and Powell, Ronald R. *Success in Answering Reference Questions: Two Studies*, Metuchen, NJ; London: Scarecrow, 1987, 139, 170.

23. Kemp, Jan and Dillon, Dennis, "Collaboration and the Accuracy Imperative: Improving Reference Service Now," *RQ* 29 (Fall 1989): pp. 62-70.

24. Gers and Seward, p. 34.

25. Whitlatch, p. 211.

26. Olszak, pp. 45-46.

27. Elzy and others, pp. 458-459, 462.

28. Benham and Powell, p. 139.

29. Elzy and others, pp. 463.

30. Dewdney, Patricia; Marshall, Joanne G.; and Tiamiyu, Muta, "A Comparison of Legal and Health Information Services in Public Libraries," *RQ* 31 (Winter 1991), 185-196.

31. Olszak, p. 41.

32. Durrance, pp. 31-36.

33. Weech, p. 120.

34. Nolan, Christopher W., "Closing the Reference Interview: Implications for Policy and Practice," *RQ* 31 (Summer 1992), pp. 518-519.

35. Elzy and others, p. 461. Gers and Seward, p. 33.

36. Benham and Powell, pp. 222, 257.

37. Ibid., p. 170.

38. Whitlatch, pp. 212, 213.

39. Ibid., pp. 212, 213.

40. Smith, Lisa L., "Evaluating the Reference Interview: A Theoretical Discussion of the Desirability and Achievability of Evaluation," *RQ* 31 (Fall 1991): pp. 77-78.

41. Nolan, p. 513.

42. Lester, "Clues or Answers?"

43. Olszak, p. 39.

44. Weech, p. 110.

45. Lester.

46. Lancaster, pp. 11-12.

47. Dervin, Brenda, "Strategies for Dealing with Human Information Needs: Information or Communication?" *Journal of Broadcasting* 20 (Summer 1976): pp. 332-333.

48. See the following citation for a discussion of the need for reference librarians to be accountable for general knowledge. D'Aniello, Charles A., "Cultural Literacy and Reference Service," *RQ* 28 (Spring 1989), pp. 370-380.

49. Olszak, p. 47.

50. Aluri, pp. 226-232.

51. Kelly, George A. *A Theory of Personality: Psychology of Personal Constructs.* New York: Norton Library, 1955.

52. Applegate, p. 532.

53. This statement is based on the author's experience while conducting two of five statewide unobtrusive tests of reference service in public libraries in Illinois. Pretest results were reported in Weech, Terry L. and Goldhor, Herbert, "Obtrusive versus Unobtrusive Evaluation of Reference Service in Five Illinois Public Libraries: A Pilot Study," *Library Quarterly* 52 (1982), pp. 305-324. Yearly results and other analyses were reported in Drone, Jeanette M., "An Index of Quality of Illinois Public Library Service, 1986," in *Illinois Library Statistical Report Number 22,* Springfield, IL: Illinois State Library, 1987. Roy, Loriene, "An Index of Quality of Illinois Public Library Service, 1984," in *Illinois Library Statistical Report Number 17,* Springfield, IL: Illinois State Library, 1985. Roy, Loriene, "An Index of Quality of Illinois Public Library Service, 1985," in *Illinois Library Statistical Report Number 20,* Springfield, IL: Illinois State Library, 1985. Roy, Loriene, "An Index of Quality of Rural Illinois Public Library Service," *ERIC* ED 337 171, 1991. Wallace, "An Index of Quality." Wallace, Danny P., "An Index of Quality of Illinois Public Library Service, 1983," in *Illinois Library Statistical Report Number 14,* Springfield, IL: Illinois State Library, 1984.

54. For example, in their study of how librarians view reference interviews, Michell and Harris asked the question, "How Confident Would You Be about Getting a Useful Answer to Your Reference Question from This Librarian?" Michell, Gillian and Harris, Roma M., "Evaluating the Reference Interview: Some Factors Influencing Patrons and Professionals," *RQ* 27 (Fall 1987), p. 101.

55. Durrance, p. 32.

56. Margaret Hutchins, quoted in Grogan, Denis, *Practical Reference Work,* London: Clive Bingley, 1979, p. 109.

57. Aluri, p. 225.

Evaluation of Reference Service
by User Report of Success

Marjorie E. Murfin

SUMMARY. The history of user evaluation of reference service is traced and related to other methods of reference evaluation, including librarian self-report of success, behavioral guidelines, and unobtrusive observation. Presently available user-report instruments are considered in light of criteria for a reference evaluation instrument. It is concluded that reference success can't be explained by any one group of factors, and that the best evaluation will utilize multiple methods.

BACKGROUND

If we look back over the history of user assessment of reference desk service, we can identify, in retrospect, a number of important turning points. In 1967, reference service had reached a pinnacle. As Rothstein wrote, studies of feedback from patrons reported 80-90% of patrons were satisfied. He noted that results could not have been bettered if we paid for testimonials.[1] By 1980, the situation had changed so dramatically that at a conference on library evaluation, a story was told by the speaker about the three greatest lies, one of which was, "I'm a reference librarian and I'm here to

Marjorie E. Murfin is Associate Professor and Reference Librarian, Information Services Department, Ohio State University Libraries, 1858 Neil Avenue Mall, Columbus, OH 43210.

[Haworth co-indexing entry note]: "Evaluation of Reference Service by User Report of Success." Murfin, Marjorie E. Co-published simultaneously in *The Reference Librarian* (The Haworth Press, Inc.) No. 49/50, 1995, pp. 229-241; and: *Library Users and Reference Services* (ed: Jo Bell Whitlatch) The Haworth Press, Inc., 1995, pp. 229-241. Multiple copies of this article/chapter may be purchased from The Haworth Document Delivery Center [1-800-3-HAWORTH; 9:00 a.m. - 5:00 p.m. (EST)].

help you."[2] What happened between 1967 and 1980 to shift opinion so strikingly in regard to reference desk service?

In the early 1970s, unobtrusive observation began to suggest that reference librarians in public libraries were only about 50-55% successful on factual questions.[3] More of the same followed swiftly when results were extended to academic libraries and a carefully researched study again showed a 50% success on factual questions.[4] In-person unobtrusive-observation studies began to be done, also with findings of 50-55%.[5] Articles began to be written about "half-right" reference service and the "age of misinformation."[6]

As a result of this puzzling discrepancy between user report and results of unobtrusive observation, confidence in user report studies dropped to a new low. Since it appeared that user ratings were considerably inflated, the general opinion came to be that users allowed their gratitude for the reference librarian's help to influence their rating and that consequently users were not able to make critical judgments on the quality of service they had received.[7] As the financial crunch tightened budgets even further and demands for accountability mounted, unobtrusive observation, formerly used as a research method, gained wider acceptance and began to be used for evaluation of individual libraries,[8] and finally even for evaluation of individual reference librarians.[9]

However, in the 1980s a number of researchers began supplying missing bits of information, that when put together like the pieces of a puzzle, suggested strongly that the inflated user ratings of the past were caused *not* by the users' lack of critical judgment but by imprecise and inadequately formulated measurement instruments. These instruments generally did not employ known techniques for control for positive bias[10] nor separate success from satisfaction.[11] Along with these findings came improvements in design of scales and the separation of reported success in finding what was wanted, from satisfaction with the service. These were important advances.[12] Studies of user success in finding what was wanted began to obtain results corresponding to those previously obtained by unobtrusive observation. This gave evidence of construct validity[13] and in addition, results demonstrated reliability.[14]

ADVANTAGES OF THE USER REPORT METHODOLOGY

As user report of success came to be regarded again as a viable method, its advantages as one important method of reference evaluation came to be realized:

There Is No Substitute for User Report of Success

User report of success is the essential component of outcome. Most experts had previously agreed, in spite of their concern over seemingly inflated user ratings, that user input should be an essential dimension of evaluation of reference service. As Tagliacozzo noted, "Perhaps we will never be able to determine what the real information needs of the users are and should therefore content ourselves with what the users believe–and tell us–that they are."[15] Lancaster defines effectiveness as "to what extent a service satisfies its user's demands."[16]

No matter how excellent the materials appear to be, or how helpful the librarian, if the user can't understand or utilize the materials or if they aren't exactly right for his/her particular purpose, then the outcome of the transaction can't be said to be successful. The user's complex pattern of needs, motivation, abilities, and personal situation are seldom all expressed in the reference interaction and can probably never be grasped in their entirety by the librarian.

Librarian Report of Success Will Not Substitute for User Report

It has been shown that librarians simply don't receive sufficient feedback to judge outcome at a high enough level. For example, Whitlatch found that on 22% of transactions little or very little feedback was received from the user.[17] Latest results from the Wisconsin-Ohio Reference Evaluation Program indicate that lack of user feedback was associated with lower success.

It is also difficult to be objective in judging the outcome of one's own performance. Results of the Wisconsin-Ohio Reference Evaluation Program indicate that when the librarian marked that the answer was found, the patron agreed 70% of the time in academic libraries and 74% of the time in public libraries. However, while this was the average, ability of individual reference departments to judge outcome correctly, varied greatly from 41% to 85% in academic libraries and from 52% to 94% in public libraries. Of 7 academic libraries scoring 50% or below in success, only one correctly identified itself at that level. Of 4 public libraries scoring 50% or below in success, one correctly identified themselves at that level.[18] For the above reasons, it appears that while feedback from the librarian is extremely useful for many purposes, the final judgment of success in finding what was wanted, should come from the user.

Behavioral Guidelines Will Not Substitute for User Report

Most reference behaviors, with a few exceptions, have not been shown by research to affect success of outcome, therefore user report methods are still necessary. Lists of desirable reference behaviors are commonly used as a method to guide staff toward more effective reference service. However, in many cases, there is no research basis for the assumption that these behaviors will assure effective service with real patrons and real questions. Unfortunately, there is seldom a perfect relationship between a list of specified reference behaviors and success of outcome. In the case of certain behaviors, there may be no relationship at all or even a negative relationship.

A certain list of prescribed behaviors/actions may not be appropriate for all situations or all patrons. Behaviors and guidelines for actions, if adhered to rigidly in all situations, may actually inhibit teamwork, lower morale and motivation, and have the end result of reducing rather than enhancing quality. This has been demonstrated, for example, with basketball teams and air defense surveillance teams. An emphasis on procedures over outcome, has caused the Joint Commission on Hospital Accreditation to be rejected by New York and California.[19] Myers, in an unobtrusive study of reference accuracy, found that some guidelines for reference service actually correlated negatively with reference accuracy.[20] Whitlatch found that an emphasis on a particular procedure was related to a lowered measure of quality.[21] These findings were not expected.

Of four libraries using the behavioral guidelines method of evaluation before participating in the Wisconsin-Ohio Reference Evaluation Program, three had lower than average success and one higher. Indications from other fields such as teaching, are that assumptions should not be made that *all* seemingly desirable behaviors are related to outcome.[22] Measurement experts caution about inferring outcome from this type of behavioral checklist. Kantor warns of a focus on behavioral guidelines as opposed to outcome evaluation.[23] Teacher evaluation has been by use of behavioral checklists and teachers have objected to this method strongly on grounds of unfairness due to lack of correspondence of behaviors to quality of outcome.[24]

The above evidence seems to indicate that behavioral guidelines should be used with care. Important concerns should be flexibility, teamwork, morale, and quality of outcome. Behavioral guidelines should be solidly based on research but only a few behaviors have been shown by research to be associated with success of outcome. These behaviors are: (1) obtaining feedback by follow-up, that is, asking the user at a later time if what was wanted was actually found; (2) going with the patron and helping with the search rather than directing; and (3) rephrasing of the user's question to pinpoint exactly what is wanted. A factor seemingly composed of librarian motivation/morale has also been indicated,[25] but this quality, in and of itself, is not a behavior and cannot be prescribed in lists of effective behaviors. It may be that motivation is as important to success as a particular group of behaviors.

These three behavioral factors appear to have solid research support. The asking for feedback has particularly strong research support from three sources: two studies by Gers and Seward, the research of Whitlatch, and the Wisconsin-Ohio Reference Evaluation Program. Gers and Seward twice found it to be significantly related to success of outcome.[26] Whitlatch found *both* the patron's report of giving feedback and the librarian's report of receiving it, to be significantly related to success of outcome.[27] The top-scoring Ohio public library in the Wisconsin-Ohio Program, when asked about its reference service, volunteered that one of its practices was that staff regularly sought feedback from patrons. Also, Wisconsin-Ohio Program results indicate that libraries who reported a high percentage of reference transactions with no feedback, (that is they reported "don't know" when asked whether the patron had found what was wanted) tended to have considerably lower success scores. This was significant at the .000 level.[28] On the basis of these results, we can say that the positive effect of this particular behavior, seeking of feedback, is well-supported by present research.

The second behavior, searching rather than directing, is supported by the first study of Gers and Seward and by Wisconsin-Ohio results. The first study found it to be related to success.[29] Wisconsin-Ohio results indicated that overall, academic libraries lost 16 percentage points of success when directing as compared to searching. Large academic libraries lost 19 percentage points of success when directing. Public libraries lost 7 percentage points of success when directing rather than searching.[30]

The last behavior, rephrasing of the question, is supported by communication research and has been found to be significantly related to success by Gers and Seward.[31] It is logical that understanding the question would be essential for success, and it is likely that the association of this particular behavior with success will be supported by further research.

However, we still do not know how important these behavioral factors are in determining outcome or how much improvement may be expected when they are practiced. One library practiced all the behavioral guidelines as outlined by Gers and Seward but did not improve its success score.[32]

Are the three research-supported guidelines mentioned above, for example, more important in determining outcome than: (1) skill and knowledge; (2) reference collection; (3) motivation and morale; and (4) environmental factors? All of the above have also been associated with success of the reference outcome. Whitlatch found that when librarians had more knowledge of the subject matter of the user's question, success of outcome was greater. In a preliminary study, Lowenthal found higher levels of reference department morale to be associated with greater success. Powell found larger reference collection sizes to be associated with increased success. The Wisconsin-Ohio Program and Whitlatch have found poor environmental conditions to be associated with failure.[33]

Even if some behaviors can be shown to be related to success of outcome, conditions outside the control of the reference librarian can prevent those behaviors from being carried out. This can be illustrated in the case of libraries where reference service points are not adequately staffed to handle the volume of patron requests. In such environments helping with the search and subsequent follow-up is simply not possible in all cases. Restating the question should usually be possible.

However, use of this method for *inferring the outcome* of reference service, assumes that *only librarian behavior* affects success or failure of a reference transaction. It is increasingly being shown that factors outside the control of individual reference librarians affect success of outcome, including volume of business, level of staffing, and books off the shelf. The Wisconsin-Ohio Program has found that when librarians report that books needed were off the shelf, success was 48% and when books in another area were needed, success was 45%. Librarians in academic libraries overall lost 11 points of success when busy and those in large libraries lost 20 percentage points of success. Public libraries lost 10 percentage points of success when busy. Whitlatch, in an analysis of 17 failed reference transactions, found that 64% of the failures were associated with library system failures that were beyond the control of individual reference librarians.[34]

Unobtrusive Observation Will Not Substitute for User Report

An excellent critique of this method, when used as an evaluation tool rather than a research method, has been written.[35] Some of the difficulties with this method are that it lacks content validity since the questions may not be representative of a library's actual questions, and nonfactual questions are omitted or are not well represented. The most recent Wisconsin-Ohio results indicate that factual questions represent, for academic libraries 21%, and for public libraries 18% of all in-person reference questions. These results, based on 9,779 transactions in 121 public libraries and 6,925 transactions in 71 academic libraries, indicate that factual questions represent less than one-fourth of all in-person reference questions.

Some libraries, who have evaluated their reference service by user report in the Wisconsin-Ohio Reference Evaluation Program, had previously used the method of unobtrusive observation. Results suggest that it is possible that sometimes the questions used are less difficult than the actual questions users bring to the reference desk. In addition, the criteria of accuracy may not be "the single crucial key to success," where there is only one acceptable answer.[36] Facts may be being compiled for purposes of illustration, to test computer programs, to carry out exercises, to acquaint students with tools, to support arguments, etc.

Also, accuracy of answer is often not possible when respected sources differ. In addition, unobtrusive observation methodology has a number of problems two of which are that proxies generally do not have the same motivations as real patrons, and that the method fails to take account of environmental factors. This last is particularly serious, since, as Maslach says, "When the brunt of blame is carried by the helper, blaming allows the contribution of the situation to be either minimized or ignored. If the appropriate situational causes are not recognized or appreciated, we can be sure that attempted solutions will be misguided or incomplete."[37] A study for Stanford University on sources of teacher effectiveness suggests that "organizational conditions more than any lack of expertise in teaching, impaired the efficiency of teachers. Much of the variance in outcome is due to factors other than the quality of teaching."[38]

Finally, accuracy of answer as the primary measure of success may result in unintended negative effects. Stress on accuracy to the exclusion of all other values may cause fewer questions to be attempted, since, technically, if the reference librarian does not attempt the question, he/she cannot be termed inaccurate. It may also affect the way in which reference work is done by more attention being paid to requests for facts arriving by telephone, than to in-person nonfactual reference questions, which are less easy to evaluate by this method.

This Methodology Has Content Validity

The user report methodology has content validity because it represents the actual work being done in the natural setting with a library's own patrons and questions. Also, nonfactual as well as factual questions can be evaluated.

This Methodology Can Easily Take Environmental Factors into Account

If librarian feedback is obtained along with user feedback, a variety of other factors can be taken into account, such as being busy, books off the shelf, weaknesses in the collection, etc. This makes it possible to suggest possible links between cause and effect. In this way areas for possible improvement can be identified.

Ethical Concerns Are Generally Not a Problem

The ethical questions raised concerning unobtrusive observation are not a problem with this method. Staff generally consider it to be a more fair method for judging the outcome of reference desk service.

DISADVANTAGES OF USER REPORT OF SUCCESS METHODOLOGY

Do-it-yourself construction of reference surveys has many problems and pitfalls. The problems of designing a reference evaluation survey, carrying it out, analyzing data, and interpreting results, are great. A danger is that scales will not be designed so as to be reliable or give evidence of validity. Inflated ratings may not be properly controlled by scale design. Also, data will not be comparable with that of any other reference department and interpretation will be difficult. However, these problems can be minimized by using an established instrument.

Telephone reference service is less easily evaluated by this method. Telephone service, however, *can* be evaluated by calling telephone reference users back after an interval, and asking them the same questions as were asked of in-person reference users. Analysis and interpretation must be done with great care. Since the natural reference situation is not controlled, as in unobtrusive observation, confounding factors can cancel each other out. Careful in-depth analysis must be done to disentangle effects of these factors, for example, by looking at libraries by size groups.

Comparisons to other libraries should be made carefully. Reference department performance cannot be compared as precisely as in unobtrusive observation where the same set of questions is used for all libraries. When comparing the performance of libraries in terms of their patrons' reports of success, it should be realized that the terms of the comparison are how well each library does *with its own patrons and questions* rather than how well they would both do with the *same set* of patrons and questions.

Results do not show how well each question *could* have been answered in terms of the best possible information/materials. This is another dimension of reference evaluation which must be left to the methodology of expert observation by an reference consultant. Another useful way might be for a reference department to work together to answer a sample set of test questions.

CRITERIA FOR AN INSTRUMENT FOR EVALUATING REFERENCE SERVICE FROM THE USER POINT OF VIEW

The first criterion for an assessment instrument should be that it demonstrates reliability and gives evidence of validity. The Wisconsin-Ohio reference transaction assessment instrument meets this criterion.[39] The scales in the instrument used by Whitlatch have also been tested for reliability.[40] One other instrument, by Mary Goulding, using the user-report-of-success method has not yet reported on reliability tests, however, it has similar features of design.

Other important criteria are that the instrument should:

1. Assess multiple factors in the reference process taking account of the environment as much as possible
2. Obtain both patron and librarian feedback for each transaction
3. Provide for comparability of data
4. Provide for interpretability
5. Separate success in finding what was wanted from satisfaction
6. Control for positive bias in scale design
7. Control for positive bias in procedures for administration of survey.

The Wisconsin-Ohio Reference Transaction Assessment Instrument is designed to be used with both public and academic libraries. It obtains both patron and librarian feedback as to the outcome of each reference transaction, along with much other information. Norms for other libraries of the same size and type are provided for each score.[41]

An academic library reference transaction evaluation instrument designed by Jo Bell Whitlatch also obtains both patron and librarian feedback. The librarian form explores some aspects not covered by the Wisconsin-Ohio Program including the librarian's opinion of whether there was enough time for the reference interview, librarian's familiarity with the question, familiarity with resources in this area, how frequently the librarian had used the resources before, whether the question involved a new type of problem, and whether they had responded to a similar question before, and how active a role the user played in resolving the information need.[42]

Another instrument designed for public libraries by Mary Goulding also obtains both patron and librarian feedback about each transaction. The success and satisfaction questions are comparable to those on the Wisconsin-Ohio forms.[43]

CONCLUSION

It is clear that reference success cannot be explained by any one single group of factors, either behavioral, motivational, skill-related, or environmental. Instead, success is probably a product of all of these factors. It is also clear that user report of success is an essential method for determining the reference outcome. The best evaluation, however, will utilize carefully chosen multiple methods to add to understanding of cause and effect.

REFERENCES

1. Samuel Rothstein, "The Measurement and Evaluation of Reference Service," *Library Trends* 12:464 (January, 1964).

2. Janine Schmidt, Comments at presentation titled "Evaluation of Reference Service in College Libraries in New South Wales, Australia," at the ALA Precon-

ference on Library Effectiveness, New York, June, 1980. Study published in *Library Effectiveness: A State of the Art,* Chicago, American Library Association, 1980, p. 265-289.

3. Kenneth D. Crews, "The Accuracy of Reference Service: Variables for Research and Implementation," *Library and Information Science Research* 10:331-355 (1988).

4. Marcia J. Myers, *The Accuracy of Telephone Reference/Information Services in Academic Libraries: Two Studies.* N.J., Scarecrow, 1983.

5. Schmidt, "Evaluation of Reference Service . . . "; Ralph Gers and Lillie Seward, "Improving Reference Performance: Results of a Statewide Survey," *Library Journal* 110:32-35 (November 1, 1985).

6. Terence Crowley, "Half-Right Reference: Is It True?" *RQ* 25:59-68 (Fall 1985). Alvin Schrader, "Performance Standards for Accuracy in Reference and Information Service: The Impact of Unobtrusive Measurement Methodology," *The Reference Librarian* 11:210 (Fall/Winter 1984).

7. Young, William F., "Evaluating the Reference Librarian," *The Reference Librarian* 11:124 (Fall/Winter 1984).

8. Crews, "Accuracy of Reference Service . . ."

9. Cheryl Asper Elzy; Alan Nourie; F. Wilfrid Lancaster, "Evaluating Reference Service in a Large Academic Library," *College & Research Libraries* 52:454-65 (September 1991).

10. L. J. Cronbach, "Further Evidence on Response Sets and Test Design," *Educational and Psychological Measurement* 10, no. 1:4-5, 22-23, 1950.

11. Helen Gothberg, "Immediacy: A Study of Communication Effect on the Reference Process," *Journal of Academic Librarianship* 2:128 (July 1986).

12. For a fuller discussion of this see: Marjorie E. Murfin and Gary M. Gugelchuk, "Development and Testing of a Reference Transaction Assessment Instrument," *College & Research Libraries* 48:317-319 (July 1987).

13. Murfin and Gugelchuk, "Development and Testing . . ." p. 329; Jo Bell Whitlatch, "Unobtrusive Studies and the Quality of Academic Library Reference Services," *College & Research Libraries,*" 50:190-191 (March 1989).

14. Murfin and Gugelchuk, "Development and Testing . . . " p. 329. Jo Bell Whitlatch, "Reference Service Effectiveness," *RQ* 30:216-220 (Winter 1990).

15. Renata Tagliacozzo, "Estimating the Satisfaction of Information Users," *Bulletin of the Medical Library Association,* 65:243 (April 1977).

16. F. W. Lancaster. *The Measurement and Evaluation of Library Services* (Washington, D.C., Information Resources, 1977), p. 1.

17. Jo Bell Whitlatch, "Client/Service Provider Perceptions of Reference Service Outcomes in Academic Libraries: Effects of Feedback and Uncertainty" (Ph.D. dissertation, University of California, Berkeley, 1987).

18. Marjorie Murfin and Charles Bunge, Unpublished data from the Wisconsin-Ohio Reference Evaluation Program.

19. *Wall Street Journal,* Wednesday, Oct. 12, 1988, p. 1.

20. Myers, *The Accuracy of Telephone Reference/Information. . . ,* p. 88.

21. Whitlatch, "Reference Service Effectiveness," p. 213.

22. Patricia Duttweiler and Maria Ramos-Cancel, *Perspectives on Performance-Based Incentive Plans* (Austin, Texas: Southwest Educational Development Labs., 1986), p. 42-51. ED272511.

23. Letter from Paul Kantor to ACRL Committee on Performance Measures, January 25, 1987.

24. Duttweiler and Ramos-Cancel, *Perspectives* ... , p. 27.

25. Ralph Lowenthal, "Preliminary Indications of the Relationship Between Reference Morale and Performance," *RQ* 29:380-393 (Spring 1990).

26. Gers and Seward, "Improving Reference Performance ... ," p. 32; Lillie Seward Dyson, "Improving Reference Services: A Maryland Training Program Brings Positive Results," *Public Libraries* 31:287 (September/October 1992).

27. Whitlatch, "Reference Service Effectiveness," p. 212.

28. Murfin and Bunge, Wisconsin-Ohio ... Unpublished data.

29. Ralph Gers and Lillie J. Seward, "Improving Reference Performance ..." p. 32

30. Murfin and Bunge, Unpublished Data.

31. Dyson, "Improving Reference Services ... ," p. 287.

32. Isenstein, Laura J. "On the Road to Stardom: Improving Reference Accuracy," *Illinois Libraries* 22:245-260 (1988).

33. Whitlatch, "Reference Service Effectiveness," p. 212. Lowenthal, "Preliminary Indications."; Ronald R. Powell, "An Investigation of the Relationship Between Reference Collection Size and Other Reference Service Factors and Success in Answering Reference Questions," In Frances Benham and Ronald R. Powell, *Success in Answering Reference Questions: Two Studies,* (Metuchen, N.J.: Scarecrow Press, 1987), p. 221; For references on the effect of environmental factors, See Footnote 34.

34. Murfin and Bunge, Unpublished Data; Whitlatch, "Reference Service Effectiveness," p. 211-212.

35. Whitlatch, "Unobtrusive Studies ... "181-194.

36. Joan Durrance, "Reference Success: Does the 55% Rule Tell the Whole Story?" *Library Journal* 114:31-36 (April 15, 1989), p. 35.

37. Christina Maslach. *Burnout: The Cost of Caring* (Englewood Cliffs, N.J.: Prentice-Hall, 1982), p.14, 20.

38. Duttweiler, *Perspectives* ... , p. 27.

39. Murfin and Gugelchuk, "Development and Testing ...", p. 322-331.

40. Whitlatch, "Reference Service Effectiveness ..." p. 216-220.

41. For further information, on the Wisconsin-Ohio Reference Evaluation Program, contact Charles Bunge at the School of Library and Information Studies, University of Wisconsin at Madison.

42. Whitlatch, "Client/Service Provider Perceptions ..."

43. Mary Goulding, *Reference Evaluation Manual for Public Libraries.* Suburban Library System Reference Service, c/o Oak Lawn Public Library, 9444 South Cook Ave. Oak Lawn, Ill.

Factors That Influence Reference Success: What Makes Questioners Willing to Return?

Joan C. Durrance

SUMMARY. Willingness to return to the same librarian at another time avoids the limitations associated with using accuracy as primary measure of success. Based on findings from the Willingness to Return Study, the article examines a variety of factors associated with the successful reference interaction.

DEFINITIONS OF REFERENCE SUCCESS

Robert Taylor's seminal 1968 article described the reference interview as "one of the most complex acts of human communication . . . [in which] one person tries to describe for another person not something he knows, but rather something he does not know" (Taylor, p. 180). Ross and Dewdney define reference as "a conversation between the librarian and the user in which the librarian asks one or more questions (a) in order to get a clearer and more complete picture of what the user wants to know, and (b) to link the user to the system" (Ross and Dewdney 1989, p. 108). When measuring reference success, therefore, one should focus on assessing

Joan C. Durrance is Associate Professor, School of Information & Library Studies, University of Michigan.

[Haworth co-indexing entry note]: "Factors That Influence Reference Success: What Makes Questioners Willing to Return?" Durrance, Joan C. Co-published simultaneously in *The Reference Librarian* (The Haworth Press, Inc.) No. 49/50, 1995, pp. 243-265; and: *Library Users and Reference Services* (ed: Jo Bell Whitlatch) The Haworth Press, Inc., 1995, pp. 243-265. Multiple copies of this article/chapter may be purchased from The Haworth Document Delivery Center [1-800-3-HAWORTH; 9:00 a.m. - 5:00 p.m. (EST)].

the quality of the interaction. "The interaction process is at the heart of the communication act . . . and thus central to the study of the reference encounter" (Whitlatch 1990, p. 47).

However, since the 1970s most library researchers have measured this complex interaction by focusing on only one aspect–the accuracy of question answering. Library researchers in the past quarter century have, for the most part, emulated the social sciences and therefore used the positivist model of research which requires researchers to design studies which can be carried out under controlled conditions. In most unobtrusive studies of reference, often tricky questions whose answers and methods of retrieval are known, are administered to librarians without their knowledge (Crowley and Childers, 1971; Hernon & McClure, 1986; Hernon and McClure, 1987).

PROBLEMS WITH USING ACCURACY AS THE MEASURE OF REFERENCE SUCCESS

Unobtrusive researchers found such a consistently similar reference performance that a decade ago. Hernon and McClure coined the phrase, "the 55% rule" to describe the performance of reference librarians (Hernon & McClure 1986). There are a number of problems associated linking success and accurate answers; several researchers have identified them (Whitlatch, 1990; Durrance, 1989; Durrance 1991). The unstated assumption behind accuracy as the measure of reference success is that librarians are in the question answering business, since accuracy focuses only on one outcome of a reference interview–a correctly answered question. If accuracy is the measure of reference success, then all questions have answers and librarians who do not answer a question correctly have failed. Reference, however, is not a unidimensional activity. It is, as Taylor described, a complex interpersonal interaction. Although interpersonal attributes have been linked with question accuracy, they are far more important to the reference interaction than just improving accuracy.

Measures of reference success need to encompass the other dimensions of reference success. Knowing that librarians have a 55% success rate at answering posed questions accurately fails to determine how "user-friendly" librarians are, nor does it tell librarians how well they are able to refer questioners to appropriate sources. The accuracy rate cannot be used to measure how successfully librarians instruct users in the use of reference resources, nor does it give librarians a tool to examine how successfully they field problem related questions (such as those which result from the need to write a term paper, research a consumer product, find out about a particular career, or contribute to the solution to a community problem).

Several fine articles and a national training campaign have been based on assumption that reference success means answering questions accurately (see Isenstein, 1992; Dyson, 1992; Gers & Seward 1985). These otherwise strong articles identify sound model reference behaviors, but relate these behaviors to providing correct answers to questions. Programs have been built around improving accuracy, which reinforces the assumption that all question have answers (Library Video Network, 1992). In sum, these efforts have chosen an appropriate set of behaviors to foster, but the findings can only appropriately be applied to question answering and not to other possible outcomes of the reference interview such as instruction, advising, or assistance in problem-solving (see Kuhlthau 1993; and Durrance 1994 for discussions of professional practice).

THE WILLINGNESS TO RETURN REFERENCE STUDY

This article is based on data from the Willingness to Return Study that I have conducted using unobtrusive methodology since 1986. The measure used in the ongoing Willingness to Return Study is to determine if the person who asks the question would return to that same staff member with another question at a later time. This measure avoids the limitations associated with using accuracy as the primary measure of success. It is supplemented by findings from a Kellogg-funded study of professional practice at job and career information centers in several states which I conducted from 1988-93 (Durrance, 1993b; Durrance 1989). Every semester each of 35 students in a class whose focus is on access factors observes two reference interactions as part of the Willingness to Return Study. Based on Dewdney's findings that most reference questions asked by patrons start with a general questions such as "Where are your books on?" or "Do you have information on?" observers in the Willingness to Return Study begin their questions in a similar manner; all initial questions to librarians expect library staff to engage in some kind of reference interview which will determine more precisely what the questioner seeks (Dewdney, 1986).

This study examines a variety of factors associated with the successful reference interaction. Each student asks a question, observes staff behavior, fills out a reference observation instrument, and writes a report on the experience. During the life of the study over 1200 interviews in public and academic libraries in a number of states have been observed. Periodically the instrument is modified to incorporate the results from previous iterations as well as the findings of other researchers. The majority of observations have been in medium sized and large public libraries. The current study (as of March 1994) includes 486 interviews conducted in public and academic libraries.

WILLINGNESS TO RETURN AS A MEASURE OF REFERENCE SUCCESS

Willingness to return to the same librarian at another time is a flexible measure of success. It takes into account the different kinds of outcomes which can be expected from a reference interaction and it incorporates the needs of the questioner into the evaluation. This measure and the extensive information provided by the instrument used to collect data for the Willingness to Return Study provide a great deal of information about a variety of factors which contribute to reference success. The sections below examine factors which influence the success of this complex interaction. Throughout the article there will be references to the factors which influence an observer's willingness to return.

THE MODEL–NOT JUST QUESTION ANSWERING, BUT WALKING, POINTING, INSTRUCTING AND (FINALLY) QUESTION ANSWERING

The Willingness to Return Study recently developed a variable called model of practice. The aim of this variable is to measure the extent to which librarians appear to be in the business of providing answers: students were asked to check the action which best described the model which the reference librarian seemed to be using. The findings described in this paragraph, based only on 128 observations, are quite preliminary. These early findings show that the reference model typically involves librarians who take one of several different actions when they are asked questions by patrons. The most common responses by librarians are walking and pointing–31% walk questioners over to resources, most often handing questioners one or more resources while 29% simply point questioners in the direction of the resources send a message that the library is a self-service operation. (See also Mellon, 1990.) Fewer than one in five library staff members engage in question negotiation and answering. Fifteen percent instruct questioners in the use of materials. These findings indicate that there is not general agreement among librarians that they are in the question answering business.

The section below, based on 486 observations, examines the contributions of several different factors to reference success. The Willingness to Return Study has found that the typical reference interview is a short, continuous interaction which is most likely to start when a questioner approaches a librarian who is near or at a reference desk and is currently not otherwise occupied. Typically it is carried on by an individual (a female) who is not clearly identified by questioners as being a librarian, and whose first words in response to the opening question are likely to be a statement. She possesses moderate interpersonal skills, but relatively poor interviewing skills.

Most librarians do not practice as though they are in the question answering business. Rather than seeking to answer questions accurately (as is assumed by most unobtrusive studies), librarians typically walk a questioner to a group of resources which they think will answer an initial question such as, "Do you have any books on. . . . " Many librarians often make it clear through words or actions that this is the extent of the help to be expected. Typically librarians fail to ask a follow-up question to find out if the assistance which has been provided is appropriate. Consistent with other studies of reference success, nearly 55% of the reference interviews observed in the Willingness to Return Study are considered successful.

The following section explains this profile in more detail. It discusses this typical reference interaction from the perspective of the behaviors and attributes which are most associated with reference success.

Dewdney found that many librarians answer the questions they are asked (Dewdney, in Durrance 1993b pp. 27-28). My research underscores Dewdney's findings. I have found that many questioners who ask "Where are your books on . . . ?", are *shown* where the books are. The response, below, reported by one of the observers, is quite typical.

> The librarian . . . came up to us and asked if we needed help. I asked, "Where are your books on health?" She never attempted to clarify my question. She asked only one question, "Do you want to take them out or use them here?"

Directing patrons to the catalog, pointing them to resources, or otherwise sending the message that the library is a self-service operation is another frequent response to the reference question. Deflecting questions, "Did you check the catalog?" and pointing users toward another area may have the effect of discouraging further interaction. One observer whose proxy was her mother, reported, "My mom was . . . somewhat embarrassed at being told to go to the catalogs and felt quite lost in the library stacks." Others have reported on this phenomenon. Murfin and Bunge as well as Mellon have identified pointing or directing as practices which result in below normal success rates (Murfin & Bunge 1984; Mellon 1986; Mellon 1990). When library staff members try to find out more precisely what patrons need they are very successful; other positive (but less successful) behavior includes instruction and walking–in that order. These findings are discussed in more detail in later sections of this article.

STAFF ACTIVITY UPON APPROACH

Does what a library staff member is doing when she is approached make any difference? This study measured the effect of each of the following conditions at the time of approach: (1) staff were free, (2) with another patron, (3) doing work away from the desk, (4) talking on the telephone or with another staff member, or (5) doing other work at the desk. My research and that of others indicates that people are often confused about the extent to which it is OK to ask a librarian questions. This confusion may be compounded by librarians who become immersed in the work they take to the reference desk to fill their time between questions. Interviews with staff who were free were far more likely to be successful (66%) than any other interviews; interactions which interrupted a librarian who was doing other work at the desk were the least successful (only 42%). Observers regularly report feeling very uncomfortable when they stand trying to get the attention of a librarian who appears to them to be far more interested in doing her own work than responding to their question. Waiting for a librarian to stop talking with a colleague may also engender an awkward feeling. Librarians should factor into reference desk management the potential impact of staffing patterns on those who attempt to approach librarians with a question.

THE ANONYMOUS ENCOUNTER

Although this is the only profession in which the professional is not identified, the fear of identification still persists and overshadows the discussion of the benefits to the questioner. Over a decade ago in "The Generic Librarian" I reported that citizen leaders who knew a librarian by name were far more likely to think highly of the library as an important information source for their "real world" public policy activities than those who did not (Durrance, 1983). Librarians still practice anonymously; this research confirms that questioners who have obtained the name of a librarian are more likely to have a successful interaction. Knowing the name of the librarian provides a mechanism to follow-up on information provided and provides a basis for trust between the questioner and the professional. The Willingness to Return study shows that 63% of those who discovered the name of the librarian would return to the librarian at another time.

The data from this study leads me to believe that lack of identification of staff may cause confusion among questioners. Questioners have difficulty distinguishing between reference librarians and para-professionals. The Brandeis experiment which trains student staff to provide the initial response to patron questions–and to refer "real" reference questions to the librarians might prove to be successful in changing the anonymous encounter (Massey-Burzio, 1992).

FIRST WORDS

When the reference interview is thought of as a conversation, it is clear that the first words which come out of the staff member's mouth are very important. Since librarians are not known to most of the people who ask them questions, they must rely on their interpersonal skills to provide the opening for the reference interview to occur. Researchers and reference librarians are in the process of developing a rich professional literature aimed at improving the interpersonal aspects of the craft of reference librarianship. In the past decade research has provided librarians with valuable knowledge as well as techniques designed to enhance the effectiveness of the interaction (Ross & Dewdney 1989, Dervin & Dewdney 1986, Murfin & Bunge 1984, Durrance 1989, Whitlatch 1990). Whitlatch has identified a number of elements which come together in the reference interview (Whitlatch 1990). The more we examine it, the better we understand that extraordinarily complex interpersonal interaction between questioners and librarians.

A number of articles and books include discussions of the use of open and closed questions and their contributions to a successful interview. We have come to accept that open questions increase success at the beginning of the interview and that closed questions help librarians focus on how to link the questioner to an appropriate resource. The Willingness to Return Study found that librarians are more likely to start interviews with a statement (37%) than either a closed (31%) or an open (27%) question. We even found that 5% of the staff responded to questioners' opening queries without words, but instead used grimaces, guttural sounds, facial expressions, or silence for an awkward period of time. During the initial silence the librarian may interact with a computer or a catalog. The impact of poorly crafted initial responses has been underestimated by librarians.

Librarians who used an open question to start an interview were far more likely to be able to find out what the individual actually needed than those who used a closed question or a statement. Open questions were the most successful first words (66%), followed by statements (50%). There has been very little work designed to help library staff make the most effective use of a statement at the beginning of an interview. Initial statements can give the questioner clues about what to expect in the interaction. Observers found that statements used to open an interview can be either welcoming or off-putting. However unintentionally negative an opening remark may be, it nonetheless can have a powerful effect on the listener. It can serve to close off further questioning. The example below illustrates off-putting first words in the form of a statement.

> The staff member was approached with the following question, "I need information on diabetes." The librarian responded by saying "The card catalog is over there, behind you." She then walked away. This woman gave me the impression that I should have looked in the card catalog before bothering her. I didn't want to bother her any more.

The initial statements below which respond directly to general questions are welcoming and helpful: "Well, with any genealogy inquiry, you will want to start with basic steps. I'll give you a couple things," or "I highly recommend that you look at the Census for that information. I'll get you started." Helpful statements such as, "That sounds interesting" or "I'd like you to tell me a little more about that" show an interest in the question and get the interview off to a good, solid footing.

Closed questions, the least effective first words, are most often system-centered. Closed questions like, "Did you check the catalog?" "Do you want a book or an article?" "Do you want to check something out?" may make perfectly logical sense to the staff member, but they may serve not only to confuse the questioner ("How should I know?") but also—and more importantly—to turn the focus away from the questioner and toward the system.

First words are a prelude to an interaction in which the reference interview "conversation" may occur. Since library staff do not have a common mental model for the reference interaction, the questioner is on his own to figure out which kind of service he is likely to receive. Of course the service or resource link is delivered through the interpersonal and interviewing skills used by the staff member. Findings of this study show the importance of including training–for librarians and paraprofessionals who have contact with the public–on the use of first words and first actions.

INTERPERSONAL SKILLS AND APPROACHABILITY

The act of approaching a stranger to ask a question is intimidating to many. This study measures several factors which increase or decrease a questioner's ability to ask a question–approachability, interest in the question, courtesy, confidence, ability to make the questioner comfortable, and a non-judgmental demeanor. Librarians who appear to be interested in the question are most likely to make the questioner feel comfortable. Other factors which contribute to raising the comfort level thereby allowing people to ask questions, are approachability and courtesy. On average, library staff appear to be moderately approachable (3.3) and show a moderate ability to listen (3.3). Staff are fairly courteous (3.6) and make questioners feel fairly comfortable (3.5). Librarians were judged to be quite non-judgmental (a mean of 4 on a scale of 1-5). This factor, however, is not positively associated with success. It may even contribute to an apparent lack of interest in the question. Even though researchers have found that interest is a very important factor in reference success, only 19% of the librarians observed appeared to be really interested in the question (5 on a scale of 1-5); 92% would return to librarians who seemed genuinely interested in the question. This underscores Gers and Seward's finding that librarians often fail to show interest (Gers and Seward, 1985).

INTERVIEWING SKILLS AND ABILITY
TO DETERMINE NEED

Interviewing skills include the ability to listen and to use open (or neutral) and closed questions effectively in order to determine what the questioner actually needs (Ross and Dewdney 1989). In this group of skills we found that librarians scored quite poorly, indicating a need for skill building in this area. Listening skills averaged 3.5 on the scale of 1-5. On average, observers ranked the use of closed questions at 2.7 and the ability to determine need at 2.5; librarians were ranked 1.5 on their ability to use open questions effectively. Only 10% were ranked at "5" or very skilled at using open questions. The ability to listen and determine need were highly correlated (.67).

THE MOVING OR DISAPPEARING LIBRARIAN

Observers fairly frequently report that the staff member's response to being asked a question is to walk rapidly away from them. Observers report being confused by this kind of behavior. They don't know whether to follow or wait for the staff member to return.

> Several times during the interview, I wasn't sure if he was still "with us." After apparently searching in the on-line catalog (he never actually explained what he was doing), he indicated he had found something and wrote down a title and a call number. He showed it, but didn't give it to the proxy. Instead he walked briskly away from the reference desk. We didn't know if we should follow or not so we didn't. He came back shortly with a book. He then said that there might be something on the CD-ROM and turned and walked away. This time we followed.

Another disturbing behavior is the disappearance. When the staff member who has left the questioner behind then disappears, the observers report wondering if they have been dismissed. The experiences of a few observers indicate the effect of the disappearing librarian on the questioner:

> The librarian we were working with suddenly left us standing at a range of books. We couldn't figure out whether she had dismissed us or whether she was still working with us and had

gone to look for something. Our only clue that she was still with us was overhearing her remark to another librarian. "Please take that patron because I am still working with these people," she said, pointing to us.

In another case a librarian had taken the questioner to the online catalog, typed in the key words which reflected his question and left before seeing the results. The observer reported:

> The librarian walked away from me, and said nothing. I felt very anxious and frustrated because I didn't want to wade through the 184 entries that showed up to find relevant information. I had more questions to ask the reference librarian, but I couldn't find her anywhere. I did not see her again while we were in the library. I left the library feeling upset.

It is not clear to the questioner whether an abrupt departure is a method of closure or a continuation of the interaction by retrieving additional materials. This poor practice which may cause confusion, resentment, or the resolve never to ask another question again, can, of course, be remedied if the staff member takes the time to inform the questioner of the action which is being taken.

FOLLOW-UP

The follow-up question serves to indicate that the librarian is interested in the outcome of the question. The follow-up question can help fix some of the problems which may occur during a reference interview (such as miscommunication, not understanding the question, faulty assumptions, etc.), yet only one in four library staff members observed actually used a follow-up questions. More than three quarters of the observers who encountered a librarian who asked a follow-up question indicated that they would return. My research suggests that the follow-up question need not be as specific as the question recommended by Gers and Seward, "Does this completely answer your question?" (Gers & Seward 1985). A variety of follow-up responses, including, "If you need further assistance, please let me know" or "Have you found what you needed?" or even, "Everything OK?" worked well because they showed that the librarian was interested.

CLOSURE. WHEN IS A REFERENCE INTERACTION OVER?

Finding that only one in four librarians actually asked a follow-up question raised the following questions: if a librarian does not ask a follow-up question, how does she signal the end of an interaction? Are there certain kinds of actions which can assure good outcomes? Likewise, are there actions which are correlated with reference failure? The Willingness to Return Study has shown that a number of librarians have chosen ineffective methods of closure. Recently we began to isolate closure as a variable and examine its impact on the questioner. Nolan's 1992 article is the first to have focused entirely on closure in the reference interview (Nolan, 1992). Nolan suggests and I concur that the lack of training in closure contributes to lack of reference success. Lacking data on the nature of closure, Nolan developed a framework for closure. He presents three categories of factors which influence closure: Knowledge-related, Interpersonal communication-related closure, and Policy and Institutional Factors. In the Willingness to Return study closure has been observed in 125 interactions. Preliminary data indicate that there are both functional and dysfunctional closure patterns. Observers found that about half of the librarians made closure fairly clear to the observers. When librarians make it clear to questioners that as far as the librarian is concerned, the interaction is over, the questioner feels that permission to ask further questions has been denied.

These words clearly signaled the end of four different interactions and discouraged further interaction.

> After the librarian gave me one source that didn't work, I said, "Is there anything else I can look at?" The librarian looked at a couple of other things, but didn't say a word. She showed me one other item and said, "That's about it" and turned her back and went back to the desk and resumed reading. I felt like I

had been dismissed and if I asked any more questions, I would be bothering her.

My proxy and I were taken over to a table and handed three books. The body language of the librarian made it clear that the interaction was over. After seating my proxy, the librarian left without further words.

The reference librarian concluded the interview in a simple, efficient manner. Without speaking a word, he handed me a slip of paper and pointed in the direction of the collection. Using this simple technique, he made it clear that I was not expected to ask anymore questions. I was dismissed.

"There ya go!" [followed by turning away]. The reference interview was clearly over.

Permission for a return interaction is given by conditional closure. One observer reported on the effective use of the conditional closure

The librarian gave us directions to various departmental libraries. However each time she referred us to a different department, she asked us to return to her to report the findings and receive further instruction.

Other conditional closures reported include:

"Go to the 640s and look. If that isn't what you need, come back."

"If the materials aren't there come back and we'll go together."

These statements and others like them were encouraging to the observers because in each case, the observers felt that they had permission to return. Closure of the reference interaction must be more carefully considered; it is an important part of professional practice. It may be a major key to reference success.

SUMMARY OF THE FACTORS WHICH
ARE MOST LIKELY TO BE ASSOCIATED
WITH THE SUCCESSFUL REFERENCE INTERVIEW

This article has identified the effects of a variety of factors which influence reference failure and discourage return. Table I shows the factors most likely to be associated with the successful reference interview.

In sum, this study clearly shows that there is no general agreement among library staff as to the nature of reference service. Most library staff in this study answered the question that was asked, rather than negotiating it. When librarians respond directly to the stated question, they are most likely to point or walk the questioner to the place where the requested materials might be located. Over 60% walked, pointed, or otherwise indicated that the way to negotiate in their libraries was through self-service. These individuals are in the question response business (i.e., they direct people to the resources that will answer the questions), but not in the question negotiation business. Pointers seem to be among the least successful of librarians because they appear not to be interested enough in the question to assure that the questioner even gains access to the resources. Only 30% of the questioners indicated they would return to those librarians who responded to their question by pointing them in the direction of the resources.

The Willingness to Return Study shows that longer interactions and those where the librarian's name is known are successful. It shows clearly that interpersonal factors dominate in the observer's willingness to return to the librarian at another time. It also shows that these skills are possessed by a minority of staff members. However, when such factors as approachability, effective use of open question, possession of an ability to listen, showing interest, or the ability to determine needs are present, they have a powerful effect on the outcome.

The predominance of walkers and pointers reinforces the message that libraries are self-service institutions serviced by librarians who provide directional assistance only. People who ask questions need to know that they have been heard and understood. There may be a strong and almost indelible effect of poor interpersonal skills

TABLE I. Factors Associated with Reference Services

FACTORS ASSOCIATED WITH MODERATELY SUCCESSFUL INTERACTIONS

%Would Return	Factor	Total%	Total
63%	Librarian used instruction	15%	N=128
63%	Staff member identified by name	14%	N=484
65%	Librarian was free at the beginning	28%	N=480
66%	Interaction lasted 5-9 minutes	24%	N=485
66%	Open question as the first response	28%	N=484
68%	Interaction lasted 9-14 minutes	8%	N=485

FACTORS ASSOCIATED WITH SUCCESSFUL INTERACTIONS

%Would Return	Factor	Total%	Total
70%	Negotiated very successfully	16%	N=128
76%	Asked a follow-up question	25%	N=484
79%	Lasted more than 15 minutes	3%	N=485
80%	Was very approachable	28%	N=480
80%	Showed a moderate interest	30%	N=485

FACTORS ASSOCIATED WITH THE MOST SUCCESSFUL INTERACTIONS

%Would Return	Factor	Total%	Total
91%	Appeared to be very interested in question	19%	N=485
92%	Possessed very good listening skills	22%	N=484
94%	Determined the need behind question	18%	N=482
96%	Used open questions very effectively	10%	N=451

NOTE: This composite table, which is brought together from a number of variables, should be read as follows, using the last factor as an example: 96% of the observers who worked with librarians who "used open questions very effectively (i.e., those who ranked 5 on a scale of 1–5)" said that they would return to that person at another time. The percent of cases where this behavior was seen was 10% of the total individuals observed.

on questioners. My guess is that library staff fail to appreciate the impact of their actions on questioners.

The examples below are based on the observation by a student in her mid-30s and her 9 1/2 year old son in a medium-sized public library. They show two very different models of practice and their impact on the questioners. The first librarian was a pointer; the second showed that she was interested in the question and would use her professional skills to see to it that the questioner got the needed information. Both mother and son asked a similar question.

Librarian One–The Pointer

After standing in line for some moments at the reference desk, it became my turn. As I stepped forward, the librarian, a man in his mid 30s moved his head from a lowered position to look at my eyes. At the same time he gestured with his head. It was clear that without words he was ready for my inquiry. I asked the question, "How does divorce affect children?" The initial response of the librarian was to lower his head and begin typing words into the computer. The computer monitor was directed in such a way that I could not view what was occurring. The lack of initial greeting was immediately discouraging. As he bent over the computer I had the sense that I was not going to be able to control any part of this interaction and was going to be at the mercy of whatever he decided to do.

He gave me the impression that he was just serving a line of people. After looking at the screen for a small amount of time, he reached for a piece of paper and wrote down two Dewey Decimal numbers. Then he said, "There are two areas. You might find more in the second one than the first." He handed me the slip of paper, showed me the location on a map on the counter, and made it clear by his actions that I was not expected to ask any more questions. Since I had observed him appearing to become annoyed with the patron directly in front of me in line who pressed him for more information, I felt that I would get the same treatment myself if I asked additional questions. I was to go to the collection and begin my quest for information. Rather than providing me with actual information, I was provided with a slip of paper. The librarian was impersonal, did not interact or negotiate with me in any way, and left me with the sense that I was simply a number.

Librarian Two–The Facilitator with Strong Interpersonal Skills

At the same library, the observer's 9 1/2 year old son approached the children's reference desk and said to the mid-40s librarian, a woman, "Excuse me, I am looking for information about how children feel when their parents get divorced." The librarian's immediate response was to stand up, smile and state, "Let's go over here." She walked with him over to a group of books. The young boy felt that this was a very encouraging response. As she looked for material, she asked him what grade he was in and chatted with him about school and his interests. Not finding what she was looking for, she said, "I'll have to look on the computer." Finding this additional information, she then led him to a couple of areas of the collection. Each time she found an appropriate book she would look through it and then hand it to him, saying things like, "You should be able to read this one," or "Honey, I hope this helps." Finally she asked politely, "Are your parents getting divorced?" He responded, "Yes."

Throughout the interview the child had the sense that he could talk with the librarian and that she was genuinely interested in assisting him. The librarian appeared not willing to end the interview until the young man had received appropriate materials and assistance. The interview itself took about 10 minutes. At the end he felt that he had really been helped and there was a sense of return obligation from him to the librarian.

In comparing the two interviews, the observer said of her son and his interview,

> They became a team working toward the goal of finding him the best sources. At the end of the interview he felt compelled to look through the suggested books. The librarian's process not only included getting him information, but making sure that he could successfully complete whatever steps he needed to successfully use the information (including asking if he had a library card). On the other hand, the goal of my librarian seemed to be to complete the interaction as quickly as possible and get me away from the reference desk! These two interviews used very different processes. Each had a profound and opposite effect on each of us.

The final section below briefly discusses professional practice which regularly incorporates longer interviews in which library staff think of themselves as professionals who facilitate problem solving. These, of course, are not the only librarians who approach their work from a need-centered perspective. Many others do. The section below, however, illustrates an emerging practice which encourages more lengthy interactions. Longer interviews incorporate the interpersonal characteristics shown in Table I and in the interview with the children's librarian described above. The practices described below acknowledge that many questions are problems in disguise and need to be treated as such.

EMERGING PRACTICE–EVIDENCE
FROM THE JOB AND CAREER CENTERS

Practitioners in job and career centers see themselves as facilitators at least as much as question answerers. My study of the emerging practice associated with providing job and career information shows that practitioners who work with job seekers use several different intervention strategies encourage interactions which are longer than the typical three minute reference interaction (Durrance, 1994; Durrance 1993a, and 1993b).

The activities of staff members in job and career information centers are likely to be need-centered rather than resource-centered. Therefore, staff have developed a variety of strategies designed to get to the problem hidden in the question. However, before people are able to ask questions about the real problems in their lives, they need to know that it is OK to ask such questions. Library staff at job information centers take action to raise the awareness of their potential clientele about the kinds of interactions to expect. They tell them that in addition to answering questions, they may be able to get help in assessing their interests and abilities so that they will know better the kind of information and help they need. Job and career center client interviews are longer than the typical reference interaction. They vary from short (5-10 minutes) interactions with "drop-ins" to one hour one-on-one sessions (Durrance 1991). Job and career center clientele are also told about workshops which are regularly held on such topics as how to prepare oneself for the job market, understand the career decision making process, put together a resume, or prepare for a job interview. They are also aware that job center staff provide referral to training, education, career counseling and other community-centered programs.

The activities described above involve a wide range of practice by librarians. In order to facilitate the activities that go on in job and career centers, staff have made changes in the environment such as creating quiet corners where private conversations can occur and locating rooms in the library where workshops can be held. While most reference interactions in libraries take place while both the librarian and the questioner are standing, job and career center staff have changed the environment in which their client contacts occur, creating a place where both can be seated to discuss the situation, the need, an approaches the questioner might take. In addition, staff often use career assessment software to help their clientele prepare for job and career changes.

Willingness to return is a less appropriate measure for this kind of professional practice, since the percentage of return will likely be higher than that of the three minute reference interaction. The expectations of the clientele have been raised. The success of these methods of practice can readily measured from the perspective of the client (Durrance 1993a; Durrance 1994). Because the interviews associated with this practice are need-based and client-centered, evaluations of these services can include stories and testimonials. Job center clientele have testified that they:

- Appreciated the help of the staff during a trying time of life–when they were trying to cope with change, get a job, or take charge of their lives.
- Were more able to take control of their situation as the result of working with Job Center staff.
- Had increased their understanding of the possibilities, become more active, and taken steps toward increasing their basic reading skills.
- Were able to make more informed decisions than they had before talking with a Job Center staff member.
- Saw their options more clearly or were better able to identify their educational needs and plan their future more realistically.
- Gained self-esteem.
- Developed new skills. (FERA; Durrance 1994)

The majority of job and career center clientele said that after using the service they increased both the number of job interviews they received and learned how to be more effective in their job search skills (Durrance 1993b). Methods used to evaluate interactions include collecting testimony, anecdotal evidence of success, and developing measures of the impact of the service on its clientele (Durrance 1993a).

Reference practice is evolving. In the process librarians need to define more carefully the different kinds of reference interactions and develop appropriate ways of helping librarians understand which of the several different methods of practice (such as pointing, walking, question answering, consultation, instruction, or problem assistance) are appropriate for the particular situation (Kuhlthau 1993, Durrance 1994). Likewise, librarians need to develop appropriate measures to evaluate each method of practice. It is not unreasonable to develop a measure to determine the success of walking or pointing questioners in terms of satisfaction with the approach or appropriateness of the information retrieved. In my study, 60% of those who worked with "pointers" and 48% of those who worked with "walkers" indicated that they were not satisfied (1 or 2 on a scale of 1-5) with that approach to responding to their question.

The intervention chosen by the library staff member should be based on an understanding of what the questioner needs as well as an ability to know when to use different intervention strategies. The considerable work which has been done by academic librarians to develop a body of literature in librarianship which helps librarians use and evaluate instruction as a method of professional practice developed only after instruction was recognized as a separate, and important, method of practice (in the mid-70s when the ACRL Bibliographic Instruction Section was formed). As a result of the work done by librarians to focus on instruction, many more staff have been deployed as instruction librarians and academic library budgets reflect the importance of this method of professional practice.

The multiple aspects of professional practice which should grow out of the reference interview cry out for the same attention which has been given to instruction. An encounter which starts at the reference desk with a question like, "Do you have any information on?" might end there by providing a correct answer or the location of a specific resource or it may continue with a consultation or instruction appointment or some other professional intervention. Librarians have not yet developed a common understanding of the range of professional intervention strategies which can appropriately be used to respond to questions. Likewise, librarians still do not agree when to apply a particular strategy (such as walking a questioner to a resource, instructing him in the use of the resource, etc.). By continuing to examine ways to evaluate the reference interview, we will add to the knowledge needed to improve this complex interaction–and will provide a more sound basis for its evaluation.

REFERENCES

Crowley, Terence and Thomas Childers. *Information Service in Public Libraries; Two Studies.* Scarecrow Press, Metuchen, NJ, 1971.

Dervin, Brenda, and Patricia Dewdney, "Neutral Questioning: A New Approach to the Reference Interview." *RQ* (Summer 1986): 506-513.

Dewdney, Patricia H. *The Effects of Training Reference Librarian in Interview Skills: A Field Experiment.* Ph.D. Dissertation, University of Western Ontario, London, Ontario, 1986.

Dewdney, Patricia. "Recording the Reference Interview." Glazier, Jack D., and Ronald R. Powell. eds. *Qualitative Research in Information Management,* Libraries Unlimited, 1992: 122-150.

Dewdney, Patricia, In Joan C. Durrance, *Education, Job and Career Information Centers in Public Libraries: Final Report on the Impact of Kellogg Funding,* March, 1993,(b): 27-28.

Durrance, Joan C., *Education, Job and Career Information Centers in Public Libraries: Final Report on the Impact of Kellogg Funding,* March, 1993b.

Durrance, Joan C. "The Generic Librarian: Anonymity versus Accountability." *RQ,* (Spring 1983): 278-283.

Durrance, Joan C. "The Influence of Reference Practices on the Client-Librarian Relationship." *College and Research Libraries,* (January 1986): 57-67.

Durrance, Joan C. *Meeting Community Needs with Job and Career Services.* Neal-Schuman, New York, 1994.

Durrance, Joan C. "Reference Success: Does the 55 Percent Rule Tell the Whole Story?" *Library Journal.* (April 15, 1989): 31-36.

Durrance, Joan C. "Research Needs in Public Librarianship." in Charles R. McClure and Peter Hernon, eds., *Library and Information Research: Perspectives and Strategies for Improvement,* Ablex, Norwood, NJ, 1991: 279-295.

Durrance, Joan C. "Public Libraries and Career Changers: Insights from Kellogg Funded Services." *Public Libraries,* (March-April 1991): 93-100.

Durrance, Joan C. et al. *Serving Job Seekers and Career Changers: A Planning Manual for Public Libraries,* American Library Association, Chicago, 1993, (a).

Dyson, Lillie Seward. "Improving Reference Services: A Maryland Training Program Brings Positive Results." *Public Libraries* 31 (Sept.-Oct. 1992): 284-289.

Formative Evaluation Research Associates (FERA), *Final Report to Pennsylvania State Library,* Ann Arbor, MI, FERA, 1990.

Gers, Ralph, and Lillie J. Seward. "Improving Reference Performance: Results of a Statewide Study." *Library Journal,* (November 1, 1985): 32-35.

Hernon, Peter and Charles R. McClure. "Unobtrusive reference testing: the 55% rule." *Library Journal* 111, (April 15, 1986): 37-41.

Hernon, Peter, and Charles R. McClure. *Unobtrusive Testing and Library Reference Service,* Ablex, Norwood, NJ, 1987.

Isenstein, Laura J. "Get Your Reference Staff on the STAR Track." *Library Journal,* (April 15, 1992): 34-37.

Kuhlthau, Carol Collier. *Seeking Meaning: A Process Approach to Library and Information Services,* Ablex, Norwood, NJ, 1993.

Library Video Network. *Does This Completely Answer Your Question?,* Towson, Md.: ALA Video/Library Video Network <distributor>, 1992.

Massey-Burzio, Virginia. "Reference Encounters of a Different Kind: A Symposium." *Journal of Academic Librarianship,* (Fall 1992).

Mellon, Constance. "Library Anxiety: A Grounded Theory and Its Development." *RQ,* (March, 1986): 160-165.

Mellon, Constance A. *Naturalistic Inquiry for Library Science: Methods and Applications for Research, Evaluation, and Teaching,* Greenwood Press, New York, 1990.

Murfin, Marjorie, and Charles Bunge. "Evaluating Reference Service from the Patron Point of View: Some Interim National Survey Results." *The Reference Librarian* 11, (1984): 175-182.

Nolan, Christopher W. "Closing the Reference Interview: Implications for Policy and Practice." *RQ,* vol. 31, (summer, 1992): 513-23.

Ross, Catherine Sheldrick. "How to Find Out What People Really Want to Know." *The Reference Librarian* vol. 16, (winter 1986): 19-29.

Ross, Catherine and Patricia Dewdney. *Communicating Professionally,* New York, Neal Schuman, 1989.

Taylor, Robert S. "Question–Negotiation and Information Seeking in Libraries." *College and Research Libraries,* (May 1968): 178-194.

Whitlatch, Jo Bell. *The Role of the Academic Reference Librarian,* Greenwood Press, New York, 1990.

Brave Newold World

James Rettig

SUMMARY. The author creates a fictional scenario of library reference service at an unspecified date in the first part of the twenty-first century. Ten major social trends for the 1990s as identified by Faith Popcorn are examined. The reference service practices in the fictional scenario and present-day reference service practice are critiqued in terms of how they fit or diverge from each of the ten trends. The fictional scenario is found to embody more of the significant trends than does present day reference practice. The need to tie into these trends is noted.

A SCENARIO OF THE FUTURE

Just after her mid-morning coffee break with several colleagues, Ariel Aquest walked towards the Arl-Fax Regional Informatique's

James Rettig is Assistant Dean of University Libraries for Reference and Information Services, College of William and Mary, Williamsburg, VA 23187-8794. jrrett@mail.wm.edu.

[Haworth co-indexing entry note]: "Brave Newold World." Rettig, James. Co-published simultaneously in *The Reference Librarian* (The Haworth Press, Inc.) No. 49/50, 1995, pp. 267-288; and: *Library Users and Reference Services* (ed: Jo Bell Whitlatch) The Haworth Press, Inc., 1995, pp. 267-288. Multiple copies of this article/chapter may be purchased from The Haworth Document Delivery Center [1-800-3-HAWORTH; 9:00 a.m. - 5:00 p.m. (EST)].

Customer Service Salon for her usual Thursday morning stint there. Moments before in the staff lounge she and Anne and Dale, both children's services specialists, had talked about the program that Anne and Dale had prepared for a group of first graders that afternoon. Their teacher had been reading Beatrix Potter's stories to them and the children were coming to the children's room of the Informatique to learn more about this British author, most famous in the previous century but still read and enjoyed by children and their parents in this modern era. Anne and Dale had explained how they had applied the hologram animator to Potter's classic illustrations of Peter Rabbit, Jemima Puddle-Duck, Benjamin Bunny, Tom Kitten, Pigling Bland, and so on to bring them to 3-D life in the children's rooms. They had also linked the animated characters' words and actions to recordings of the books as read by professional actors. They explained that a hologram Beatrix Potter would greet each child as the class entered and then introduce her characters. The hologram characters would then act out the stories before and amidst the children, always remaining true to Potter's early twentieth-century text. Afterwards the children would have an opportunity to ask Peter how he felt when Mr. McGregor was chasing him or ask Tom Kitten what he thought as the rats prepared to cook him.

The children's rooms were the showcase and strategic symbol of the Informatique. In one of its rooms a combination of comfortable chairs, tables, and sofas in a range of just-right sizes interspersed among holding units brimming with books, video recordings, sound recordings, and interactive multimedia programs. Another room was a large state-of-the-art virtual experience chamber wired to bring in any machine-transmittable information from anywhere on the globe and equipped with all the tools the staff needed to combine and integrate information from disparate sources to provide rich experiences for youngsters exploring the world through a wide array of media. The third public room consisted of smaller chambers with simplified versions of the same tools the staff used; these chambers allowed individual children or small groups of children collaborating with one another to create their own experiences. When the Informatique was constructed as the successor to the local libraries, the staff decided that the children's services area had to make a strong statement to compete with the many diverting but intellectually hollow multimedia experiences available to children through their 700-plus channel cable infotainment systems and specialized and increasingly sophisticated virtual experience games that had been the hot Christmas season sellers the past several years. Even though these were pricey toys, they had a staying power unlike any other toy fad, making the video games of Ariel's youth look like a fleeting flash-in-the-pan fad. If this younger generation did not develop a loyalty to the Informatique and its unique services whereby its members could tap the Informatique's vast storehouse of information stored in media that, once state-of-the-art, had shrunk to serve narrow niches, the future of the Informatique would be bleak and the ideals it stood for–especially access to information for all–would lose their most ardent defenders and promoters.

Print on paper accounted for the largest amount of this information. In this modern era it had little sway any longer outside of a series of paperbound books published under the imprint of Beach Books–and information that individual information consumers elected to print for their convenience. However, fewer and fewer people had reason to create prints since their InfoLink devices (produced to international standards by a variety of manufacturers in the United States, Vietnam, India, Macedonia, Angola, and several other countries) allowed easy hand-written and even easier voice annotation and revision of information. Since, despite millions and millions of Universal Currency units spent in R&D, engineers had yet to come up with a hand held, satellite-linked, battery or solar powered InfoLink device that could display text and images without glare from the seaside sun and immune to the ruinous effects of a spill in the sand or surf, Beach Books held their market niche securely and offered seaside entertainment-seekers a variety of texts from throughout the centuries and the world. Every resort town had at least several outlets that allowed vacationers to browse catalogs; watch and listen to other readers comment on the books, explaining the strengths and flaws of each; and then, after making their selections, insert a credit/debit card and just moments later the bound book–hot off the press, as they used to say–would be ready. (Seaside ice cream parlors and coffee houses found that sales of their principal products increased after installation of a Beach Book vending machine.)

Beach Books offered a wide range of titles, however they made up but a minuscule percentage of the titles preserved and available in the nation's Informatiques, successors to the libraries of Ariel's youth. It was ironic that in its greatest legislative success, the American Library Association had managed to transform every library in the nation and at the same time spell its own doom. Never a nimble organization, due to the chronic complexity of its internal structure, the ALA had managed to work with Congress to draft a bill to create a national network of libraries, formerly known parochially as school, public, academic, and special libraries, and to broaden the mission of each. Working in partnership with other groups, especially the Virtual Experience Trade Association, libraries became Informatiques. A few of the larger public and academic libraries had managed this transition on their own, but most needed the help of a Congressionally mandated program. That program assured that every Informatique (formerly library) would continue to preserve the books and other media it had collected, but would also be equipped with needed communications links to tie into the well established commercial OmniMedia transmission network and would in return make its retrospective resources available over the network. The law had saved libraries from becoming mausoleums for forsaken media and placed them at the center of their communities' information needs. However Informatiques required a much wider range of expertise than most libraries could boast back in the early years of the century and the ALA, unable to reposition itself as quickly as its members and their institutions, went bankrupt after it lost members precipitously to the upstart but responsive American Informatiques Coalition, a group that welcomed librarians, electronic information specialists, intellectual property rights and use negotiators, government officials, museum curators, communications executives, and others who worked together to make the Informatique concept a reality and a success for the educational, recreational, and economic benefit of the entire society. The authors of the law that authorized the Informatiques wisely recognized that the minds of the past were a terrible thing to waste and, therefore, also recognized the need to make libraries' rich retrospective collections readily available and thereby revivify their role in education, government, and commerce.

Ariel had lived through the transition, the last reference librarian ever hired at one of the local public libraries that had preceded the Informatique. After two years on the job–frustrated that fading funding for the library denied her and her colleagues access to the commercial services that superseded the 1990s' Compuserve, America Online, GEnie, and Prodigy services that had skimmed the high-volume, quick-return information market–Ariel was ready for the brave new world of the Informatique which would integrate the library's values of access for all with the power and reach of modern virtual experience technology. Indeed, it was, she discovered to her delight, "a sea change/Into something rich and strange" and most welcome.

Instead of sitting at a reference desk waiting for a patron to approach or for the phone to ring or for an e-mail message to arrive as she had done eighteen hours a week at the old library, at the Informatique Ariel enjoyed greater variety; but most of all she reveled in the satisfaction of seeing the results of her work as she collaborated with clients from many fields of education, business, government, and industry. As she settled into her chair in the Customer Service Salon, she remembered hearing a radio commentator in her youth talking about one of the political corruption scandals involving a president's spouse and how the commentator had said, "The Smiths have come to Washington and have learned that it is a place where appearances becomes reality." So, too, she thought, on the south bank of the placid Potomac, for here in the Customer Service Salon she could conjure up all wonders of information on invisible, immaterial screens adjusted and arranged for her comfort and subject to quick, easy rearrangement as she judged one more significant than another. Upon her command these screens displayed videos; text from databases; still pictures; descriptions of materials in the CapitalCat; and customized combinations of information from all of these sources. CapitalCat–the integrated database of information available on-site in non-electronic media; non-electronic media in all other Washington-area Informatiques; artifacts in museums; texts, images, videos, audio recordings, and mixed-media products available from various sources via the OmniMedia network; information in locally developed files describing community resources (also made available to the world

at large through the OmniMedia network), regardless of format–
was a basic tool for staff and clients of the Informatique. And today
Ariel would have another tool at her disposal for the first time. A
task force composed of members of the American Informatique
Coalition and the information/entertainment conglomerate that
owned Beach Books had developed a system for hologramic reproduction of entire books and their contents.

Ariel had completed her training on this system, called the
Whole-a-Grammar, and was ready to use it. It would mean she no
longer had to wait for printed materials to be retrieved by robot
from book stacks and delivered to her, but could now have them
retrieved and displayed from their storage site, almost instanta-
neously and project their contents, page by page, on one of the
screens at her command. Links were in place between the Whole-a-
Grammar and the InfoIntegrater, the electronic tool she used in the
Customer Service Salon to extract relevant sections from items
regardless of format or location on the OmniMedia network. The
next step in development of the Whole-a-Grammar would be to
extend its reach to all of the print materials at the various sites
covered by CapitalCat. However the Whole-a-Grammar would
truly fulfill its potential once it was integrated into the OmniMedia
network environment and its use was simplified to the point where
anyone could use it without special training.

After checking with Jamie on how busy she and Sam had been
during the first half of the morning, Ariel greeted Robert, her team-
mate in the Salon that morning, as he took his place beside her at the
Salon's second station. Ariel double checked to make sure that the
Whole-a-Grammar was in service, adjusted her communications
headset that allowed her to keep both hands free, rearranged screens
before her on different focal planes, closed some Jamie had been
using but that she didn't need now, and, in the moment before the
first request for information came in, reflected that indeed "What's
past is prologue." With the arrival of the Whole-a-Grammar the
Informatique staff had decided to disband the Print Promotion
Team, a staff committee charged with making sure that the old
printed materials in the collection were used whenever possible and
in any way possible lest valuable information in them be over-

looked. And now here she was, as much in touch with those printed sources as she had been in her two years at the public library.

The first request was from a local government official who needed information on environmental regulations as they would apply to utilities needed for the county's new government building which would allow citizens the same sort of connections to government officials that the Customer Service Salon gave them to the Informatique and its riches. Ariel and the official agreed that it would be best to collaborate during the initial part of the information search, so she kept his image on the customer screen, just as her image was available to him in a window on the screen of his Info-Link. While he fielded a phone call from a colleague, Ariel searched CapitalCat and other resources. Then she created a second screen and on it displayed in parallel the texts of current state and federal regulations; on another she displayed a summary video of a longer production describing the process whereby a local government in Montana had developed its new facility and complied with environmental mandates; on another she displayed descriptions of items related to the issue of utilities and government regulation and available through the OmniMedia network. Together they discussed each screen full of information; then the official confirmed that all of this looked useful and asked Ariel to package it and transmit it to his InfoLink at the county building. Ariel said good-bye, evaporated the screen the official had been on and ran the information from the others through a relevance filter selected to fit the inquirer's needs, and issued the edit/send command. This told a computer elsewhere in the building to arrange the information into a standard report format that the county and the Informatique had designed for county official's convenience and to send it to the government official's InfoLink as soon as it was ready.

Ariel glanced over at Robert and saw he was busy with another inquirer and was adjusting his communications headset and creating a new screen; another query came in to her station, this one from a college student who had to prepare a multi-media program "about the Spanish colonies." Ariel questioned him to clarify what he had to learn about the Spanish colonies. No matter what approach she tried, he remained vague; and, despite his frequent use of "you know," Ariel didn't. Ariel asked if his electronic notebook included instructions from the professor that might explain the project requirements. He said he had instructions and promised to upload them for Ariel's perusal.

As he did that, Ariel checked to see how much activity HAWK was registering. HAWK was the online system that allowed Informatique clients to answer many questions without the assistance of a staff professional. It had replaced the overgrown, minimally organized gophers that so many libraries developed in the 1990s and, because of declining funding, had been stuck with during the early years of the century as sleek, swift commercial services sped past them in popularity and convenience. She saw that, in response to the huge jackpot of the night before, the most frequently requested bit of information over HAWK was Wednesday's winning lottery numbers, a bit of information Ariel herself had checked earlier in the day to her disappointment. Since snow threatened and Washingtonians persisted in considering it more an invader than an inconvenience, weather information had been in high demand, as had been airline schedules for Florida flights. There appeared to be the usual number of inquiries about community service and organization schedules and calendars, the usual number of inquiries about stock market and other financial news; the usual inquiries about sports results, etc.

Meanwhile the student had uploaded his assignment instructions and Ariel learned that he was supposed to identify key events in the history of Spanish colonies in the Americas as these events related to the rise of nationalism. She queried CapitalCat, identified books, databases, and other resources that seemed to apply. She searched one database, a chronology of world history, and displayed results of that search on a screen. Then she used the Whole-a-Grammar to display the contents of a book that looked promising. Together she and the student looked at its table of contents and the index. She asked him if it looked useful and he said it was at best marginal. So they looked at another and he said it was much more useful. Ariel used a tool from the Whole-a-Grammar's tool kit to highlight the relevant index entries; the Whole-a-Grammar then culled passages (plus at least 1,000 words either side of each passage so as to provide some context) allied with the index entries and had them transmitted to the student to judge their value individually. They also examined a historical maps file and an encyclopedia since Ariel's questioning had revealed that the student was not at all sure what territory had composed Spain's American colonies. His image on the customer screen visibly brightened when Ariel displayed these for him and he said that they would be very helpful. Ariel arranged an appointment for him to contact her the next day to let her know if he needed additional information. He promised to examine everything she had found for him thus far, assess it, compare what he had on hand to what he needed, and let her know how his project stood at the appointed time. (The next day he asked for images of conquistadors and native peoples as well as information about trade between the colonies and Spain during the sixteenth through eighteenth centuries.)

After handling other queries, a number of which she or Robert asked the other to help with, Ariel's assigned three hours in the Customer Service Salon were over. Before leaving the Salon she reviewed her schedule. She joined several colleagues who braved the thirty-four degree cold to walk down the street to a restaurant for lunch. As they passed the children's rooms, they heard Peter Rabbit sneeze "Kertyschoo!" accompanied by the laughter of children, followed by Mr. McGregor's heavy footsteps in pursuit, accompanied by the suddenly silent audience's tension. After lunch Ariel spent an hour in the On-Site Customer Service Salon, the counterpart to the Customer Service Salon that served those clients who chose to come to the library in person rather than connect to it through an InfoLink. The pace there was much slower with only one professional on duty at any time. However since both salons were equipped the same way, Ariel was able to work collaboratively with each client, exploring options and allowing the client, with her professional counsel, to judge the value of each. She could then transmit results of a collaborative session to an on-site private salon or virtual experience chamber where the client could further manipulate and make use of those results. One thing remained a constant from the old library to the new Informatique—meetings! Ariel ended her Thursday with a meeting of most of the staff to see the unveiling of the Informatique's new advertising and public relations campaign to introduce to the public its expanded service made possible by the Whole-a-Grammar. The campaign would run on radio, tele-

vision, the What's New Locally sections of the OmniMedia network and other networks, in the OmniMedia news system's advertising nooks, and on placards posted in public transportation. She
left the meeting and the Informatique thinking excitedly about how
the campaign and the new services would strengthen the Informatique's quarterly report of its economic impact. This report docu-
menting the Informatique's contribution to local job growth, corporate profits, academic grant procurement, and cost cutting in
government was the instrument whereby the Informatique received
funds beyond its basic budget so that it could continue to contribute
to cooperative resource development projects locally, nationally,
and worldwide; implement new tools such as the Whole-a-Grammar; and provide better service. She made a mental note to raise that
point at the meeting Friday morning when she and other members
of the management team examined the report for the past quarter.
She would have made a note in her Personal Electronic Assistant,
but she discovered that she had forgotten to recharge its batteries
while at work. Some things just hadn't changed from her college
days when she would get to the library in the evening to study or
search CD-ROM databases and discover that her DiscMan batteries
were dead!

Will Informatiques replace libraries sometime in the first part of
the twenty-first century? Not likely–and almost assuredly not as a
result of Congressional action. For one thing, libraries are in the
process of transforming themselves (although not, perhaps, into
Informatiques) and the changes will appear to be a sea change, rich
and strange, only if they are sudden, which they will not be. Nevertheless, libraries and their services must respond to changes in
society if they are to continue to play a significant role in supplying
information to people to help them make informed decisions about
issues they face in their lives. If libraries abdicate (or allow others to
snatch) this role and become little more than sources of popular
fiction, free videos, children's book collections, and meeting rooms
for local civic organizations, then the future of libraries and reference services looks bleak. No one knows what the future will be
like; yet everyone knows it will be different. How? One could glibly
say that one person's guess is as good as another, but that would
ignore the people who have refined tools and techniques used to

examine the present to identify the emerging trends that will shape the future. Truly, "what's past is prologue," so it is important to examine these trends and then assess whether or not the course on which librarianship and reference service are set is in line with these trends or in conflict with them. If the latter, adjustment–perhaps minor, perhaps radical–is necessary.

For the sake of convenience, I have sketched the scenario about the Informatique and its services as marketing and future trends specialist Faith Popcorn and her staff at BrainReserve might if they were asked to chart a thriving future for reference service. (Brain Reserve is a New York City marketing consulting form established in 1974; the focus of its business is predicting consumer behavior for the company's clients, mostly Fortune 500 corporations.) The scenario of the Informatique sketched above will not come to pass just so; however it embodies key characteristics that, however the library/reference scenario plays out in the next two decades, must be present if reference service is to remain relevant. And if reference service loses its value to society and to the communities that individual libraries (of every type, although type of library is not a significant variable here) serve, they will become little more than "free" sources for popular fiction, free videos, children's book collections, and meeting rooms for local civic organizations.

In *The Popcorn Report** Popcorn identifies ten trends that she says will characterize American society through the present decade. She names these:

Trend 1:	Cocooning in a New Decade
Trend 2:	Fantasy Adventure
Trend 3:	Small Indulgences
Trend 4:	Egonomics
Trend 5:	Cashing Out
Trend 6:	Down-Aging

---

*Faith Popcorn. *The Popcorn Report* (New York: Doubleday, 1991). All further references to *The Popcorn Report* are made parenthetically in the text; references consist only of page numbers. Any italics within quotes appear in the original.

Trend 7:   Staying Alive

Trend 8:   The Vigilante Consumer

Trend 9:   99 Lives

Trend 10:   S.O.S. (Save Our Society)

How much faith should one place in Faith Popcorn's predictions? At least as much as in one's own predictions and perhaps a bit more since Ms. Popcorn's business, especially her repeat customer business, depends upon the acuity with which she can identify and articulate trends. She does not claim omniscience and applies these trends to problems in a measured, flexible way. When dealing with corporate clients hoping to ride the next societal wave to success in the marketplace, BrainReserve staff test product and service ideas against these trends. If an idea fits with at least *four* of these trends, it shows promise for the 1990s. Products and services that don't match up well with these trends may not survive the 1990s.

Libraries and reference service operate in the same society as Coca-Cola, Ford Motor Company, and Apple Computer, albeit for different purposes. Nevertheless major trends affect all enterprises in the society, so libraries need to be alert to them and capitalize on these trends whenever possible. How, then does reference service fit these trends? And how does the Informatique scenario exemplify key trends and suggest positive directions for reference librarianship? The answer to those questions can be suggested by testing both reference service as it is today and its embodiment in the Informatique scenario against Popcorn's trends of the 90s.

TREND 1: COCOONING IN A NEW DECADE

Popcorn describes cocooning, a 1980s trend becoming intense in the 1990s, as a "retreat into the last controllable (or sort of controllable) environment–your own digs" (p. 27). In the 1990s she predicts three varieties of cocooning–the "armored" cocoon in which personal security concerns are paramount in the face of increasing (or the perception of) increasing crime and violence in society, the "wandering cocoon" in which automobiles offer an environment for more than transportation, and the "socialized" cocoon in which in their own digs people selectively entertain "people you feel comfy with to help weather the storm" (p. 32).

Reference service today is not well suited to any form of cocooning. The general expectation is that library patrons will come to the library for reference service. The exception is telephone reference service, but many libraries severely limit the extent of service offered by telephone. Some libraries also offer limited service via e-mail, but this medium has not yet become widespread in society nor is it heavily used for this purpose in most of the libraries that now offer it. In the language of BrainReserve, reference service in 1994 is definitely "off-trend," especially in urban libraries (regardless of type) that expect patrons to reach that service by sharing city streets with armed criminals.

The Informatique, in contrast, offers cocoon residents, whether they are ensconced in their cocoons out of fear or exhaustion, the sort of service they want. The "wired" cocoon can connect to the world beyond in many ways. Interactive television, a service currently in its experimental phase but one that may have significant implications for reference service, will allow the flow of information to go two ways. With the exceptions of electronic mail (usually through commercial vendors such as Online America or Compuserve), the telephone, and the fax machine, wired communication comes today into the cocoon but doesn't go out. The future promises a much more versatile, much more robust, and much more interactive exchange between the cocoon and the outside world, including the library.

TREND 2: FANTASY ADVENTURE

Popcorn's "Fantasy Adventure" trend fits well with the armored cocoon; people want the thrill of adventure but not the risks associated with it. She says it is "vicarious escape through consumerism, catharsis through consumption. It's a momentary, wild-and-crazy retreat from the world into an exotic flavor, a 'foreign' experience, some product-assisted derring-do of the imagination . . . it's an escapist identification with a hero who's gutsier than you are, able to get rid of all the bad guys and still get you back home to dinner. It's video rentals and aggressively foreign cuisines and perfumes named Safari, and mountain bikes you ride to the mall" (p.34). In other words, it is a lot like the television commercials that promise a more exciting life to anyone who just uses their credit card or buys their four-wheel drive vehicle, etc.

Reference service today and in the future is not likely to be strongly "on-trend" with fantasy adventure. Libraries cannot succeed if they try to be all things to everyone. Fantasy adventure is probably best left to Hollywood, Madison Avenue, and Stephen King.

The Informatique offers promise of some on-trend tie-in to fantasy adventure, although fulfilling fantasy adventure yearnings is not its mission. If the tools that allow for integration of diverse media into new, customized information packages created to fulfill a particular person's or group's needs are too complex to use or too costly for consumers, libraries will have a role in making them available. These tools will allow library patrons to indulge in some fantasy adventure as they capture and manipulate elements in a variety of media from the library's collections. However a trip to the library is never likely to be equated to a trip to Disneyworld.

TREND 3: SMALL INDULGENCES

Small indulgences are a response to the excesses of buying and living on credit in the 1980s and amassing debt to be paid off during the 1990s. Consumers cannot afford to indulge themselves in big-ticket items, but they can allow themselves, without serious risk, a small indulgence now and then.

The tradition of public library service, replicated in analogous ways within schools and colleges and universities for their respective communities, means that library service in this society is viewed more as an entitlement than an indulgence. Librarians would be foolish to desire any change in this view. It may be off-trend, but it works to libraries' and society's advantage. Neither library service today nor the library service of the Informatique fits this trend.

TREND 4: EGONOMICS

Yes, that is "egonomics," *not* ergonomics! Describing it as a "nicer narcissism" than the narcissism of the 1980s, Popcorn says it is "a little recognition of the *no-one's-quite-like-me* self. It's about individuating, differentiating, customizing. And it's a major force to reckon with . . . Egonomics means simply this: there is profit to be reaped in providing for the consumer's need for personalization–whether it be in product concept, product design, 'customability,' or personal service" (pp. 43-44). In line with the trend towards Total Quality Management in service industries, Popcorn points out that "egonomics shifts the emphasis from the manufacturer's priorities to the consumer's" (p. 44). She cites as an example of this trend the proliferation of new magazines serving narrow market niches defined by special interests. One need only scan a list of Usenet newsgroups or Internet listservs to see compelling verification of this trend.

Reference service today is, for the most part, on-trend. Reference librarians strive to meet the individual information needs of individual patrons. It is a service that, no matter how high tech it becomes, always has the possibility of also being very "high touch." However in some libraries policies limit how much reference service is offered and in nearly all libraries staffing levels create ceilings beyond which reference service cannot rise. Solutions to policy impediments are easy–once the staff recognizes them as impediments. Dialogue with patrons about the quality and level of service– through questionnaires, through focus groups, or through other means–can be very useful in identifying policies that hinder good service. Once identified, library staff need to change those that can be changed and then work to secure the resources needed to change others. Internal reallocation of resources must, of course, also be looked at.

A librarian can also limit the depth of service he or she offers through personal, rather than institutional, policy. It does not matter whether this personal policy is founded on philosophical tenets or something less noble; a personal policy that sets standards lower than the institution's creates problems. Ideally the depth of service offered by the reference librarians in a given institution does not vary from individual to individual. In practice, it always will vary due to differences among individuals' knowledge and experience. However if a librarian consistently chooses to offer a level of service less than that identified as the institution's goal, supervisory personnel must work with that individual to improve the situation. If, on the other hand, a librarian consistently chooses to offer a level of service greater than that identified as the institution's goal, that individual is likely to become a favorite among patrons; and, if all goes well, the benefits of this deeper service will be evident to others in the library, resulting in an upward revision of service goals.

While sidestepping the contentious debates about the role of the academic library and the responsibilities of the students its serves, it is worth noting that bibliographic instruction programs in many university libraries, in both intent and design, are decidedly off-trend when it comes to egonomics. Because they are designed for groups, these programs do not acknowledge the many differences among individual students and their needs.

Vigorous, proactive reference service has the potential in every community served by a library (regardless of type) to cement the library's central role in the life of that community. Every county supervisor, every school superintendent, every mayor, every dean, every college president pays lip service to the importance of the library. Strong, individualized, thorough reference service with a personal touch can create enduring, powerful allies in the community, allies who can force those officials to live up to their words of praise for the library.

The service provided by the Informatique could hardly be more in sync with this major trend. Each client receives customized service, delivered in a collaborative way that lets each client know he or she is indeed special. This must be a significant characteristic of reference service in the future, regardless of the type of library (if such distinctions continue to hold meaning and value).

TREND 5: CASHING OUT

Telecommuting and abandoning the city for the country typify the cashing-out trend of the 1990s. Most people, however, lack the resources or the courage to give up the security of a steady job for the uncertainty of a cottage industry operated out of their home or the risk and long hours of running a country inn in New England. Most people content themselves with vicarious versions of cashing out, and so, in our desire "to incorporate small-town values into the lives that still hold us in the cities. . . we wear flannel shirts and hiking boots . . . and buy cookbooks devoted to 'country cooking'" (p. 54). Popcorn says that "we definitely want life to be folksy and straightforward; to be plain and explainable" (p. 55).

"Plain and explainable." One could say that reference service is librarians' valiant attempt to put very off-trend institutions on-trend! Think of how cumbersome many OPACs make access to serials holdings information or of how user-hostile the interfaces of most CD-ROM bibliographic files are! Reference librarians cannot fix these problems on their own. As Popcorn says, "The future is a collective effort. You can't decide on the future alone, and especially you can't create it alone" (p. 12). Reference librarians need to establish stronger communications channels with information service and product vendors to let those vendors know how their products and services can be improved and can be made "plain and explainable." And those vendors ought to be working even harder than the librarians to establish such channels. It is in everyone's interests to try to get libraries on this trend.

It appears that with regard to cashing out, the Informatique is on-trend–but only because of mediation. Information, especially when it is considered and collected and collated from diverse media, is messy and confusing. With the right tools employed by knowledgeable professionals (i.e., reference librarians!), information can be made manageable and intelligible. The universe of information and the media used to convey it will continue to grow and proliferate. This means the tools used to organize and retrieve it will need to become more complex, counter to the cashing out trend. Initially, at least these probably will not be tools for the masses, but for the experts. It will always be possible for library patrons to find something they can use in (or from) a library; however as libraries become increasingly complex and as they can retrieve information from a wider variety of sources and retrieve it more expeditiously, it will be more important for an expert to collaborate with patrons to help them find the best possible sources. Ultimately only the patron can judge the value of a source and the information it conveys; however a good reference librarian can do much to make plain and (at least seemingly) simple the process of identifying and gathering those sources so that the patron can then perform the important task (indeed, the most important task) of evaluating it. The Informatique is as on-trend as it possibly can be in the messy, confusing world of recorded information and access systems to that information.

TREND 6: DOWN-AGING

A "refusal to be bound by traditional age limitations is the trend we are calling Down-Aging: redefining *down* what appropriate age-behavior is for your age" (p. 57). A cynic might say that down-aging is really an epidemic of Peter Pan-ism among Baby Boomers. Popcorn cites as manifestations of this trend the continuing careers of rock 'n rollers now past fifty, the galloping increases in sales of skin care products and hair colorings, and the popularity of Nintendo games among adults.

Like small indulgences, it is difficult to link this trend to reference services.

TREND 7: STAYING ALIVE

Staying alive is "the trend that represents our hyper-quest for health" (p. 62). The national concern about the health care system, a key issue in the last presidential campaign and an ongoing issue in Congress, validates this trend.

Reference service has only a peripheral relationship to this trend. To the extent that consumers of health services want to be better educated about health and health policy issues, reference librarians can help them and thereby allow libraries to ride this trend. However most of the public's information about diseases, health insurance plans, and public policy issues come from the popular press (in its manifestations in all media), not from libraries. Could the Informatique change this situation? Perhaps–but not likely. As they say at BrainReserve–off-trend.

TREND 8: THE VIGILANTE CONSUMER

Vigilante consumerism is the demand for quality. Smart companies, Popcorn, says realize that "What will make us buy one product over another in this decade is a feeling of partnership with the seller, and a feeling that we're buying for the future. Anonymous, impersonal selling–the old-style K mart–is over ... We want to buy from a *person* ... a person whom we trust. Trust will be implicit in every purchase" (p. 76). And in every reference transaction.

Reference service as it is practiced today offers a mixed picture on this trend. Most reference service is offered anonymously and it is not consistently a partnership. Some reference librarians can be identified by name, through name plates or name tags, or other means, but most are anonymous functionaries of their institutions, undifferentiated in the public mind from other library staff who perform different roles. Reference service often consists of a set of suggestions on how a patron might find needed information; after these suggestions are given, the patron his left to act on them alone. Overall library patrons rate reference service highly. However as more and more consumers of reference service become consumers of other information services such as America Online or Prodigy, there is no reason to assume that these satisfaction levels will remain as high. The chronic problems of insufficient staff resources noted above in the discussion of egonomics apply here as well; so do the prescriptions for the future.

The Informatique is strongly on-trend with this important social phenomenon. Quality has become a national concern, connected to every issue imaginable from health care to school reform, from the way standardized tests for college admission are scored to trade competition with Japan. It remains to be seen if quality becomes a national obsession; nevertheless the service providers who monitor and continually improve the quality of their services will come out of the 1990s winners. The collaborative nature of the reference service provided by the Informatique staff is designed to instill trust in the client. Follow-up by the Informatique professional with the client strengthens that trust and builds a partnership.

The Informatique has "salons" rather than "desks" to emphasize this collaborative meeting of minds in partnership to solve a problem. Even in the Customer Service Salon where the librarian has face-to-face contact with the client only electronically, there is the opportunity, as in a Parisian salon, to explore alternatives, to test them, and to identify the best choices. Definitely on-trend!

TREND 9: 99 LIVES

We are all just too, too busy with too, too many things to do! "We're pleading to the big time clock in the sky: 'Give me *fewer* choices, far fewer choices. Make my life easier. Help me make the most of my most valued commodity–the very minutes of my life' " (p. 81).

Reference service as it is practiced today generally promotes this trend, but not always. Some practitioners strive to make patrons aware of every possibility and thereby risk overwhelming them in an age characterized by "information overload" in which the amount of information most people need and the amount they receive is often (even to the point where it has become a cliché) compared to trying to quench one's thirst by drinking from a fire hose. Generally, however, reference service does help people limit the universe of information sources they have to choose among from a undifferentiated galaxy of unnamed possibilities to an identified set of specific sources that the patron can judge for value. S.R. Ranganathan's Fourth Law of Library Science, "Save the time of the reader," codifies this and shows that what today is a trend for others, has long been a basic value for reference librarians.

Popcorn says that "The biggest technological achievement of the 99 Lives era will be a way to *edit down* all the information that assaults us daily" (p. 84). The Informatique, employing educated librarians trained in the use of sophisticated tools such as those in the Customer Service Salon and the On-Site Customer Service Salon fulfills this desire at the same time it responds to the strong cocooning, egonomics, and vigilante consumer trends. To the extent that reference service in the future can help patrons edit down the wealth of information available to them, it will respond to their basic needs and their deep desire to manage their time more efficiently.

TREND 10: S.O.S. (SAVE OUR SOCIETY)

"What is the S.O.S. trend exactly? It's an effort that contributes to making the '90s our first truly socially responsible decade: the Decency Decade, dedicated to the three critical E's, Environment, Education, and Ethics" (p. 86). It is characterized by a concern for the future and for the welfare of future generations.

It would be very easy to belabor the point, but with the possible exception of environmental concern, librarians have been riding this trend for more than a century. It is good to see that the rest of society has bought into these fundamental values. The Informatique is more environmentally friendly than the present day library in that it offers greater options for information delivery that require fewer natural resources than present methods. At the same time, it is as committed to education and to ethical principles as the libraries of today and yesterday. And it was designed to give special service to the up-and-coming generation and the generations after it. On-trend, even before it was trend!

CONCLUSION

Whatever one's cherished beliefs about the role of libraries in society and "philosophies" of reference service, deeply rooted social trends are "can't-beat-'em, better-join-'em" phenomena; and there is no "if" in front of that. Libraries and librarians (despite innumerable ineffectual ALA resolutions that imply as much) cannot remake society to fit any beliefs or philosophies; libraries and reference services have to develop in sync with these trends.

Faith Popcorn's ten trends may not accurately characterize American society in the 1990s. However her major trends–cocooning, egonomics, vigilante consumerism, 99 lives, and save our society–seem right on the mark. Librarianship will ignore them at its peril. The Informatique, despite its centralization of and compression of roles formerly assigned to specific types of libraries and despite its linkages to a far more comprehensive universe of information sources than any library today is linked to, manages on the one hand to combine the intimacy and personal attention, to convey the feelings of security and personal attention, of a boutique with, on the other hand, the best services of today's information providers (among whom are reference librarians). If reference librarians work to develop their services in line with these trends, they as a profession can emerge in the new century as not just one of the best information providers in American society, but as the very best.

Reference service as it is practiced today has weak connections with these trends. Reference service needs to be redesigned, not necessarily to create Informatiques, but to capitalize on these key trends so that it is a vital force for good in society, a source that daily reminds individuals of all ages and from all walks of life of the inestimable value of libraries and of society's considerable return on its relatively modest investment in its libraries. Reference librarianship can (and should) move into this brave new world without forsaking its fundamental values of equity of access, of not imposing personal value judgments on information, and so on. The skills contemporary reference librarians apply every day will continue to serve them well in the future, although they will have to develop additional skills (such as a better sense of public relations and promotion). Much of the new world will be familiar from the old world. But it has the potential to be a more exciting world, a world in which librarians provide even better service to society, a world in which society, in return, values librarians more highly.

Index

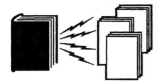

Haworth
DOCUMENT DELIVERY
SERVICE

This new service provides a single-article order form for any article from a Haworth journal.

- *Time Saving:* No running around from library to library to find a specific article.
- *Cost Effective:* All costs are kept down to a minimum.
- *Fast Delivery:* Choose from several options, including same-day FAX.
- *No Copyright Hassles:* You will be supplied by the original publisher.
- *Easy Payment:* Choose from several easy payment methods.

Open Accounts Welcome for . . .
- Library Interlibrary Loan Departments
- Library Network/Consortia Wishing to Provide Single-Article Services
- Indexing/Abstracting Services with Single Article Provision Services
- Document Provision Brokers and Freelance Information Service Providers

MAIL or *FAX* THIS ENTIRE ORDER FORM TO:

Haworth Document Delivery Service
The Haworth Press, Inc.
10 Alice Street
Binghamton, NY 13904-1580

or FAX: (607) 722-6362
or CALL: 1-800-3-HAWORTH
(1-800-342-9678; 9am-5pm EST)

PLEASE SEND ME PHOTOCOPIES OF THE FOLLOWING SINGLE ARTICLES:
1) Journal Title: _____
   Vol/Issue/Year:_____Starting & Ending Pages:_____
   Article Title:_____

2) Journal Title: _____
   Vol/Issue/Year:_____Starting & Ending Pages:_____
   Article Title:_____

3) Journal Title: _____
   Vol/Issue/Year:_____Starting & Ending Pages:_____
   Article Title:_____

4) Journal Title: _____
   Vol/Issue/Year:_____Starting & Ending Pages:_____
   Article Title:_____

(See other side for Costs and Payment Information)

COSTS: Please figure your cost to order quality copies of an article.

1. Set-up charge per article: $8.00
   ($8.00 × number of separate articles) _____

2. Photocopying charge for each article:

                   1-10 pages: $1.00 _____

                   11-19 pages: $3.00 _____

                   20-29 pages: $5.00 _____

                   30+ pages: $2.00/10 pages _____

3. Flexicover (optional): $2.00/article _____

4. Postage & Handling: US: $1.00 for the first article/
                   $.50 each additional article _____

                   Federal Express: $25.00 _____

                   Outside US: $2.00 for first article/
                   $.50 each additional article _____

5. Same-day FAX service: $.35 per page _____

                    GRAND TOTAL: _____

METHOD OF PAYMENT: (please check one)

❑ Check enclosed   ❑ Please ship and bill. PO # _____
                (sorry we can ship and bill to bookstores only! All others must pre-pay)

❑ Charge to my credit card: ❑ Visa; ❑ MasterCard; ❑ American Express;

Account Number:_____ Expiration date:_____

Signature: X_____

Name: _____ Institution: _____

Address: _____

_____

City: _____ State:_____ Zip:_____

Phone Number: _____ FAX Number: _____

MAIL or *FAX* THIS ENTIRE ORDER FORM TO:

Haworth Document Delivery Service	**or FAX:** (607) 722-6362
The Haworth Press, Inc.	**or CALL:** 1-800-3-HAWORTH
10 Alice Street	(1-800-342-9678; 9am-5pm EST)
Binghamton, NY 13904-1580	